WITHDRAWN

THREE PLAYS
BY
HEBBEL

ALSO BY MARION W. SONNENFELD

Kleist's *Amphitryon* (translator)
Wert und Wort (editor)
The Prose of Conrad Ferdinand Meyer (co-translator with George
 F. Folkers and David B. Dickens)

THREE PLAYS
BY
HEBBEL

Translated and with an Introduction
by
Marion W. Sonnenfeld

Lewisburg
BUCKNELL UNIVERSITY PRESS

DALE H. GRAMLEY LIBRARY
SALEM COLLEGE
WINSTON-SALEM, N. C.

PT
2295
A2
E58
1974

© 1974 by Associated University Presses, Inc.

Associated University Presses, Inc.
Cranbury, New Jersey 08512

Library of Congress Cataloging in Publication Data

Hebbel, Friedrich, 1813–1863.
   Three plays.

   CONTENTS: Judith.—Herod and Mariamne.—Gyges and
his ring.
   I. Sonnenfeld, Marion, tr.
PT2295.A2E58   1973   832′.7   72-3531
ISBN 0-8387-1239-8

PRINTED IN THE UNITED STATES OF AMERICA

In loving memory of
Kurt Sonnenfeld
To
Sibylla Sonnenfeld
with all my love and gratitude

Contents

Translator's Preface

These three plays were chosen for translation because they are among the best—perhaps even *the best*—of Hebbel and because of their thematic connection and development. In translating, I have tried to preserve as much of the flavor of Hebbel's language and syntax as possible. Hebbel has a predilection for long involved sentences, and, wherever possible, I have tried to preserve this aspect of his style as well.

In the introductory material, I have quoted considerable amounts of Hebbel's dramatic theory and tried to analyze the plays in accordance with it, not because the plays are not readable and lucid without it, but rather to expose the reader to as much of Hebbel's thought as possible. There are, of course, many other aspects in each play which are of interest and worthy of discussion, among them the structure of each play, its style, and its symbolism. These each reader will note for himself and I hope that the plays will be enjoyed in the process.

Acknowledgments

Very special gratitude is herewith expressed to the outstanding photographer Rosemarie Clausen for generously making available for this book her pictures of the Hamburg Theater productions of *Judith* and *Gyges and His Ring*. Thanks are also in order to INTERNATIONES and the Westdeutscher Rundfunk for making available the photographs of the television performance of *Herod and Mariamne*.

DALE H. GRAMLEY LIBRARY
SALEM COLLEGE
WINSTON-SALEM, N. C.

Short Biographical Sketch of Friedrich Hebbel

Christian Friedrich Hebbel was born in Wesselburen in Holstein in 1813. His childhood, about which he reminisces in *Aufzeichnungen aus meinem Leben,* was marked by the poverty of the lower middle class family. His father, a mason by trade, had little money to spend on the education of his children. Young Hebbel was employed as a mason's helper at age twelve. When he was fourteen, his father died, and Hebbel entered the employ of the local church official for whom he worked for eight years, first as servant, then as secretary with servant's pay. During these years he read voraciously what little he could find and began to write lyric. The publication of some of his poems brought him new friends, one of whom wrote to him in 1834 that she had obtained money to finance his "study."

In 1835, Hebbel moved to Hamburg to make up the high school studies prerequisite to entering a university. There, he met a seamstress, Elise Lensing, who was to become his common-law wife and the mother of his first two children. Elise was nine years older than Hebbel. She mothered him and compensated to some extent with her understanding and devotion for the igno-minies which were attached to Hebbel's eating as a charity boarder and studying as a charity student. After one year in Hamburg, Hebbel received the rest of the charitable fund, completed the examinations for admission to the university, and went to Heidel-berg. To finance this, he was forced to borrow money from Elise.

Later, having heard that life was cheaper in Munich, Hebbel moved there and spent three years studying literature after abandoning his original intention to study law. Although he lived as frugally as possible, he found it necessary to avail himself of additional funds provided by Elise. During these years, he wrote and published some narrative prose.

After three years in Munich, he ran out of financial resources altogether and returned to Hamburg and Elise in 1839. In 1840, his first drama, *Judith,* was presented in Berlin. It was followed by a number of other dramas and prose works. The ensuing reputation he enjoyed encouraged him to appeal, in 1842, to King Christian of Denmark, his king, for a travel grant or a professorship. The two-year travel grant he received in 1843 took him first to Paris and then to Italy. An essay on dramatic theory, part of which is to be found in *My Word Concerning the Drama,* was approved by the University of Erlangen as a Ph.D. thesis, and only lack of funds prevented Hebbel from picking up his diploma. In 1845, his application for renewal of his grant resulted in a payment for his return trip.

In November of 1845, Hebbel arrived in Vienna, where he met Christine Enghaus, an actress with the famous Burgtheater. She was most interested in portraying his dramatic heroines and persuaded him to stay in Vienna. After the exchange of tortured letters with Elise, from whom study and travel had completely estranged him, he decided to stay in Vienna and marry Christine. After his marriage in 1846 began the happiest time in Hebbel's life. Because of Christine's understanding, a friendship with Elise was possible, and, after the death of her second child, Elise spent a year in the Hebbel household in Vienna. During this year, Hebbel began the drama *Herod and Mariamne.* The remaining years of his life were spent in continuing his dramatic work and absorbing the frustrations caused by a public not ready to receive the thought content of his dramas. His body, weakened by years of poverty and deprivation, hard work and frustrations, succumbed in 1863, and Hebbel died at age fifty and at the height of his productivity.

Hebbel's Best-Known Dramas

JUDITH (1840)

The Maccabean heroine undertakes what she considers her God-inspired mission: to free her people from the threat of the Babylonian tyrant Holofernes by killing him. Because she is very beautiful, she arouses his amorous interest. He has certain aspects of greatness, however, and Judith suddenly finds herself in danger of falling in love with him. What restores her ability to carry out her mission is her realization that he has no human respect for her. After the assassination, Judith fears that she may be carrying his child, and if this is so, she will seek death.

GENOVEVA (1841)

Falsely accused of unfaithfulness to her husband, Siegfried, by Golo, a knight secretly in love with her, Genoveva undergoes seven years of trials and sorrows, all of which she bears nobly. Golo is finally driven to assume responsibility for his crime, and Siegfried finds and restores his wife and child just before Genoveva dies.

MARIA MAGDALENA (1844)

Klara, the daughter of Meister Anton, has been forced by her fiancé, whom she does not love, to prove her love for him by

15

giving herself to him before marriage. When she discovers her pregnancy, neither the man she loves nor her fiancé will have her. Her father has made it clear to her that he could not survive such shame and has forced her to swear that she has never been violated. Thereupon Klara commits suicide. When her upright, stern father hears of this, he sighs, "I no longer understand the world!"

HEROD AND MARIAMNE (1849)

King Herod, responsible for the death of his Maccabean brother-in-law, whom he has suspected of plotting against him, is very much in love with his wife, whom he regards as his most precious possession, and is also very jealous. Because he is unsure of her love, he makes provision that she should be killed if he fails to return from war. Mariamne is appalled and deeply offended when she learns of his lack of trust in her love and completely outraged when he makes a similar arrangement a second time. Upon his return, Mariamne convinces him that she had hoped for his death and does not love him and is executed on Herod's command. When he learns, after her execution, that she had indeed loved him and been faithful to him, Herod is shattered. Upon learning of the birth of the King of kings, he decides to fight for the survival of himself and his world by having the infants in Bethlehem killed.

AGNES BERNAUER (1852)

The daughter of a middle class artisan loves and marries the young Duke Albrecht, who will someday fall heir to his father's realm of Munich-Bavaria. The father, Duke Ernst, refuses to acknowledge his son's bride until she has been condemned and executed as a threat to the state. The young Duke, about to avenge the death of his beloved wife by killing his father, is given the duchy which he is now ready to rule because he has learned that his personal interest must be subordinated to that of the state.

GYGES AND HIS RING (1856)

The Lydian king, Candaules, wants to show the full beauty of his wife, Queen Rhodope, to Gyges. While wearing a ring which will make him invisible, Gyges is to observe Rhodope in her bedroom. Overcome by her beauty and the feeling of baseness in thus deceiving the queen, Gyges removes a piece of jewelry from her neck and turns the ring so that she will have to see him. She demands of Gyges that he kill the king in order that she may be restored to purity and innocence. Gyges complies with her demand because he loves her. She gives Gyges her hand, and, purified because only her husband has seen her, she then kills herself.

THE NIBELUNGEN (Trilogy, 1861)

The plot is that of the Middle High German epic, with successful humanization of the characters. A grandiose epic background shows the dual transition from titanism to paganism and from paganism to Christianity. The main characters are titans who are atavisms in the pagan world and pagans who are on the decline without realizing it. Their successor is a Christian.

DEMETRIUS (Fragment)

The pretender to the Russian throne learns at the height of his political success, when he is very close to attaining the throne, that he is a bastard. He is confronted by the ethical conflict: whether to continue in his quest for the throne with full knowledge of the illegitimacy of his claims or whether he should desert and disappoint his followers.

Excerpts from Hebbel's
My Word Concerning the Drama
(1843)

Art has to do with life, both internal and external, and one may well say that it depicts both life's purest form and its highest meaning. The main genres of art and its laws derive immediately from the diversity of the elements it takes from life and uses in each case. But life appears in two-fold form, as being and as becoming, and art fulfills its task most perfectly if it maintains itself in proper balance between the two. Only in this way does it assure itself of the present as well as of the future, which have to be of equal importance to art. Only in this way does it become what it is supposed to become: life within life; for what is enclosed in circumstance stifles the creative spirit without which art would remain ineffectual, and what flashes into embryonic existence excludes form.

Drama represents the process of life itself, not only by presenting life in all its breadth to us, which, after all, epic poetry presumes to accomplish likewise, but also by bringing the situation to be considered before our eyes, the situation in which the individual, released from his original context, confronts the whole, a part of which he still remains in spite of his incomprehensible freedom. Accordingly, the drama, as befits the highest form of art, is directed equally to what exists and to what is to be: to that which exists, because it may not tire of repeating

the eternal truth that life, as an individuation which does not
know how to preserve a mean, does not accidentally produce
guilt, but of necessity, and essentially must include and cause
it; to that which will be, because it shows with ever new subject
matter, offered by time in its eternal movement and its record,
history, that man, no matter how the objects in his environment
may change, eternally remains constant in nature and fate. Here
one should not overlook that dramatic guilt, unlike Christian
original sin, does not derive solely from the direction of human
will, but that it derives directly from the will, from the rigid,
arbitrary expansion of the Ego, and that it is therefore a matter
of total indifference to the drama whether the hero fails at an
excellent or reprehensible aspiration.

The dramatic subject matter is formed by plot and characters.
We shall disregard plot here, for it has become, at least among
more modern dramatists, a subordinate force, as anyone who
doubts it may see clearly by picking up a Shakespearean drama
and asking himself whether the writer was inspired by history or
by the human beings he places on the stage. The treatment of the
characters is of the greatest importance, however. Under no
circumstances should they appear to be completely formed, merely
acting throughout a set of circumstances, enabling them to win
or lose external happiness or unhappiness but not internal core
and essence. That is the death of the drama, death before birth.
The drama only comes alive for us when it visualizes for us
how the individual gains his form and focus in the conflict between his personal will and the universal one which keeps modi-
fying and transforming the deed, the expression of freedom, by
the event, the expression of necessity, and by thus clarifying the
nature of all human action which, as soon as it tries to manifest
an inner motive, always simultaneously releases an opposing
external one which is calculated to restore equilibrium. And,
although the basic idea, on which the presupposed dignity and
value of the drama depend, is the ring, inside of which everything must move in planetlike fashion, the writer must still
properly see to it that the interests are manifold, or, more properly put, that the totality of life and the world are realized without harming the true unity of the drama, and he must guard
against placing all his characters equally near the center, which
is often done in the so-called lyric drama. The most perfect
depiction of life is achieved if the main character becomes for
the subordinate characters and the antagonists what fate, with

which he is in conflict, is for him, and if everything down to the lowest substrata is thus developed, caused, and mirrored with total reciprocity.

The question arises now: what is the relationship between drama and history, and to what degree must drama be historical? I think, to the degree to which it already is historical in itself and to which art may already be considered the highest historiography, since it can not depict the grandest and most significant of life processes without also depicting the decisive historic crises which produce and cause them, the loosening or gradual tightening of the religious and political mores of the world as the main transmitters and representatives of all developments, in a word, the atmospheres of the times. Material history, which Napoleon already called the plot of congruence, this colorful, vast chaos of dubious facts and characterizations which are either one-sided or not at all defined, will, sooner or later, surpass the human ability to comprehend; and the modern drama, especially Shakespearean drama, and not only that which is especially designated historical, could, thus, naturally have the same position for more remote posterity as ancient drama has for us. Then, and probably not before then, people will stop narrowmindedly trying to find a common identity for art and history and to compare actual and treated situations and characters exactly, for they will have come to understand that, through it, the almost-indifferent agreement between art and history can be shown but not that between depiction and truth as such; and they will come to see that the drama is symbolic, not only in its totality, where that is obvious, but in each of its elements, and must be seen as symbolic. In the same way, the painter does not distill the colors with which he gives his figures red cheeks and blue eyes from real human blood but, calmly and without being attacked for it, employs red and blue paints.

But the content of life is inexhaustible and the medium of art is limited. Life knows no end; the thread from which it spins phenomena extends to infinity, while art must twist the thread into a circle as well as possible, and this must be the point Goethe intended to make when he stated that all its forms have something untrue about them. This untrue element may indeed even be traced to life itself, for it too does not show a single form in which all its elements come out evenly; e.g., it can not develop the most perfect man without denying him the advantages which produce the most perfect woman, and the two pails in the well, only one of which can be full at any one time, are the most significant symbol of all creation. This basic deficiency shows up much more strongly and questionably in art than in life, however, for in life, the whole always steps into the breach created by the part and compensates for it, while in art, the breach on one side must absolutely be balanced by an overabundance on the other.

I want to explain this thought and apply it to the drama. The most excellent dramas of all literatures show us that the writer often could only create the invisible ring, within which his depiction of life moves, by endowing one or several of his main characters with a degree of world- and self-confidence which far exceeds reality. I shall not cite the ancients, for their treatment of characters was different. I only want to remind one of Shakespeare and, without mentioning *Hamlet,* since one can perhaps find better examples, cite only the monologues in *Macbeth* and *Richard III,* as well as the Bastard in *King John.* By the way, people have at times desired to see a virtue, a special advantage, in this obvious weakness of Shakespeare (even Hegel in his aesthetics) instead of letting the proof suffice that it does not have its basis in the writer but in the art itself. But what, according to them, is found as a consistent trait in whole characters in the works of the greatest dramatists is also found in a single character in the moments of culmination when the word moves alongside the action, indeed even hastens ahead of it, and this is, to draw a most important conclusion, what differentiates the conscious depiction in art from the unconscious one in life, that the former, in order to be effective, must set sharp and total limits, while the latter, which does not need to struggle for credibility and which, in the end, need not care whether or how it is understood, may be satisfied with the halfway expression, the sigh or the oh, a facial expression or a gesture. Goethe's words which dared to touch on the most dangerous secret of Art have often been repeated, but generally only in regard to that external which is called *form.* In the most profound verse of Scripture, the schoolboy sees only his good friends, the twenty-four letters in which it is written.

German drama seems to be making a new beginning. What task must it accomplish now? The question could be confusing, for the most obvious answer must be, of necessity, *the same that the drama had to accomplish at all times.* But. one can go on with these questions: Should it reach into the present? Should it turn back to the past? Or should it concern itself with neither of these, i.e., should it be social, historical, or philosophical? Respectable talents have already taken these three directions. . . . Now there is also a fourth possibility, a drama which unites these three . . . directions and, for just that reason, lets no single one dominate decisively. This drama is the goal of my own efforts. . . . a drama is possible which pursues the stream of history to its most mysterious sources, the positive religions, and which, since it depicts in dialectic form all the consequences of the innermost principles of those individuals who first had them, whether conscious of them or not, erects a symbol of all the historic and social conditions which had to develop from these ideas in the course of centuries. . . .

. . . The task of art and philosophy is one and the same, but they seek to carry it out in different ways. If philosophy tries to grasp the immediate idea, then art finds it sufficient to destroy everything which contradicts it in the phenomenal world. Philosophy has not as yet lived up to its share of the common task; it has contracted the periphery surrounding the mysterious center more and more tightly but has not succeeded in the leap from the periphery to the center, for *individuation* has not been traced to its *inner necessity*. Art, on the other hand, has always carried out its task at the right time; in older and more recent works of art, it has, again and again, known how to dissolve the individuation through the lack of balance implanted in the individuation itself and how to free the idea from its deficient form. Guilt lies in lack of balance but, at the same time, (since the individual is only unbalanced because he is imperfect, hence he has no claim to permanence and must work toward his *destruction*) so does reconciliation, in so far as it can be demanded in the circle of art. This guilt is original, not to be distinguished from the concept of humanity, and hardly conscious on man's part, for it is a hypothesis along with life. As the darkest thread, it moves through the traditions of all peoples, and original sin is nothing more than a consequence derived from it with Christian modification. It does not depend on the direction of the human will; it accompanies all human action; whether we incline toward good or evil, we can be imbalanced there as here. The highest drama has to do with it, and it is not merely a matter of indifference whether the hero perishes as a result of his excellent or reprehensible aspiration, but it is necessary that it be the former to depict the most moving scene . . .

. . . As I construct it, drama by no means *ends* with a dissonance, for it resolves in itself the dualist form of existence as soon as it appears too dominantly, and it represents, if I am permitted a comparison, the two circles in the water which, precisely by expanding toward each other, destroy each other and dissolve into a single large circle which smoothes out once more the broken reflection of the sun. But one dissonance does remain unresolved, to be sure, the original one which was passed over in the beginning in accepting the individuation, without looking for the *causa prima,* as an immediate fact with or without creation; therefore it does not end with the *abrogation* of guilt, but with the inner cause of the guilt *unrevealed.* But this is the aspect in which the drama loses itself into one and the same night with the mystery of the world. Its highest attainment is the satisfaction it brings to the idea by the destruction of the individual who resists the idea either by his actions or by his very existence; a satisfaction which is, at times, incomplete because the individual perishes sullenly and defiantly and announces thus, ahead of time, that, at another time, he will reappear in the universe and fight once again; at other times, the satisfaction is complete because, in his very destruction, the individual gains a purified view of his relationship to the whole and dies in peace. But, in the second instance, this also satisfies only halfway, for even though the breach is healed, why did it have to occur? I have never found the answer to this, and no one will who seriously asks the question.

. . . I have not forgotten what I said above concerning the possibility of a symbolic drama which pursues the stream of history to its innermost sources, the religious ones, but perhaps I should now state explicitly that I was not by any means thinking of creating a dialogue from the dogmatic section of church history, but of a grandiose depiction of the few characters who, in their role as organic transmitters pass on the centuries, indeed millennia, and who, at times, like Luther for instance, themselves come into conflict with the ideas for which they are protagonists because they begin to shudder before the consequences of these ideas, which they had not suspected in the beginning. This drama could become universal since it would be of equal interest to all peoples; and it is not too daring to think of such a drama at a time when national differences are disappearing more and more. . . .

THREE PLAYS
BY
HEBBEL

PART ONE

Judith

Introduction to *Judith*

SUMMARY OF HEBBEL'S SOURCE:
THE APOCRYPHAL BOOK OF JUDITH

In the eighteenth year of his rule, the Assyrian King, Nebuchadnezzar, met with his ministers to plan the destruction of those peoples who had refused to aid him during his five-year war against Arphaxad. Holofernes, second in the realm, was to force the surrender of these people or destroy them. Wherever he marched in, he destroyed the local gods and introduced the worship of Nebuchadnezzar.

The Israelites, who had been living in Judea since their return from captivity and had reconsecrated their temple, now fortified their borders, villages and mountain summits. Joakim, the high priest in Jerusalem, wrote to Bethulia and Betomesthaim to urge the two cities to fortify themselves against attack by setting up guards in their mountain passes. The Israelites dressed in sackcloth and strewed ashes on their heads, praying for the safety of their land.

When Holofernes heard that Israel was prepared for war, he was enraged and summoned the leaders of the Canaanites to learn what he could about the Israelites. Achior, the commander of the Ammonites, told him that the Israelites were descended from the Chaldeans but had moved to Mesopotamia in order to worship a god in heaven rather than the Chaldean gods. Their god had then ordered them to move to Canaan, where they had lived and become rich. After a great famine had begun, they had moved to Egypt, where they had lived for a long time, had

29

become a very large people, and had finally been enslaved by the king. They had cried out to their god, and he had sent plagues to Egypt and helped them to flee. He had made the Red Sea dry up for them, led them through the desert, and they had eventually crossed the Jordan and settled in the mountain region. All was well with them while they did not sin against their god, but when they left him, they were destroyed or captured in many wars and their temple was razed. But now they had returned to their god and had come back together, had taken Jerusalem and the mountainous region, and the only way to defeat them would be to wait until they incurred the displeasure of their god. Holofernes refused to take the God of the Israelites seriously and ordered Achior taken to the mountains to be found and killed there with the Israelites. The latter found Achior there and he informed them of Holofernes' plans.

On the next day Holofernes began moving his troops toward Bethulia and cut off the water supplies of that city. The Israelites, faced with the prospect of languishing to death, were asked by Uzziah, one of the three magistrates to wait for five days before they surrendered to Holofernes, which some of them thought would be preferable.

When Judith, the beautiful rich widow of Manasse, who had lived in seclusion since her husband's death three years and four months before, and who fasted except on the Sabbath and feast days, heard of the five-day waiting period, she sent for the Elders to urge them not to set God any limits and to state her conviction that God would save them in His time. The Elders replied with the request that she pray for rain, but she answered that she would act to save Israel within these five days.

Judith put ashes on her head and prayed for the strength to destroy the Assyrians. Then she bathed and perfumed herself, dressed in beautiful clothes and jewelry, packed some food, wine, and dishes, and, accompanied by her maid, went outside the city gate. When the Assyrians found her, she told them that she would show Holofernes a safe entry into Bethulia, and they, admiring her great beauty, took her to Holofernes.

She told Holofernes that the sin of the Israelites would bring about their defeat, for they were planning to eat the food and drink the wine which had been consecrated to God, and this sacrilege would be punished by their destruction. As soon as they began, Judith would lead Holofernes into Judea. Holofernes was taken by her beauty and intelligence and promised to accept her god and establish her in the house of Nebuchadnezzar in return for her help. She refused his offer of food and wine, saying that she must use her own. When he asked what she would do when her supply gave out, she replied that God would permit her to carry out her mission before it did. The next morning, she received Holofernes' permission to leave his camp in order to pray. She stayed outside camp for three days and nights and prayed for His help in raising up the sons of her people. On the fourth day, Holofernes had a banquet, to which Judith, who had been invited, brought her own food. Holofernes drank too much wine, and, at the end of the evening, he was lying on his bed in a drunken stupor; everyone left; only Judith stayed behind. After she had prayed for divine help, she took Holofernes' scimitar and cut off his head. She gave the head to her maid, who put it in the foodbag. Then, as they had done on other days in order to pray, they left the Assyrian camp without attracting any attention.

In Bethulia, Judith showed the people the head of Holofernes and told them that he had never touched her but had been deceived by her beauty. She told the men to hang the head on the city wall and to go out to attack the Assyrians in the morning. Achior identified the head of Holofernes, and after he had heard Judith's story, was converted to faith in the God of Israel. In the morning, the Assyrians found Holofernes dead and fled before the attacking Israelites, who plundered the camp of Holofernes and gave Judith his canopy and dishes. The High Priest and the Senate came to Bethulia from Jerusalem to honor and bless Judith. The women came to her and danced and sang with her. Judith sang a song in praise of God, recounting God's greatness, Holofernes' threats, her feat, and her gratitude to God, Who can do all things for those who fear Him.

Finally, they all went to Jerusalem, where Judith dedicated Holofernes' canopy and dishes to God and then stayed to celebrate for three months.

Having returned to Bethulia, Judith, who never married again, became great and renowned, lived until the age of one hundred and five, and was mourned for seven days on the occasion of her death. "No one could terrify the Israelites in Judith's days, nor for a long time after she died."[1]

---

1. Retold from Edgar Goodspeed (translator), *The Apocrypha*, New York: Random House, 1959. The quotation is found on page 164.

ANALYSIS

Although, if I succeeded in carrying out my task, Judith and Holofernes are true individuals, they are also, at the same time, representatives of their peoples. Judith is the dizzying pinnacle of Judaism, of that people which believed that it had a personal relationship with the Deity; Holofernes is paganism hurtling into destruction; in his abundance of strength, the ultimate idea of history is contained, the idea of the god born from a human womb, but he attributes demiurgic power to his thoughts; he believes that he is what he thinks. Judaism and paganism are only representatives of humanity as it was split into an unresolvable dualism since the beginning of time, and thus, the conflict in which the elements of my tragedy crush each other has the highest symbolic meaning, although it is kindled by passion and brought to an end by emotion and confusion of the senses. The appearance of the prophet is, in a way, the thermometer of the whole. It indicates the level of the world's development at that time and it shows that created life had not been liberated sufficiently to be beyond the immediate interference of the power of the Highest, the Divine, and to be able to do without this power. A critic who failed to penetrate to the core of my work might ask how it could happen that Judith could be destroyed in her mind for doing what God had announced through his prophet and thus marked as necessary; such a critic might see a contradiction in the ending. But this is the working of the curse which rests on all mankind; even when he dedicates himself in the holiest enthusiasm to be a sacrifice to the Deity, man is never a totally pure sacrifice; his sinful birth conditions his sinful death, and, even if Judith truly perishes for the guilt of all men, in her consciousness she still only perishes on account of her own guilt. That is the basis for the absolute necessity of this ending. Because no human reconciliation is conceivable, the two sides of the scale must be absolutely equal, and the poet must leave undecided whether the invisible hand above the clouds will add another weight or not.[2]

In these words, Hebbel characterizes the basic elements of the drama: the conflicts within Judith, the conflict between two individuals, a man and a woman, and beyond that, the conflict between two cultures; all of these are symbolic of the conflict

2. From a letter to Madame Stich, April 3, 1840.

arising from the dualism of human nature itself, which leads to Judith's tragic end: that she will be punished as a woman for doing a man's deed which absolutely had to be done.

When we first encounter her, Judith is a young, beautiful girl who has apparently been cheated and deprived of leading a normal life through a combination of circumstances; Manasse's refusal to consummate the marriage, which she had apparently approached with modest but normal expectations, and his untimely death without ever explaining his lack of husbandly behavior. Judith has spent the time since his death in devout piety, has honored all the religious traditions and given alms to the poor, but has lived completely withdrawn from the world around her. For this reason, she is deemed a holy person by the community. But she herself knows that she has withdrawn because she feels that she has no share in normal life. She is neither a girl nor a woman in her own eyes; she is merely an animate object. She sees no point to her own life: "A woman is nothing; she can only develop into something through the man; she can become a mother through him. . . . Cursed are the unfruitful; doubly cursed am I, who am neither a virgin nor a woman! . . . My beauty is like that of the deadly nightshade; enjoyment of it leads to madness and death!"

Her experiences with her husband, who seemed to fear her, and with Ephraim, who is too much of a coward to win her respect, and her observation of the despair of the Bethulians frustrate her further, for she sees men as creatures who fail to use their strength and prerogative, while she is hampered by being a woman and forced by circumstances to lead a completely passive, useless existence. She has always envied men their more active role in life and now feels that Ephraim's unmanliness, typical as it is of the reactions of the Bethulians to Holofernes' appearance, gives her the right, indeed the duty to act, to rid her people of this godless aggressor.

After three days of praying and fasting and concentrating on her mission, she suddenly realizes, however, that she will only be able to carry out this mission *as a woman*. Her body must be the means by which she can approach Holofernes. She suddenly sees a divine reason for her virginity and her beauty. It is no longer hers, for it must be perfect if her mission is to succeed; it must be the sacrifice she brings to kill Holofernes. She realizes her own limitations as a woman when she begs God to protect her from seeing anything good about Holofernes. Only if he outrages her humanity with acts of inhumanity will she have the strength to kill him.

Holofernes is, without doubt, an ogre. His atrocities, which he proudly recounts, are endless; his excesses are incredible, and the world will be well rid of him when he is killed. His attitude toward women is that they offer a man satisfaction as do food and drink, no more, no less, and that this is all that they themselves want to do. But Holofernes has some good qualities. He has insuperable courage; he is capable of being generous; he spends himself in pursuit of greatness. But then, these good qualities are canceled by his arrogance, his seeing himself as a god.

When Judith asks, "Why am I a woman?" after his first kiss, we see her inner conflict very clearly. What she means is: why do I have to approach Holofernes in this way? Instead of facing him in open combat, I have to submit to him when I want to kill him! Why must I be subject to responding to the man in him? Why must I feel an attraction when I want to hate and kill. The theme of her ambivalence towards him is sustained until he orders her to kneel before him and worship him; from this point on, the hatred theme rises and dominates to the end. Her account of the rape leads her directly to murder. She feels violated, not only as a virgin, but, even more, as a woman, and, most of all, as a human being. She condemns Holofernes for using her, for making her into a counterintoxicant to wine, for his readiness so to debase a human being.

What fascinated Hebbel about the original story was the fact that a woman carried out an assassination:

> This most terrible contrast, this wanting and not being able, this doing which is still no action.[3]

To explain this act, he stated:

> The kind of courage which is ready to confront the most monstrous man can only emanate from the soul of a virgin; this is grounded in conviction in the human mind, is congruent with universal faith, is attested to by history. Therefore, the widow [of the Apocrypha] must be cut out. But a virgin's soul can sacrifice everything except itself, for, with its purity,

---

3. Hebbel's diary, November 24, 1839.

the basis of its strength is destroyed; it can no longer draw on its innocence once that innocence has been lost.[4]

His Judith had to be a virgin, for the woman in her had to be roused in order to be totally debased. She had to be demolished inwardly in order to become a tragic figure. When she first appears childish after her deed, this is not yet her tragic end; she is merely expressing her understandable horror at what has been done to her and at her own deed. It is not until she realizes that she might be carrying Holofernes' child that she becomes tragic. Hebbel wrote in the same entry:

> I can't use the Judith of the Bible. That Judith is a widow who lures Holofernes into the net with her trickery and cunning; she is happy to have his head in her sack and sings and expresses her jubilation with all of Israel for three months. That is mean; such a character is not worthy of success, Acts of this sort may be successfully committed by an enthusiasm which later feels its punishment within, but not by a deceitful nature which sees merit in good luck. My Judith is paralyzed by her deed; she is petrified at the possibility that she might bear the son of Holofernes; it becomes clear to her that she has exceeded beyond her limits, that, at the very least, she has done what is right for the wrong reasons.

Hebbel's Judith assumes tragic guilt in three ways: first, she feels an attraction for her enemy, for the monster who would destroy her people and her God; second, when she does kill him, her pure motive, her divine mission, is not the main drive, but, rather, she is impelled by deep, passionate hatred for the man who has violated her personal sanctity; third, by committing this act, she has overstepped her natural limitations, has reached beyond the limits of her sex. In transgressing these limits, she has upset world order as much as Holofernes, who overstepped his human limits by seeing himself as a god. In order to restore world equilibrium, or harmony to the universe, Hebbel's Judith must die, and must do so to expiate her personal guilt. This guilt is tangibly evident, if indeed she is bearing a son. He too must be killed, for he is the product of two human beings who overstepped their limits and constituted threats to the survival of universal order. The inevitability of personal guilt in indi-

---

4. Diary, January 3, 1840.

viduation, of being guilty of upsetting the order of the universe by committing the very act necessary for its restoration, the perfect balance of innocence and guilt in the tragic hero or heroine, is basic to Hebbel's conception of tragedy, to his image of "the two pails of the well, only one of which can be full at any one time."

Because Holofernes is killed in his sleep, he can neither aver nor condemn his individuation, although his final statement surely indicates that he would cling to it with stubborn defiance. In the case of Judith, however, there is self-abhorrence as soon as she has committed the murder: she speaks childishly; she wants no credit; while she gives God the glory for the liberation of her people, she clearly feels that this same God will inflict deserved punishment on her. Thus, Hebbel balances the spectator's reaction between moral satisfaction and moral vacuum. Whether his Judith bears a child or not, she has forfeited the opportunity of leading any kind of normal life; she is broken *by* and *because of* her individuation.

There is still another element basic to Hebbel's concept of tragedy. Since life is "being and becoming," the world is constant in its existence and constantly undergoing change. Hebbel likes to pitch his dramas against the background of changing times. Any given period of history, any present, belongs with its past in respect to change and thus forms a transition for the future. In *Judith,* Holofernes has rejected the old faith of the pagans, does not believe in any pagan gods, rejects Nebuchadnezzar's divinity, and considers himself more divine than his ruler; he understands the longing of mankind to immortalize itself and sees the culmination of this longing in the birth of a god from a mortal mother. Thus, in his readiness to overthrow the old religion, he is transitional to the new. But he is not ready to submit to the God of the new monotheism; he is too exuberant and sanguine, and strays into the error of desiring to be worshipped himself. He is not ready to move into the new era; in fact, while he lives and conquers, he endangers the existence of monotheism.

Judith

DRAMATIS PERSONAE

JUDITH
HOLOFERNES
HOLOFERNES' OFFICERS
HOLOFERNES' VALET
EMISSARIES FROM LYBIA
EMISSARIES FROM MESOPOTAMIA
SOLDIERS AND HERALDS
MIRZA, *Judith's maid*
EPHRAIM
THE ELDERS OF BETHULIA
THE PRIESTS OF BETHULIA
CITIZENS OF BETHULIA *including:*
AMMON
HOSEA
BEN
ASSAD *and his brother*
DANIEL, *mute, blind, inspired by God*
SAMAJA, *Assad's friend*
JOSHUA
DELIA, *Samaja's Wife*
ACHIOR, *Captain of the Moabites*
ASSYRIAN PRIESTS
WOMEN
CHILDREN
SAMUEL, *an ancient man*
SAMUEL'S GRANDSON
   The action takes place near and in the city of Bethulia.

ACT I

*Holofernes' camp. In the foreground, on the right, the tent of
the general. Other tents. Soldiers and crowds. The background
is enclosed in a range of mountains in which a city is visible.
General Holofernes enters from the open tent with his officers.
Music is heard. After a while, he signals. The music stops.*

HOLOFERNES: Make sacrifice!

HIGH PRIEST: To which god?

HOLOFERNES: To whom did you make offering yesterday?

HIGH PRIEST: We cast lots, as you had commanded, and the lot
decided for Baal.

HOLOFERNES: Then Baal isn't hungry today. Then make your
offering to one whom you all know and still don't know at all!

HIGH PRIEST (*with loud voice*): Holofernes commands us to
make offering to a god whom we all know and still don't know
at all.

HOLOFERNES (*laughing*): That is the god I respect the most.
    (*Offering is made*)

HOLOFERNES: Herald!

HERALD: What does Holofernes command?

HOLOFERNES: If anyone among my soldiers desires to complain
about his commanding officer, let him step forward. Announce it.

HERALD (*going through the formations of soldiers*): Whoever
desires to complain about his commanding officer, let him step
forward. Holofernes will hear him.

A SOLDIER: I have a complaint about my officer.

HOLOFERNES: Why?

SOLDIER: In yesterday's offensive, I captured a slave who was
so beautiful that I felt shy when I looked at 'her and did not
dare to touch her. The officer enters the tent in the evening

when I'm away, sees the girl, and strikes her down when she resists him.

HOLOFERNES: The accused officer is condemned to death! (*To a soldier*) Hurry! But his accuser as well. Take him along! But the officer is to die first.

SOLDIER: You want to have me killed along with him?

HOLOFERNES: Because you are too bold! I had the announcement made to test you men. If I permitted the likes of you to complain about your officers, who'd protect me from the complaints of the officers?

SOLDIER: I'd saved the girl for you! I was going to bring her to you!

HOLOFERNES: If a beggar finds a crown, he knows, of course, that it belongs to the king. The king doesn't waste much time in thanking him when he brings it. But I will award your good intentions since I am in a merciful mood this morning. You may get yourself drunk on my best wine before your execution. Take him away!

(*The soldier is led to the background*)

HOLOFERNES (*to one of the officers*): Have the camels tethered.

OFFICER: It's been done.

HOLOFERNES: Had I already commanded it?

OFFICER: No, but I could anticipate that you'd command it next.

HOLOFERNES: Who are you that you presume to steal my thoughts out of my head? I don't like this aggressive servility. My will is number one; your action, number two, not the other way around. Don't forget it!

OFFICER: I beg your pardon! (*Off*)

HOLOFERNES (*alone*): That's the real art: not to let yourself be calculated, but always to stay a mystery. Water does not know this, so they've dammed the sea and dug a bed for the river. Fire hasn't mastered the art either; it's fallen so low that the kitchen boys have investigated its nature and now it has to boil cabbage for any rascal who wants it. Not even the sun knows it: they've spied out its path and shoemakers and tailors measure time by its shadows. But I have mastered the art! They lurk about me and peer into the cracks and crevices of my soul, and, out of every word I utter, they try to forge a wrench to open up the chambers of my heart. But my present is never consistent with my past; I am not one of those fools who fall flat on their faces in cowardly vanity and make each day the other's fool; no, I cheerfully hack up today's Holofernes into little pieces and feed him to tomorrow's Holofernes. I don't see merely a dull feeding process in life, but rather a steady transformation and rebirth of existence. Indeed, at times, I feel among all these fools that I am alone, as though they could only become aware of themselves if I cut off their arms and legs. They notice this more and more, but, instead of climbing up on top of me, they wretchedly withdraw from me and flee like a rabbit who flees from fire which might singe his whiskers. If I only had one enemy, just one, who'd dare to confront me! I'd kiss him; indeed, after I'd made him bite the dust, in hot battle, I'd throw myself upon him and die with him! Nebuchadnezzar is, unfortunately, nothing but an arrogant cipher who passes the time by eternally multiplying himself. If I subtract myself and Assyria, nothing remains but a human skin stuffed with fat. I want to conquer the world for him, and, when he has it, I want to take it away from him!

AN OFFICER: A messenger from our great King is arriving.

HOLOFERNES: Lead him to me at once. (*To himself*) Neck, are you still agile enough to bow? Nebuchadnezzar sees to it that you don't forget how it's done.

MESSENGER: Nebuchadnezzar, before whom the earth cringes and to whom power and dominion has been given from ascent to descent sends to his general, Holofernes, the greetings of power.

HOLOFERNES: I humbly await his command.

MESSENGER: Nebuchadnezzar does not wish that other gods be honored with him in the future.

HOLOFERNES (*proudly*): He probably decided this when he received news of my latest victories.

MESSENGER: Nebuchadnezzar commands that sacrifice be offered to him alone, and that the altars and temples of the other gods be consumed by fire and flames.

HOLOFERNES (*to himself*): One instead of many; that's quite convenient. But it is most convenient for the king himself. He just takes his shiny helmet in hand and worships before his own image. But he must avoid stomach cramps, lest he grimace and startle himself. (*Aloud*) Nebuchadnezzar surely had no more toothaches last month?

MESSENGER: We thank the gods for that.

HOLOFERNES: You mean, you thank him.

MESSENGER: Nebuchadnezzar commands that sacrifices be brought to him every morning at sunrise.

HOLOFERNES: Unfortunately, it's too late today. We'll think of him at sunset.

MESSENGER: Finally, Nebuchadnezzar commands you, Holofernes, to take care of yourself and not risk your life so carelessly.

HOLOFERNES: Indeed, my friend, if only swords could accomplish something worthwhile without men. And then—look, I don't abuse my life with anything as much as drinking the King's health, and I certainly can't stop that.

MESSENGER: Nebuchadnezzar says that none of his servants could take your place and that he still has much for you to do.

HOLOFERNES: All right. I'll love myself because my King commands it. I kiss his footstool.

(*Messenger off*)

HOLOFERNES: Herald!

HERALD: What does Holofernes command?

HOLOFERNES: There is no god but Nebuchadnezzar. Make it known.

HERALD (*going through the formations of soldiers*) : There is no god but Nebuchadnezzar.

(*A high priest passes*)

HOLOFERNES: Priest, have you heard what I've had proclaimed?

PRIEST: Yes.

HOLOFERNES: Then go and destroy the Baal which we're dragging along with us. You may keep the wood.

PRIEST: How can I destroy what I've worshipped?

HOLOFERNES: Let Baal defend himself. There are two possibilities: either you destroy the god or you hang yourself.

PRIEST: I'll destroy him. (*To himself*) Baal wears golden bracelets.

HOLOFERNES (*alone*) : Cursed be Nebuchadnezzar! Cursed, because he had a great idea, an idea which he does not bring to the honor due it, which he can only cripple and make a laughing stock! It's true, I've felt it for a long time: humanity has only one great purpose: to give birth to a god; and the god which it creates, how can he show that he is a god except by opposing mankind in eternal conflict, by suppressing all the foolish emotions of pity, of shuddering before himself, of fainting in the face of his gigantic task, by crushing humanity to dust and forcing it to cry with jubilation, even in the very hour of death. Nebuchadnezzar knows how to make it easier for himself. The herald must designate him as god, and I am to provide the world with proof that he is.

(*The high priest passes*)

HOLOFERNES: Is Baal destroyed?

PRIEST: He is going up in flames; I hope he'll forgive me.

HOLOFERNES: There is no god but Nebuchadnezzar. I command you to find the reasons for this. I shall pay with an ounce of gold for each reason, and you have three days to come up with them.

PRIEST: I hope to live up to your command. (*Off*)

AN OFFICER: Emissaries of a king beg to be received.

HOLOFERNES: Which king?

OFFICER: Forgive me. It's impossible to remember the names of all the kings who humble themselves before you.

HOLOFERNES (*throws him a golden chain*): The first impossibility I like! Bring them in.

EMISSARIES (*prostrate themselves*): Thus the king of Lybia will prostrate himself in the dust before you if you will be merciful enough to occupy his capital.

HOLOFERNES: Why didn't you come yesterday or the day before?

EMISSARIES: Lord!

HOLOFERNES: Was the distance too great or your respect too small?

EMISSARIES: Woe on us!

HOLOFERNES (*to himself*): Rage fills my soul, rage against Nebuchadnezzar. I must be merciful so that this race of worms does not flatter itself that it is the source of my rage. (*Aloud*) Rise and tell your king—

OFFICER (*enters*): Emissaries from Mesopotamia!

HOLOFERNES: Bring them in.

MESOPOTAMIAN EMISSARIES (*prostrate themselves*): Mesopotamia offers its subjection to the great Holofernes if it can attain his mercy by so doing.

HOLOFERNES: I give my mercy away! I don't sell it.

MESOPOTAMIAN EMISSARIES: Not thus. Mesopotamia accepts all conditions. It only hopes for mercy.

HOLOFERNES: I don't know whether I can fulfill this hope. You've waited a long time.

MESOPOTAMIAN EMISSARIES: No longer than the long road demanded.

HOLOFERNES: No matter. I've vowed that I'll annihilate the last people to humble itself before me. I must keep my vow.

MESOPOTAMIAN EMISSARIES: We are not the last. On the way we heard that the Hebrews, the only ones among all, want to offer you resistance and have barricaded themselves.

HOLOFERNES: Then bring your king my message that I accept his capitulation. As to conditions, he will learn about those from my officer, whom I'll send to him for implementation. (*To the*

Lybian emissaries) Tell your king the same. (*To the Mesopotamian emissaries*) Who are the Hebrews?

MESOPOTAMIAN EMISSARIES: Lord, they are a people of madmen! You can tell that by the very fact that they presume to resist you. You can tell it even more clearly by the fact that they worship a god whom they can neither see nor hear, of whom no one knows where he dwells, and to whom they still make offering as though he looked down upon them with a wild and menacing face like our gods. They live in the mountains.

HOLOFERNES: What cities do they have? What can they do? Which king rules them? How many soldiers do they have?

MESOPOTAMIAN EMISSARIES: Lord, these people are hidden and distrustful. We don't know much more about them than they know about their invisible god. They shun contact with foreign peoples. They don't eat or drink with us; at best, they fight against us.

HOLOFERNES: Why speak if you can't answer my question? (*Signals; the emissaries bow, prostrate themselves; off*) The officers of the Moabites and Ammonites are to appear. (*Herald off*) I respect a people that offers me resistance. Too bad, that I must destroy everything I respect.

(*Officers enter, among them Achior.*)

HOLOFERNES: What kind of people lives in these mountains?

ACHIOR: Lord, I know this people well, and I'll tell you all about it. They are full of scorn when they go out with spears and swords; the weapons are useless toys in their hands, toys which their own god shatters, for he does not want them to fight and stain themselves with blood. He alone will destroy their enemies. But this people is awe-inspiring when it humbles itself before its god as he demands. They fall on their knees, strew their heads with ashes, utter laments, and curse themselves. Then it is as though the world were transformed, as though nature had forgotten its own laws. The impossible becomes real; the sea parts so that the waters stand firm on both sides like walls between which a street is placed, bread falls from the heavens, and, out of the desert sands, fresh drink gushes forth.

HOLOFERNES: What is the name of their god?

ACHIOR: They consider it robbing him to express it and would surely kill the stranger who tried.

HOLOFERNES: What kind of cities do they have?

ACHIOR (*points to the city in the mountains*): Bethulia is the name of their nearest city, which you see over there. They have barricaded it. But their capital is called Jerusalem. I've been there and seen the temple of their god. It is unequalled on earth. When I stood before it and gazed at it with admiration, I felt as though something were fastening itself around my neck and pushing me to the ground. Suddenly, I lay upon my knees and didn't even know myself how it had happened. They almost stoned me, for, when I rose again, I felt the irresistible urge to enter the sanctuary, and that's punishable by death.—A beautiful girl stepped in my path and told me so; I don't know whether she felt sorry for me because I was so young or feared that the temple would be defiled by a pagan. Now, listen to me, Lord, and do not scorn my words; try to learn whether this people has sinned against its god; if so, let us go there; then their god will surely place them in your hands, and you'll grind them underfoot easily. If they have not sinned against their god, turn back, for their god will protect them and we will become a laughing stock everywhere. You are a powerful hero, but their god is too mighty. If he can not confront you with an opponent who is your equal, he can force you to rise up against yourself and to eliminate yourself by your own hand.

HOLOFERNES: Do you prophesy out of fear or cunning of heart? I could punish you for presuming to fear anyone but me. But I shall not; I'll let your own judgement stand. Whatever awaits the Hebrews awaits you too! Seize him and lead him there in safety. (*This is done*) And I shall match the weight of his head in gold as payment to the man who kills him and brings it to me when we occupy the city! (*Raises his voice*) We're off to Bethulia! (*Procession*)

ACT II

Judith's room. Judith and Mirza at the loom.

JUDITH: What do you make of this dream?

MIRZA: Come now, I wish you'd take my advice.

JUDITH: I walked and walked, was in quite a hurry, and still didn't know where I felt impelled to go. At times, I stopped and thought, and then I felt as though I were committing a great sin; 'keep going,' I said to myself and walked even faster.

MIRZA: Ephraim just passed by. He looked very sad.

JUDITH (*without listening to her*) : Suddenly I stood on a high mountain; I was dizzy at first, but then I felt proud; the sun was so close to me, I nodded to it and kept looking upward. Suddenly, I noticed an abyss at my feet, just a few steps away, dark, fathomless, full of smoke and fumes. I could not go back, neither could I stand still,—I staggered towards it; 'God! God!' I cried out in my terror; 'I am here!' came the reply from the abyss, a kind voice, a sweet one; I leapt; soft arms caught me; I thought I was resting in the embrace of one I could not see. I felt more wonderful than I can say. But I was too heavy; he could not hold me. I sank and sank and heard him weep, and something that felt like hot tears dropped on my cheek—

MIRZA: I know an interpreter of dreams. Shall I have him come?

JUDITH: Unfortunately, it's against the law. But I know one thing; one should not take such dreams lightly! I think it's this way: When a human being sleeps, relaxed, no longer inhibited by his self-consciousness, then a feeling of the future pushes all thoughts and images of the present away, and the things which are to come glide through the soul as shades; they prepare it, warn it; console it. That's why we are so rarely or never truly surprised, and why we confidently hope for the good before it happens and instinctively tremble before any evil occurs. I've often wondered whether we also dream just before we die.

MIRZA: Why don't you ever listen when I mention Ephraim to you?

JUDITH: Because I am afraid of men.

MIRZA: But you were married, after all—

JUDITH: I must confide a secret to you. My husband was insane.

MIRZA: That's impossible! How could I have failed to notice?

JUDITH: He was, though; I have to call it that, if I am not to be afraid of myself, if I am not to believe that I am a dreadful, terrifying creature. You see, I was not even fourteen years old when I was brought to Manasses; you'll remember that evening, for you followed me. With each step I took, I became more frightened; at times, I thought I should soon stop living altogether; then, at other moments, that I was just about to begin. Oh, and the evening was so beguiling, so tempting, one could not resist it. The warm wind raised my veil as though it wanted to say: it's time now; but I held on to it, for I felt my face glow and was ashamed of it. My father walked by my side. He was very serious and said some things to which I did not listen; at times, I looked up to his face and thought: Manasses surely looks different. Didn't you notice any of this? You were with me.

MIRZA: I was sharing your feeling of shame.

JUDITH: Finally, I arrived at his house, and his old mother came to meet me with a somber expression. I had difficulty in addressing her as mother because I thought that my own mother must feel that in her grave and be hurt by it. Then you anointed me with nard and oil, and that made me feel as though I were dead and being anointed as a corpse. You even said that I was turning pale. Then Manasses came, and when he looked at me, first shyly, then more and more boldly, I felt as though I were being set on fire and as though tall flames were shooting forth from inside me. Forgive me for saying that.

MIRZA: You pressed your face between your hands for a few moments; then, you got up very quickly and threw your arms around his neck. I was quite startled.

JUDITH: I saw it and laughed at you, and I suddenly believed myself to be vastly more clever than you. Now listen, Mirza. We went into the bedroom; the old woman did all sorts of strange things and said something like a blessing. I felt depressed and frightened again when I was alone with Manasses. Three lights were lit, and he wanted to put them out. 'No, no,' I said pleadingly. 'Little fool,' he said and wanted to take hold of me— then, one of the lights went out; he hardly noticed; he kissed me—and the second went out. He shuddered and I after him; then he laughed and said: 'I'll put out the third myself!' 'Quickly!', I said, for I felt chills; he did. The moon shone brightly into the room; I slipped into bed, and the moon shone right in my face! Manasses exclaimed: 'I see you as clearly as by daylight!' and came towards me. Suddenly he stopped; it was as though the black earth had stretched forth a hand and seized him from below. It seemed weird to me; 'Come, come!' I cried and wasn't even ashamed to do so. 'I can't,' he replied with a dull, leaden tone, 'I can not!' he repeated and stared at me terrifyingly with his eyes wide open. Then he staggered to the window and said, perhaps ten times, 'I can not!' He did not seem to see me at all, he seemed to see something strange and terrifying.

MIRZA: You poor girl!

JUDITH: I began to cry violently. I felt defiled; I hated and abhorred myself. He said tender, loving words to me; I held out my arms to him, but, instead of coming to me, he began to pray quietly. My heart stopped beating! I felt as though I were freezing in my very blood! I burrowed into myself as though I were something strange, and, when I finally, gradually, lost myself in sleep, I felt as though I were awaking. On the next morning, Manasses stood in front of my bed; he looked at me with infinite pity. I felt depressed to the point of suffocation; then it was as though something snapped inside me. I broke out into wild laughter and could breathe again. His mother looked at me darkly and scornfully; I could tell that she had listened, but she didn't say one word to me, but went to a corner of the room with her son and whispered to him. 'No, indeed not!' he suddenly shouted angrily; 'Judith is an angel,' he added and wanted to kiss me; I refused him my mouth; he nodded strangely, seemed to agree that this was best. (*After a long pause*) I was his wife for six months—he never touched me!

MIRZA: And—?

JUDITH: We walked along, side by side, and felt that we belonged together, but it was as though something stood between us, something dark and unknown. At times he looked at me with an expression which made me shudder. I could have choked him to death at such a moment, out of fear, in self-defense. His eyes bored into me like a poison arrow. You know, it was three years ago, during the barley harvest, that he came home from the field and was sick, and then dying after a day and a half. It seemed to me that he was going to steal away after robbing me of my innermost self. I hated him because of his illness. I felt as though he were threatening to violate me with his death. 'He must not die'—was the cry within me—'he must not take his secret to the grave; you must find the courage to ask him at last.' 'Manasses,' I said, bending over him, 'what happened on our wedding night?' His dark eyes had already closed; he opened them with difficulty—I shuddered, for he seemed to raise himself out of his body as though it were a coffin. He looked at me for a long time; then he said: 'yes, yes; yes, now I may tell you, you—' but quickly, as though I should never be permitted to learn the answer, death stepped between him and me and closed his mouth forever. (*After a long silence*) Tell me, Mirza, must I not go mad myself, if I stop considering Manasses mad?

MIRZA: This makes me shudder!

JUDITH: You've often noticed that I've suddenly collapsed completely and begun to pray when I've been quietly sitting at the loom or some other work. For this reason, I've been called pious and God-fearing. I tell you, Mirza, if I do that, it is because I

JUDITH
Deutsches Schauspielhaus Hamburg, May 28, 1966
Director: Gerhard Klingenberg
Joana Maria Gorvin as Judith
Photo by Rosemarie Clausen

JUDITH
Deutsches Schauspielhaus Hamburg, May 28, 1966
Director: Gerhard Klingenberg
Rolf Boysen as Holofernes
Photo by Rosemarie Clausen

JUDITH
Deutsches Schauspielhaus Hamburg, May 28, 1966
Director: Gerhard Klingenberg
Joana Maria Gorvin as Judith and Andrea Grosske as Mirza
Photo by Rosemarie Clausen

don't know how to save myself from this thought. Then my prayer is a submersion in God; it is only a type of suicide; I leap into the Eternal like a despairing man who leaps into deep water—

MIRZA *(deliberately changing the subject)* : During such moments, you ought to stand in front of the mirror. The nighttime ghosts would disappear shyly and be blinded by the glow of your youth.

JUDITH: Oh, you fool, do you know of a fruit that can eat itself? It would be better not to be young and beautiful if one has to be so for oneself alone! A woman is nothing; she can only develop into something through the man; she can become a mother through him. The child she bears is the expression of thanks she can give to Nature for her own life. Cursed are the unfruitful; doubly cursed am I who am neither a virgin nor a woman!

MIRZA: Who would prevent you from being young and beautiful for others, even for a beloved young man? Haven't you the choice among the very best?

JUDITH *(very seriously)* : You haven't understood anything I've said! My beauty is like that of the deadly nightshade; enjoyment of it leads to madness or death!

EPHRAIM *(enters hastily)* : How can you two be so calm when Holofernes stands at our gates!

MIRZA: Then may God be merciful to us!

EPHRAIM: Indeed, Judith, if you had seen what I saw, you'd be trembling! One could swear, the pagans have everything in their employ to inspire fear and horror. This great number of camels and horses, of wagons and battering rams! It's fortunate that walls and gates have no eyes! They would collapse with fright if they could see all these horrors!

JUDITH: I think you've seen more than everybody else.

EPHRAIM: I tell you, Judith, there is no one in all of Bethulia now who does not look as though he had a fever. You seem to know little about Holofernes; I know much more about him. Every word his mouth speaks is like a raging beast! When it's dark at night—

JUDITH: He calls for the lanterns to be lighted.

EPHRAIM: We do that, you and I! He has his men set fire to entire villages and says: 'These are my lanterns! I get them cheaper than others.' and he thinks he is very gracious indeed when he has his sword polished or a roast cooked in the fire that's burning a city! When he saw Bethulia, he is said to have laughed and asked his cook scornfully: 'Do you think that you can roast an ostrich egg in that?'

JUDITH: I'd like to see him! (*To herself*) What did I say?

EPHRAIM: Woe unto you, if you were ever seen by him! Holofernes kills women with kisses and embraces as he kills men with spears and swords. If he had known that you were within these walls, he would have come just for you.

JUDITH (*smiling*): I wish it were that way! Then I'd just have to go out to meet him, and our city and country would be saved.

EPHRAIM: You alone have the right to imagine such things!

JUDITH: And why not? One for all, and, at that, one who has always asked herself in vain: 'Why do I exist?' Ha, and even if he had not come for me, could one not get him to the point of believing that he had? If the giant's head towers so far into the clouds that you can't reach him, then throw a precious stone at his feet. He'll stoop to pick it up, and then you can easily overpower him.

EPHRAIM (*to himself*): My plan was naive. What was supposed to frighten her and drive her into my arms makes her courageous instead. I feel condemned when I look into her eyes. I hoped she would look for a protector during these hard times, and who was closer to her than I? (*Aloud*) Judith, you are so courageous that you stop being beautiful!

JUDITH: If you are a man, you may say that to me!

EPHRAIM: I am a man and may say more to you. Look, Judith, bad times are coming, times during which no one is safe except those who inhabit graves. How will you survive them since you have no father, no brother, no husband?

JUDITH: You aren't trying to have Holofernes plead your case for you, are you?

EPHRAIM: Make fun of me, but listen. I know that you've rejected me, and if the world around us had not changed so threateningly, I'd never have come to you again. Do you see this knife?

JUDITH: It's so shiny, I can see myself reflected in it.

EPHRAIM: I sharpened it the day you rejected me with a scornful laugh, and, honestly, if the Assyrians were not standing at our gate, it would now be in my heart! Then you could not use it as a mirror, for my blood would have made it rusty.

JUDITH: Give it to me. (*She points it toward his hand, which*

he pulls back) Come now! You dare to mention suicide and fear
a cut in your hand.

EPHRAIM: You are standing before me: I see you, I hear you.
Now I love myself, for I no longer feel myself. I am full of you!
Such an act is only successful in the dark of night, when nothing
is awake in my heart but pain, when death shuts the soul, as
sleep shuts the eyes, and when one believes that one is doing
instinctively what an invisible force demands. Oh, I know it
well, this feeling, for I had come to such a point that I don't
know myself why I did not finish it! That has nothing to do
with courage or cowardice; it's like bolting a door when one
wants to sleep.

(*Judith extends her hand to him*)

EPHRAIM: Judith, I love you, but you don't love me. You can't
help the one; I can't help the other. But do you know what
it means to love and to be rejected? That's like no other suffering.
If you take something away from me today, I'll learn tomorrow
that I can do without it. If someone wounds me, I have a chance
that the wound may heal. But if my love is treated like folly,
then what is most sacred in my heart is made into a lie. After
all, if the feeling which draws me to you deceives me, what
assurance is there for me that it is the truth which makes me
kneel before God?

MIRZA: Don't you feel it, Judith?

JUDITH: Can love be a duty? Must I give him my hand to
make him drop his dagger? I almost believe it!

EPHRAIM: Judith, I ask you once more, that is, I ask for permission to die for you. I only want to be the shield which will
dull the swords which threaten you.

JUDITH: Is this the same man whom the mere sight of the
enemy camp seemed to have defeated? Who seemed like someone
to whom I'd have to lend one of my skirts? His eyes flame; his
hands form fists! Oh God, I like to respect people; I feel as
though I were cutting into myself when I must despise someone!
Ephraim, I've hurt you! I'm very sorry! I wanted to stop seeming
worthy of your love to you, for I could give you nothing; that's
why I spoke scornfully to you. I want to reward you now, and
I can! But woe unto you, if you fail to understand me now, if
as soon as I speak the words, the deed, as demanding as necessity
itself, does not confront your soul, if you don't feel that you
are only alive to carry it out! Go and kill Holofernes! Then—
demand the reward you wish from me.

EPHRAIM: You are mad! Kill Holofernes in the midst of his soldiers! How could that be done?

JUDITH: How that can be done? Do I know? If I did, I'd do it myself. I only know that it's necessary to do this.

EPHRAIM: I've never seen him, but now I do!

JUDITH: I see him too, with his face which is all eyes, commanding eyes, and his feet before which the earth upon which he walks seems to shrink away. But there was a time, when he was not; therefore, a time can come, when he will no longer be!

EPHRAIM: Give him the thunder and remove his army from him, and I'll try it, but now—

JUDITH: Just will it! And up from the depths of the abyss and down from the firmament of heaven you will summon holy, protecting forces and they will bless and shield your deeds, if not you! For you want what is universally wanted: that about which God broods in his first rage and which Nature plans while gnashing her teeth in torturing dreams, she who trembles before the gigantic creature born from her own womb and will not create the second man like him unless she does it to have him annihilate the first.

EPHRAIM: You demand the unthinkable from me only because you hate me and want to kill me.

JUDITH (*glowing*): I did not misjudge you! What's this? Such an idea does not inspire you? Doesn't even intoxicate you? I, whom you love, and who wish to raise you beyond yourself so that I should be able to return your love, I place this thought into your soul, and it means nothing to you but a burden which presses you more deeply into the dust? You see, if you had received the idea exultantly, if impulsively you had reached for your sword, and had not even taken the time for a quick farewell, then, oh, I feel it, then I would have cried and thrown myself in your path; I'd have elaborated on the danger with the fear of a heart which trembles for the one it loves most; I'd have kept you from it or followed you. But now—ha! I am more than justified; your love is your punishment for your impoverished nature; it is your curse that you be consumed by it; I'd be enraged at myself if I were ever to catch myself feeling even a little sorry for you. I understand you completely, even understand that what is loftiest must seem lowest of all to you; that you must smile when I pray!

EPHRAIM: Despise me! But first show me the one who makes the impossible possible!

JUDITH: I shall show him to you! He will come! He has to come! And if your cowardice is that of your entire sex, if all men see nothing in danger but the warning to beware of it—then a woman has attained the right to perform a great deed, then—ha! I've demanded it of you; I'll have to prove that it's possible!

ACT III

Judith's room. She sits huddled in rags, strewn with ashes.

MIRZA *(enters and looks at her)* : She's been sitting like this for three days and nights. She won't eat; she won't drink; she won't speak. She does not even sigh or lament. I screamed at her last night, 'the house is on fire!' and acted as though I had gone mad, but she didn't even move a muscle. I think she wants to be placed inside a coffin, have the cover nailed down, and be carried off. She hears everything I'm saying, but replies nothing. Judith, shall I call the grave digger?

(Judith signals for her to leave)

MIRZA: I'm leaving, but only to return immediately. I'm forgetting all about our enemy and all the danger because of you. If someone aimed an arrow at me, I'd not notice it as long as I see you sitting there, alive and yet dead. At first you showed so much courage that all the men were ashamed, and now—Ephraim was right; he said: 'she's challenging herself in order to forget her fear.' *(Off)*

JUDITH *(falls to her knees)* : Oh God! I feel as though I'd have to catch at the very edge of Your garment, as though You were threatening to leave me forever! I didn't want to pray, but I have to, as I have to breathe if I am not to suffocate! God! God! Why do You not look down upon me; I am too weak to rise up to meet you! Behold, I lie here as though outside of the world and of time; I anxiously await a signal from You which will command me to rise and act. I rejoiced to see danger approaching us, for to me it was merely a sign that You wanted to glorify Yourself among Your chosen people. With shuddering joy, I realized that what elevated me threw everyone else to the ground, for it appeared to me as if Your finger were mercifully pointing at me; as though Your triumph were to emanate from me! Enraptured, I realized that the man, for whose sake I had renounced the great deed in order to make the greatest sacrifice with humility, was cowardly and trembled, indeed crawled into hiding in the slough of his wretchedness like a worm. 'You are the one!' I cried to myself and prostrated myself before You and vowed with a precious vow never to rise again unless You showed me the way which leads to the heart of Holofernes. I kept listening within because I believed that the lightning of annihilation would have to leap up from my soul; I've also listened to the outside because I thought a heroic man has made me superfluous; but, within and without, darkness remains. Just *one* thought has come to me, just *one,* which I've entertained and which keeps returning to me; but it did not come from You. Or did it?—(*She leaps up*) It did come from You! The path to my deed crosses sin! Thank You, thank You, my Lord! You give light to my eyes. The impure becomes pure in Your sight; if You place a sin between me and my deed, who am I to quarrel with You about it, to withdraw from You because of it! Is not my deed worth as much as it will cost me? Am I permitted to love my honor, my pure body more than You? Oh, I feel something loosen inside me like a knot. You've made me beautiful; now I know why. You denied me a child; now I feel for what reason, and I'm glad that I don't have doubly myself to love. What I've always considered a curse now appears to me as a blessing! (*She steps before a mirror*) I greet you, my image! Be ashamed, cheeks, for not glowing as yet; is the road between you and my heart such a long one? Eyes, I praise you; you've drunk fire; you are intoxicated! My poor mouth, I don't blame you for being pale; you are about to kiss horror itself! (*She leaves the mirror*) Holofernes, all this is yours; I no longer have any share in it. Take it, but tremble when you have it; I shall leap out of myself, like a sword out of a sheath, when you least expect it, and I shall be paid for with your life! If I have to kiss you, I shall imagine that my lips are poisoned; if I embrace you, I'll think that I am choking you to death! Oh God, have him commit monstrous acts before my eyes; let him shed blood atrociously, but protect me from seeing anything good about him!

MIRZA (*enters*): Did you call me, Judith?

JUDITH: No, yes. Mirza, you are to help me dress up.

MIRZA: Won't you eat?

JUDITH: No, I want to be dressed up.

MIRZA: Eat, Judith. I can't stand it any longer.

JUDITH: You?

MIRZA: You see, when you refused to eat and drink, I vowed

that I wouldn't either! I did that to force you. If you didn't
have pity on yourself, you were to have it on me. I told you
about it, but you probably did not hear me.

JUDITH: I wish that I were deserving of so much love.

MIRZA: Let's eat and drink. It will soon be for the last time
anyway, at least as far as drinking is concerned. The pipes that
were connected to the well have been cut off. No one can
reach the small wells near the wall either, because they are
guarded by soldiers. But some people have already gone out
there because they preferred being killed to remaining thirsty
any longer. They tell about one man who was dying and still
managed to crawl to the well to have a final drink, but, before
he could bring the water in his hands to touch his lips, he died.
No one expected this cruelty from the enemy and for that reason,
there is not enough water anywhere in the city. If anyone has
a little left, he hides it like a treasure.

JUDITH: How monstrous to take what is necessary for life
instead of the life one can't take. Kill, singe, and burn, but do
not deprive man who lives in the abundance of nature of that
which is essential to life! Oh, I've already waited too long!

MIRZA: Ephraim brought me water for you. You can see by
that how great his love for you is. He'd denied it to his own
brother.

JUDITH: How horrible! He is one of those people who even
commit a sin when they want to do good.

MIRZA: I didn't like that either, but you are still too hard
on him.

JUDITH: No, I tell you, no! Every woman has the right to
demand from every man that he be a hero. When you see a
man, don't you feel as though you were seeing what you'd like
to be and should be? One man may forgive another for his
cowardice, but a woman may never do this. Do you forgive a
support for breaking? You can hardly forgive the fact that you
need the support.

MIRZA: But could you really expect Ephraim to obey your
command?

JUDITH: I could expect it of one who had made an attempt to
kill himself and therefore had deprived his life of a master. I
struck him, as I'd have struck a stone, not knowing whether to
keep it or throw it out; if he had had a spark—the spark would
have leapt into my heart; but now I step on that useless stone.

MIRZA: But how could he have done it?

JUDITH: The bowman who asks how he is to shoot will not

hit the mark. The mark—the eye—the hand—there it is! (*With a glance to heaven*) Oh, I saw it hovering over the world like a dove seeking a nest to brood on, and the first petrified soul which began to glow had to receive the idea of redemption. But, Mirza, go and eat and then help me to dress.

MIRZA: I'll wait as long as you wait.

JUDITH: You look at me so sadly. Well, I'll go with you. But afterwards, collect all your talents and dress me up as though for a wedding. Don't smile! To be beautiful has now become an obligation for me. (*Off*)

Public Square in Bethulia. Many people. A group of young citizens bearing arms.

ONE CITIZEN (*to the other*): What did you say Ammon?

AMMON: I'm asking you, Hosea, what's better, death by the sword, which comes so rapidly that it allows you no time to dread it or even feel it, or this gradual drying out which awaits us?

HOSEA: I'd answer you if my throat weren't so dry. One gets thirstier by talking.

AMMON: You are right.

BEN (*third citizen*): One gets to the point of begrudging one-self the few drops of blood oozing within. I'd like to tap myself like a cask!

(*Puts his finger in his mouth*)

HOSEA: The best thing about it is that we forget how hungry we are because we are so thirsty.

AMMON: Well, we still have food.

HOSEA: How much longer, do you suppose? Especially, if we keep on tolerating people like you in our midst who can carry more food in their stomachs than on their shoulders.

AMMON: I'm eating my own food. That's nobody else's business!

HOSEA: In time of war everything is public. They should place you and others like you in the area where most of the arrows hit. In fact, they always should put those who overeat in the front lines. If they win, one need not thank them but the oxen and calves whose marrow strengthens them; if they perish, that's an advantage too.

(*Ammon slaps his face*)

HOSEA: Don't think that I'll return what I receive. But remember this; if you are in danger, don't expect any assistance from me. I'll leave it to Holofernes to avenge me.

AMMON: Ingrate! To beat a man means forging him armor of his own skin. Today's slap in the face inures you against the one which awaits you tomorrow!

BEN: You are fools! You quarrel and forget that you are to occupy the wall at once.

AMMON: No, we're clever; as long as we quarrel, we forget the danger we're in.

BEN: Come along. We have to go.

AMMON: I don't know if it weren't far better to let Holofernes enter. He surely would not kill the man who'd do that!

BEN: But I would!

(*Two older citizens in conversation*)

THE ONE: Have you heard any more about Holofernes' atrocities?

THE OTHER: Of course.

THE ONE: Where do you hang about to get hold of them! But tell me about it.

THE OTHER: He rises and speaks with one of his officers. All sorts of secrets. Suddenly, he notices a soldier nearby. 'Did you hear what I was saying?' he asks the soldier; 'No,' the latter replies. 'You're lucky,' says the tyrant, 'otherwise, I'd have your head chopped off because there are ears on it!'

THE ONE: You'd think you'd be struck dead when you hear such a thing! That's the most vicious thing about fear, that it kills halfway, not completely!

THE OTHER: God's patience is inexplicable to me. If He doesn't hate a pagan like that, whom does He hate?

(*They pass by*)

(*Samuel, a very ancient old man, enters, led by his grandson*)

GRANDSON: Sing a new song unto the Lord, for His goodness is everlasting!

SAMUEL: Everlasting! (*He sits down on a rock*) Samuel thirsts, grandson. Why don't you go and get him a fresh drink?

GRANDSON: Grandfather, the enemy is standing in front of our city! He's forgotten again!

SAMUEL: The psalm! Louder! Why are you hesitating?

GRANDSON: Bear witness of the Lord, oh youth, for you do not know whether you'll live to old age! Praise him, old man, for you did not live in order to hide what the merciful Lord has done for you!

SAMUEL (*angrily*) : Doesn't the well have enough water anymore for Samuel's last drink? Can't my grandson draw water even though the noon is hot?

GRANDSON (*very loudly*) : Swords guard the well; spears stare; the pagans have great power over Israel.

SAMUEL (*rises*) : Not over Israel! Whom was the Lord seeking when he gave the waves and the wind power over the little boat so that it flew up and down? He was not looking for the helmsman nor for any one but obstinate Jonah alone, who was sleeping calmly. From the secure boat, He drove him into the raging sea; from the sea into the jaws of Leviathan; from Leviathan's jaw through his jagged teeth into his dark belly. But when Jonah repented, was the Lord not strong enough to save him from the belly of Leviathan? Arise, you secret malefactors, who are asleep to your own selves as Jonah slept; do not wait until the lot is cast over you! Step forth and speak saying: 'We are they,' lest the innocent be consumed with the guilty! (*He takes hold of his beard*) Samuel struck Aaron; the nail was sharp; the brain was soft; deep was Aaron's sleep in the embrace of his wife. Samuel took the wife of Aaron and begot Ham, but she died of horror when she saw the child, for his head bore the mark of the nail, like the dead man's head; and Samuel repented and turned his face against himself!

GRANDSON: Grandfather, Grandfather! You yourself are Samuel, and I am the son of Ham!

SAMUEL: Samuel shaved his head and stood before his door, waiting for vengeance as one waits for good fortune, for seventy years and more, until he could no longer number his days. But the pestilence bypassed him and did not stop at his house; suffering went past, and did not stop at his house, and death went past and did not touch him. Vengeance did not come of itself, and he lacked the courage to summon it.

GRANDSON: Come now! (*He leads Samuel to the side*)

SAMUEL: Aaron's son, where are you, or his son's son, or his brother, that Samuel does not feel the thrust from your hand nor the weight of your foot? An eye for an eye, said the Lord; a tooth for a tooth, blood for blood!

GRANDSON: Aaron's son is dead and his son's son, and his brother, and the whole family.

SAMUEL: No avenger has survived? Are these those final days

when the Lord permits sin to stand like a tall weed and breaks the scythes? Woe! Woe! (*The grandson leads him off*)

(*Two citizens*)

THE FIRST: I tell you, not everyone lacks water. There are people among us who don't only drink their fill but even wash several times a day.

THE SECOND: Oh, I believe it! I'll tell you something in confidence. My neighbor, Assaph had a goat which grazed cheerfully in his yard. My house faces that yard and each time I looked at that animal with its full udders, I felt like a pregnant woman. Well, yesterday, I went to Assaph and asked him for a little milk. When he refused to give me any, I took my bow and killed the goat with a quick shot and sent him what it's worth. I did the right thing, for the goat misled him into hardening his heart against his neighbor.

THE FIRST: I'd expect a trick like that of you! After all, you were but a tiny child when you'd already turned a virgin into a mother.

THE SECOND: What?

THE FIRST: Indeed! Aren't you the firstborn?

(*They pass by*)

(*One of the Elders enters*)

THE ELDER: Hear me, hear me, men of Bethulia! (the people gather around him.) Hear what the pious High Priest, Jehoiakim, makes known to you.

ASSAD (*a citizen, leading his brother Daniel, who is mute and blind, by the hand*): Pay attention! The High Priest wants us to be lions so that he can be a better rabbit!

ANOTHER: Don't malign him.

ASSAD: I'll accept no consolation but the one I can get from the well.

THE ELDER: You are to think of Moses, the servant of the Lord, who slew Amalek, not with the sword but by prayer. You are not to tremble before the shield and the spear, for a word from the holy ones will put them to shame.

ASSAD: Where is Moses? Where are the holy ones?

THE ELDER: You are to take courage and remember that the sanctuary of the Lord is in danger.

ASSAD: I thought that the Lord wanted to protect us; now it turns out that we are to protect him.

THE ELDER: And above all, you are not to forget that the Lord, if he lets you perish, can make up your death and suffering to you in children and children's children to the tenth generation.

ASSAD: Who can tell me how my children's children will turn out. Couldn't they be fellows of whom I'd have to be ashamed, who would make me a laughing stock? (*To the Elder*) Man, your lips are trembling; your eyes aren't focussing; your teeth would like to tear into the resounding words behind which your fear is hidden. How can you demand from us the courage you yourself lack? Let me speak to you in the name of all these people. Give the order that the gates of the city be opened up. Surrender will find mercy! I don't say this for my sake, I say it for the sake of this poor mute; I say it for the sake of the women and children. (*Some bystanders make signs of approval*) Give the command at once, or we'll do it without your command.

DANIEL (*forcibly freeing himself from his brother's hold*): Stone him! Stone him!

PEOPLE: Was this man not a mute?

ASSAD (*looking at his brother in horror*): Mute and blind! He is my brother! He is thirty years old and has never spoken a word!

DANIEL: Yes, he is my brother. He has refreshed me with food and drink. He has clothed me and has let me live in his house! He has taken care of me by day and by night! Give me your hand, my faithful brother! (*Just as he takes it, he drops it violently, seized with terror*) Stone him! Stone him!

ASSAD: Woe! Woe! The spirit of the Lord speaks out of the mouth of the mute! Stone me!

(*The people pursue him, stoning him.*)

SAMAJA (*hurrying after them, frightened*): What are you doing? (*Off*)

DANIEL (*enthusiastic*) I am coming, I am coming, says the Lord, but you must not ask from where! Do you think it is time? I alone know when it is time!

PEOPLE: A prophet, a prophet!

DANIEL: I permitted you to grow like grain in the summer! Do you think that I shall leave My harvest for the pagans? Truly, I say unto you, that shall never happen!

(*Judith and Mirza appear among the people*)

PEOPLE (*throwing themselves on the ground*): We are blessed!

DANIEL: And no matter how great your enemy may be, I but need a small thing to demolish him! Sanctify yourselves! Sanctify yourselves! For I want to dwell with you and will not leave you unless you leave me— (*After a pause*) Your hand, Brother.

SAMAJA *(returning)* : Your brother is dead. You have killed him! That's how you thanked him for all his love! Oh, how I wanted to save him! We've been friends since our youth. But what could I do against so many whom your folly had driven mad? 'Look after Daniel!' he called out to me when his dying eyes recognized me. I place these words into your soul as a burning testament.

(Daniel wants to speak but can not; he whimpers)

SAMAJA *(to the people)* : You should be ashamed to be kneeling, and even more ashamed that you've murdered a good man who intended the best for all of you! Indeed, so violent was your rage as you pursued him, as though you could stone your own sins to death in him! Everything he said to the Elder, not from cowardice but from pity with your suffering, was planned between us this morning. This mute sat with us, immersed in himself and totally indifferent, as always; by no change of facial expression did he reveal his abhorrence. *(To the Elder)* I still demand everything my friend demanded; open the gates quickly; surrender unconditionally.—*(To Daniel)* Now show us that the Lord spoke through you. Curse me as you cursed your brother.

(Daniel is most frightened; he wants to speak, but can not)

SAMAJA: Behold the prophet! A demon of the abyss who wanted to lead you into temptation unsealed his lips, but God has sealed them again, sealed them forever. Or can you believe that the Lord makes the mutes to speak so that they can become their brothers' murderers?

(Daniel beats himself)

JUDITH *(steps into the midst of the people)* : Do not let yourselves be tempted. Were you not seized as though by the closeness of God and thrust to the ground by sacred annihilation? Will you tolerate having your deepest feelings accused of being lies?

SAMAJA: Woman, what do you want? Don't you see that he despairs? Don't you realize that he must despair if he is a human being? *(To Daniel)* Tear your hair; crush your head against the wall, so that the dogs will lick up your brain. That is the only thing left for you in the world! What is against Nature, is against God!

VOICES AMONG THE PEOPLE: He's right!

JUDITH *(to Samaja)* : Will you prescribe to the Lord the path He is to take? Does He not cleanse any path by choosing it?

SAMAJA: What is against Nature, is against God! The Lord

has performed miracles among our fathers; they were better than we. If he wanted to perform miracles now, why doesn't he send rain? And why does he not perform a miracle in the heart of Holofernes and move him to leave?

A CITIZEN (*attacks Daniel*): Die, sinner, you who misled us to stain ourselves with the blood of a just man!

SAMAJA (*steps between them*): No one may kill Cain! Thus spoke the Lord. But Cain may kill himself! Thus speaks a voice inside me! And Cain will! Let this be a sign for you: if this man lives until tomorrow, if he can tolerate his crime a whole day and a whole night, then act according to his words and wait until you sink dead to the ground or a miracle saves you. If not, do what Assad told you: open the gates and surrender. And if, burdened down by your sins, you do not presume to hope that the Lord will move the heart of Holofernes, then lay hand on yourselves, kill each other, and spare only the children. The Assyrians will spare them, for they themselves have children or wish to have them. Make it murder on a gigantic scale, where the son kills his father, and a friend proves his love to his friend by cutting the latter's throat without waiting to be asked. (*Takes Daniel by the hand*) I shall take the mute to my house. (*To himself*) Indeed, the city his brother wanted to save shall not perish on account of his madness! I shall lock him into a room, put a sharp knife into his hand, and talk to his very conscience until he does what I have prophesied in the name of Nature and as her prophet. Thank God that he is only mute and blind and not deaf as well! (*Off with Daniel*)

PEOPLE (*all at once*): Why are our eyes opened only so late? We'll not wait any longer! Not even one more hour! We want to open the gates! Now!

JOSHUA (*a citizen*): Who was to blame for our refusal to humble ourselves like other peoples? Who misled us so that we defiantly raised again the necks we had already bent for the yoke? Who told us to gaze into the clouds and to forget about the earth?

PEOPLE: Who but the priests and the Elders!

JUDITH (*to herself*): Oh God, now the wretched souls are quarreling with those who made something out of them from nothing!—(*Aloud*) Do you only see in your misfortune the challenge to deserve it by your meanness?

JOSHUA (*walking about among the citizens*): When I heard

of the campaign of Holofernes, my first thought was that we should go out to meet him and plead for his mercy. Who among you thought differently? (*All keep silent*) Why did Holofernes come? Only to make us surrender! If he had seen us surrender along the way, he would not have gone the rest of the way and would have turned back, for he has enough to do. Then we'd sit in peace now, and we'd enjoy food and drink; now our wretched lives have become nothing but a promissory note for all possible sufferings.

PEOPLE: Woe! Woe!

JOSHUA: And we are innocent; we've never been defiant; we've always trembled! But Holofernes was still far away and the Elders and priests were close by and threatened us; so we forgot one fear for another. You know what? Let's drive the Elders and priests out of our city and say to Holofernes: 'These are the rebels.' If he has mercy on them, well and good; if not, it would be better to mourn for them than for ourselves.

PEOPLE: Will this save us?

JUDITH: That is like killing the man who forged the weapon and gave it to you because you don't know how to defend yourself with it.

PEOPLE: Will it help?

JOSHUA: How could it fail? It means cutting off our heads, not our feet or hands.

PEOPLE: You're right! That's the way!

JOSHUA (*to the Elder who has watched somberly*) What do you say to this?

THE ELDER: I'd advise you to do it, if it could help. I've just turned seventy-three today and would like to join my fore-fathers; a few breaths more or less make no difference. To be sure, I believe that I've earned an honest burial and would prefer resting in the earth to resting in the belly of a wild beast; but if you think that I can serve in the place of all of you, I'm ready; I make a present to you of this gray head; but hurry, lest death anticipate you and throw my present into a ditch with scornful laughter. Only, permit me to use this head which now belongs to you just one more time. You spoke not only of me, but of all the Elders and priests. Won't you take the trouble to count your sacrifices before you begin the sacrifice?

JUDITH (*wildly*): You can listen to that and not beat your breasts and not fall down and kiss the feet of this old man?

I'd like to take Holofernes by the hand now and lead him inside our city, and sharpen his sword for him myself if it became dulled before it finished mowing down all these heads!

JOSHUA: The Elder spoke cleverly, very cleverly. He could not oppose us, he realized that, so he gave in, and in such a way as to—I bet if lambs could speak, not a single one would be slaughtered!—(*To Judith*) Certainly, you are not the only one he moved.

JUDITH: He could not have opposed you, but he could still have ruined your wicked plan by killing himself. And he frantically did reach for his sword, I noticed that and came closer to prevent him from doing so; but, all at once, something like an inner victory shone forth from his face; he withdrew his hand from his sword as though ashamed and looked up to heaven!

THE ELDER: You think too highly of me. I had not intended it for myself but for him.

PEOPLE: Your advice is bad, Joshua; we won't follow you.

JUDITH: I thank you!

JOSHUA: But you do still insist on opening the gates, don't you? Consider the fact that an enemy you let in yourselves can never be as cruel as one who must let himself in—(*to the Elder*) Command this! I shall beg your pardon for my suggestion tomorrow, that is to say, if I'm still alive then!

JUDITH (*to the Elder*): Say no!

ELDER: I say yes, for I don't see myself where we can get help.

ACHIOR (*steps into the crowd of people*): Open up, but expect no mercy from Holofernes. He has vowed that he will annihilate from the face of the earth that people which last surrenders to him, so that no trace of it will remain. You are the last people!

JUDITH: He has vowed this?

ACHIOR: I was present at the time. And you will be sure that he will keep his vow when I tell you this: He was enraged with me when I told him about the power of your God, and his rage means death! But instead of killing me at once, he commanded, as you know, that I be brought to you. You see, he is so sure of your defeat that he lets go the man he hates, and the weight of whose head he will match with gold, because he'll only take his vengeance on him at the same time he'll take it on you. And any thought of mercy is so remote from his mind that he can think up no worse punishment for his enemy than the one he has planned for you.

PEOPLE: The gates must not be opened. If we are to perish by the sword, we have our own swords!

JOSHUA: Let's set a time limit. Everything has to come to an end!

PEOPLE: A time limit! A time limit!

ELDER: Dear brothers, have patience for five more days then, and wait for the help of the Lord.

JUDITH: But what if the Lord needs another five days?

ELDER: Then we are dead! If the Lord wants to help us, the help must come during these five days; at any rate, not all of us will survive this time limit!

JUDITH (*solemnly, as though pronouncing a death verdict*) So he has to die within five days!

ELDER: We shall have to go to extremes to survive even that long. We must distribute our offering to the Lord, the sacred wine and oil, among ourselves. Woe unto me, that I must advise such measures!

JUDITH: Woe unto you, indeed! Why don't you rather advise another extreme?— (*To the people*) Men of Bethulia, have the courage to attack! The small wells are close to the wall; divide into two groups; one will cover the withdrawal and the gate, while the other attacks as a body; you can't fail, and you'll bring water in!

THE ELDER: You see that no one replies.

JUDITH (*to the people*): How am I to understand this? (*After a pause*) But I am glad about it. If you lack the courage to fight against a few hundred soldiers, you are even less likely to presume to challenge the Lord to vengeance by sacrilegiously reaching for the food of the altar!

ELDER: But this is necessary, and it shall be restored a hundred-fold. The other extreme is questionable; an opened gate could mortally wound our city. David too ate the holy bread and he did not merit death for it.

JUDITH: David was sanctified by the Lord. If you want to eat like David, you must first become like him. Eat and drink, but first sanctify yourselves!

ONE OF THE PEOPLE: Why do we listen to her?

ANOTHER: Whoever does not, should be ashamed. Is she not like an angel?

A THIRD: She is the most God-fearing woman in the city. As long as we were well-off, she sat quietly in her room; has anyone ever seen her in public except when she went to pray or offer sacrifice? But now that we are about to despair, she leaves her house, walks with us and consoles us!

THE FORMER: She is wealthy and has many goods. But do you know what she said one time? 'I am only the steward of these goods; they belong to the poor.' And she doesn't just say that; she lives it! I believe that she has not remarried because, if she did, she'd have to stop being a mother to the needy! If the Lord helps us, He will do it for her sake!

JUDITH (*to Achior*): You know Holofernes. Tell me about him.

ACHIOR: I know that he thirsts after my blood, but don't think that I despise him for that! If he were to stand before me with his sword raised and were to call out to me: 'Kill me, or I'll kill you!' I don't know what I'd do!

JUDITH: You feel that way only because he had you in his power and let you go.

ACHIOR: Oh no; it's not that! That could rather enrage me! Blood rushes to my cheeks when I stop to think how little he must value a man whom he himself sends to the enemy.

JUDITH: He's a tyrant!

ACHIOR: Yes, but he was born to be one. One sees no value in oneself or in the world if one is with him. Once I was riding in the most desolate mountains with him. We came to a wide chasm which was dizzyingly deep. He spurs his horse; I reach for his reins, point to the depth, and say: 'It's unfathomable!' 'I don't want to fathom it; I want to cross it!' he exclaims and risks the terrible leap. Before I can even follow him, he has turned and is back beside me. 'I thought I saw a spring over there,' he said, 'and wanted to drink, but there isn't any after all. Let's get over our thirst by sleeping!' and he throws the reins to me, leaps from the horse, and goes to sleep. I could not help myself; I got off my horse too, touched his clothes with my lips, and stationed myself in the sun so he'd have shade. Shame on me! I am so much his slave that I praise him whenever I speak of him.

JUDITH: He is fond of women?

ACHIOR: Yes, but in the same way as he is fond of food and drink.

JUDITH: Curses on him!

ACHIOR: What did you expect? I knew one woman among my

people who went mad, because he had spurned her. She secretly
entered his quarters and, when he had just gone to bed, she
approached him threateningly with a bare dagger.

JUDITH: What did he do?

ACHIOR: He laughed and laughed until she finally stabbed
herself.

JUDITH: Thank you, Holofernes! I need only think of her,
and I'll have courage like a man!

ACHIOR: What's the matter with you?

JUDITH: Oh rise up before me from your graves, all you whom
he has murdered, so that I may look into your wounds; come
before me, all of you whom he has violated, and open your
eyes one more time, your eyes which are closed for ever, so
that I may read in them how much he owed to you. You are
all to be paid for! But why do I think of you and not of the
young men whom his sword can still consume and the maidens
whom his arm can still crush. I wish to avenge the dead and to
protect the living.— (*To Achior*) I'm beautiful enough to be a
sacrifice, am I not?

ACHIOR: No one has ever seen your equal!

JUDITH (*to the Elder*) : I have business with Holofernes. Will
you have the gate opened for me?

ELDER: What are you planning?

JUDITH: No one may know that but the Lord God!

ELDER: Then may He be with you! The gate will be open for
you!

EPHRAIM: Judith! Judith! You can never do it!

JUDITH (*to Mirza*) : Do you have the courage to accompany
me?

MIRZA: I lack even more the courage to stay behind.

JUDITH: And you've done what I commanded?

MIRZA: Bread and wine are here. There's very little.

JUDITH: It's too much.

EPHRAIM (*to himself*) : If I'd thought that, I'd have done
what she asked of me! I'm cruelly punished!

JUDITH (*takes a few steps, then turns again to the people*) :
Pray for me as you would for a dying woman. Teach the little
children my name, and ask them to pray for me. (*She approaches
the gate; it is opened; as soon as she is outside, all but Ephraim
fall to their knees*)

EPHRAIM: I don't want to pray that God may protect her. I

want to protect her myself! She is going into the lion's den—I think, she's doing it in the expectation that all the men will follow her. I shall follow her. After all, if I die, I'll just die a little sooner than the others. Perhaps she'll turn back! (*Off*)

DELIA (*comes into the crowd of people; she is very upset*) Woe! Woe!

ONE OF THE ELDERS: What is the matter?

DELIA: The mute has strangled my husband!

ONE OF THE PEOPLE: That's Samaja's wife!

THE PREVIOUS ELDER (*to Delia*): How could this happen?

DELIA: Samaja came home with the mute. He went into the back room with him and locked the door behind them. I heard Samaja speak loudly, and the mute groan and weep. 'What is going on?' I think and steal to the door and look through a crack. The mute sits there and holds a sharp knife in his hand; Samaja stands next to him and reproaches him severely. The mute turns the knife towards his heart; I scream with terror when I see that Samaja does not try to prevent his violence. But suddenly, the mute throws away the knife and attacks Samaja. As though he possesses superhuman strength, he throws him on the floor and seizes him by the throat. Samaja can't defend himself; he wrestles with him; I scream for help; neighbors come and ram in the door, locked from the inside. Too late. The mute has already strangled Samaja. Like a beast, he still rages against the dead man and laughs when he hears us enter. When he recognizes my voice, he quiets down and comes toward me on his knees. 'Murderer!' I scream; then he points toward heaven with his finger, then hunts for the knife on the floor, picks it up, hands it to me, and points to his heart as though begging me to kill him with it.

A PRIEST: Daniel is a prophet. The Lord has permitted the mute to speak; He has performed a miracle so that you may believe in the miracles He is still planning to perform. Samaja has been destroyed along with his prophecy! He has committed sacrilege, and he has received his reward at Daniel's hand.

VOICES FROM THE PEOPLE: Let us go to Daniel lest harm come to him.

THE PRIEST: The Lord has sent him; the Lord will protect him. Go and pray! (*The people disperse in various directions*)

DELIA: They have no consolation to offer me except to tell me that the man I loved was a sinner! (*Off*)

ACT IV

Holofernes' tent. Holofernes and two of his officers.

ONE OF THE OFFICERS: The General looks like a dying flame.

THE SECOND: One has to beware of such a flame! In order to feed itself, it will consume whatever it can reach!

THE FIRST: Did you know that Holofernes came close to killing himself last night?

THE SECOND: That's not true!

FIRST: It is! He has a nightmare and believes in his sleep that someone is throwing himself upon him and will strangle him. Caught up in his dream, he reaches for his dagger, and thinking that he's stabbing his enemy in the back, he actually stabs into his own chest! Luckily, the iron slips on his ribs. He wakes up, sees it, and, when the valet wants to bandage the bleeding wound, exclaims with a laugh: 'Let it run! It's cooling me off; I have too much blood anyway!'

SECOND: That sounds fantastic!

FIRST: Ask the valet.

HOLOFERNES (*turns quickly*): Ask me! (*They are startled*) I called to you because I like you and don't like to have two brave men whom I find useful toss back and forth all sorts of idle observations and gossip. (*To himself*) They are surprised that I heard their conversation; it is quite disgraceful that I had time and attention to listen! A head that does not know how to occupy itself with its own thoughts, one which has room for the whims and ideas of others is not worthy of nourishment; the ears are the almsmen of the mind; only beggars and slaves need them, and a man who uses his ears will turn into a beggar or a slave! (*To the officers*) I'm not reproaching you. It's my fault that you have nothing to do and so have to talk in order to keep up the pretense that you are alive. What was food yesterday is waste today. Woe unto us that we have to wallow in it! But, tell me, what would you have done anyway if you'd really found me dead in my bed this morning?

OFFICERS: Lord, what should we have done?

HOLOFERNES: Even if I knew, I would not tell you that! The man who can think of himself as dead and can name his replacement no longer belongs among the living! I am grateful to my ribs for their being made of iron. That would have been a farcical death! And surely this error, made by my hand, would have served to fatten some skinny god, for example, the God of the Hebrews! How Achior would have boasted about his prophecy and how much self-respect he would have acquired!—I'd like to know one thing: what is death?

ONE OF THE OFFICERS: A thing on account of which we love life.

HOLOFERNES: That's the best answer. Indeed, only because we can lose it at any moment, do we hold on to it, squeeze it dry, and suck it in until we are about to burst. If it always moved as it did yesterday and today, we'd see value and purpose in its opposite; we'd rest and sleep and fear nothing in our dreams but the awakening. But now we try to protect ourselves from being eaten by eating, and, with our teeth, we fight against the teeth of the world. Therefore the only beautiful death is through life itself. To let the stream swell up so that the vein which is to receive it bursts! To fuse the greatest enjoyment with the shudders of destruction! Often I think that I must have said to myself at some point: 'I want to live now!' At that point, I was released as though out of a most tender embrace; it became light around me; I felt chills, a thrust, and—I was there! In the same way, I'd like to say to myself at some time: 'Now I want to die!' And if, as soon as I utter this, I am not dispersed into the winds and am not sucked in by all the thirsty lips of creation, I shall be ashamed and admit to myself that what I had considered to be my roots was, in fact, my fetters. It's conceivable that someone could kill himself at the mere thought of such a possibility!

ONE OF THE OFFICERS: Holofernes!

HOLOFERNES: You think one should not get carried away! That's true, for he who is not acquainted with intoxication does not realize how insipid sobriety is! And still, intoxication is wealth in the midst of our poverty, and I enjoy it so much when it bursts out of me like the sea and floods every dam and limit! And if there were ever such an urging and flooding in every living creature at the same time, should it then fail to break through and become one flood, and, like a great thunderstorm, to triumph over the wet, cold, tattered clouds which the wind chases according to its whims and pleasures. Oh, certainly! (*To the Officers*) You are surprised that I use my head as a spindle to wind the yarn of dreams and whims like a bundle of flax. Of course, the thought steals from life; the seedling, pulled out of the ground and exposed to light can not go on growing; I know that very well, but, today, after I've let blood, it may be possible! After all, we have time right now, for the people of Bethulia don't seem to know that a soldier goes on sharpening his sword for as long as he is prevented from using it.

ANOTHER OFFICER (*enters*): Lord, a Hebrew woman whom we've captured in the mountains stands at the door.

HOLOFERNES: What kind of woman?

THE OFFICER: Lord, every moment spent without seeing her is a lost one! If she were not so beautiful, I should not have brought her to you. We were lying near the well, waiting to see if anyone would dare approach it. Then we saw her coming; her maid, behind her like a shadow. She was veiled and, at first, was walking so quickly that her maid could hardly stay behind her; then she suddenly stopped as though she wanted to turn back, turned toward the city, threw herself on the ground and seemed to pray. One of the guards approached her; at first, I thought that he was going to harm her, for the soldiers are mean since they've been idle for so long, but he leaned over, scooped up some water, and offered it to her. She took it without thanking him and held it to her lips, but, before she had drunk it, she took it away from her mouth and slowly poured it on the ground. This annoyed the guard; he pulled out his sword and raised it towards her, but she lifted her veil and looked at him; he almost fell down at her feet, but she said: 'Lead me to Holofernes. I have come to humble myself before him and to reveal the secrets of my people to him.'

HOLOFERNES: Bring her in. (*Officer off*) I enjoy seeing every woman in the world but one, and I've never seen her and never shall.

ONE OF THE OFFICERS: Which one is that?

HOLOFERNES: My mother! I'd have as little desire to see her as to see my grave! I am happiest about the fact that I don't know where I came from! Hunters found me in a lion's den when I was an uncouth boy; a lioness had nursed me; no wonder then, that I once crushed the lion himself with my bare arms! What is a mother to a son, after all? The mirror of his impotence of yesterday and tomorrow! He can't look at her without recalling the time when he was a wretched worm who paid for the few drops of milk which he swallowed by smacking his lips. And, if he forgets that, he sees a ghost in her which brings him visions of old age and death and makes his own form, his flesh and blood, abhorrent to himself.

JUDITH (*enters accompanied by Mirza and the officer, who remain at the door; she is confused at first but composes herself quickly, approaches Holofernes and falls at his feet*) : You are he whom I seek. You are Holofernes!

HOLOFERNES: You think that the man on whose clothing the most gold shimmers has to be master of this place?

JUDITH: Only one man can look like that!

HOLOFERNES: If I found a second man, I'd place his head at his feet, for I believe that I have the sole right to my face.

ONE OF THE OFFICERS (*to the other*) : A people that has such women is not to be despised.

THE SECOND: One should wage war on them for their women alone. Now Holofernes has found a diversion. Perhaps she will stifle his entire rage with her kisses.

HOLOFERNES (*lost in contemplation of her*) : Doesn't one feel while one is looking at her as though one were taking a luxurious bath? One becomes what one sees! The great rich world could not be compressed into the bit of taut skin which contains us; we received eyes so that we could swallow it piecemeal! Only the blind are wretched! I swear, I'll never have anyone blinded again! (*To Judith*) You are still kneeling? Rise. (*she does so; he sits down on his prince's chair under the canopy*) What is your name?

JUDITH: My name is Judith.

HOLOFERNES: Do not be afraid, Judith; you appeal to me as no woman ever has before.

JUDITH: That is the direction of all my wishes.

HOLOFERNES: Tell me now why you've left the city and come to me?

JUDITH: Because I know that no one can escape you. Because our own God will place my people in your hands.

HOLOFERNES (*laughing*) : Because you are a woman, because you rely on yourself, because you know that Holofernes has eyes, isn't that it?

JUDITH: Be so kind as to listen to me. Our Lord is enraged with us; He has been telling us through his prophets for a long time that he wants to punish our people for their sins.

HOLOFERNES: What is sin?

JUDITH (*after a pause*) : One time, a child asked me that. I kissed the child. I don't know how to answer you.

HOLOFERNES: Go on.

JUDITH: Now they are placed between the rage of God and

your rage and are trembling greatly. In addition, they suffer from hunger and languish from thirst. And their great hardship is misleading them to a new sacrilege. They want to eat the holy sacrifice which they are forbidden even to touch. It will turn into fire inside them!

HOLOFERNES: Why don't they surrender?

JUDITH: They lack the courage! They know that they have deserved the worst; how could they believe that God would avert it from them! (*To herself*) I'll test him. (*Aloud*) They go further in their fear than you can go in your rage! Your vengeance would crush me if I were to tell you how their fearfulness presumes to stain the hero and man you are! I look up to you; I see the noble limits of your rage in your face; I find the point beyond which it can't burn in its wildest stage. And then I have to blush, for, in doing so, I remember that they are brazen enough to expect from you every kind of atrocity which a guilty conscience is at all capable of thinking up in cowardly self-torture, that they are presuming to see an executioner in you because they themselves are worthy of death. (*She falls down before him*) On my knees, I beg your forgiveness for this insult from my blinded people.

HOLOFERNES: What are you doing? I don't want you to kneel before me!

JUDITH (*rises*): They think that you want to kill all of them! You smile instead of being enraged. Oh, I've forgotten who you are! You know the human disposition; nothing can surprise you; if your image appears distorted and defaced in a dull mirror, this only arouses your scorn. But I must say one thing in defense of my people; they themselves would never have thought up such a thing. They wanted to open the gate for you when Achior, the Moabite officer, came among them and frightened them. 'What are you doing?' he cried, 'do you know that Holofernes has vowed to annihilate you?' I know that you've given him his life and freedom; you've generously placed him among your enemies because you did not want to take vengeance on an unworthy man. He thanks you by painting your picture in blood and by turning every heart away from you. I'm right, am I not? It is presumptuous of my little people to consider itself worthy of your rage? How could you hate those whom you've never known, whom you've just met along your path, and who only failed to get out of your way because fear petrified them and robbed them of life and thought? And even if something resembling courage had really inspired them, could that tempt you to be untrue to yourself? Could Holofernes persecute and be hostile to that in himself or in others which makes him great and unique? That is contrary to Nature and can not ever happen. (*She looks at him; he remains silent*) Oh, I'd like to be you! Just for a day! Just for an hour! Then, by merely putting my sword in its sheath, I'd celebrate a triumph greater than any ever celebrated by the sword. In my city thousands are now trembling at the thought of you; 'You've defied me,' I'd shout to them, 'but just because you've offended me, I'll give you your lives; I want my vengeance on you but it is to be through you yourselves. I'll let you go unscathed so that you'll be completely enslaved to me.'

HOLOFERNES: Are you aware of the fact, woman, that you make all this impossible for me by asking me to do it? If the thought had originated within me, I might have carried it out. Now it is yours and can never be mine. I'm sorry that Achior will turn out to be right!

JUDITH (*breaks out in wild laughter*): Forgive me; permit me to jeer at myself. There are children in my city who are so innocent that they will smile when they see the shiny iron that is to stab them to death. There are virgins in this city who tremble when a ray of light is about to penetrate their veils. I thought of the death which awaits these children and the shame which threatens these virgins; I imagined the horrible happening and thought that no one could be so strong as not to shudder at such scenes. Forgive me for attributing my own weakness to you.

HOLOFERNES: You wanted to decorate me and that deserves my thanks, even if the type of decoration you chose does not suit me. Judith, we should not argue with each other. I am destined to inflict wounds; you, to heal them. If I were negligent in pursuing my calling, you'd have nothing to help pass your time. You also must not be too hard on my soldiers. People who don't know today whether they'll be around tomorrow must take brazenly, after all, and overload their bellies somewhat if they are going to get their share of the world.

JUDITH: Lord, you surpass me as much in wisdom as in courage and strength. I had strayed within myself and have only you to thank for being able to straighten myself out again. Ha, how foolish I was! I know that they've all deserved their death, that they were told that a long time ago. I know that the Lord, my

God, has given to you the office of avenger, and still, overcome by wretched pity, I throw myself between you and them. Blessed am I that your hand stayed firmly on the sword, that you did not drop it to dry the tears of a woman! How much that would have encouraged them in their exuberance! What would remain for them to fear if Holofernes by-passed them like a thunderstorm which fails to break out! Who knows whether they would not see cowardice in your generosity and whether they would not lampoon your mercy! Now they sit in sackcloth and ashes and do penance, but they would probably compensate with a day of wild pleasure and madness for every hour of abstinence! And all their sins would be on my account, and I'd just die from regret and shame. No, Lord, be mindful of your vow and destroy them. The Lord, my God, commands through me that you do this; He will be your friend to the degree that you are their enemy.

HOLOFERNES: Woman, it seems to me that you are playing games with me. But no, I'm insulting myself by even thinking that such a thing is possible. (*After a pause*) You harshly accuse your people.

JUDITH: Do you think that I find it easy to do that? It is my punishment for my sins that I must accuse them of theirs. Don't think, I've fled from them merely because I wanted to ecape the general destruction which I saw coming. Who would feel so pure that he'd presume to escape the great judgement of the Lord? I have come to you because my God commanded me to come. I am to lead you back to Jerusalem; I am to place my people into your hands as though they were a herd lacking a herdsman. He told me to do this when I was kneeling before Him one night, praying in despair, and begged Him to visit thousandfold destruction upon you and your men. When each of my thoughts tried to trap you and strangle you, His voice resounded. I was jubilant, but He had rejected my prayer, condemned my people to death, and burdened my soul with the executioner's office. Oh, that was a transformation! I was petrified, but I obeyed. I left the city hurriedly and shook it's dust off my feet; I came before you and admonished you to annihilate those for whose rescue I'd have offered my body and blood a short time ago. Behold, they will despise me and brand my name forever; that is worse than death, and still, I am firm and do not waver!

HOLOFERNES: They won't do that. Can anyone despise you if

I let no one survive? Truly, if your God accomplishes what you have said, He shall be my God too and I shall exalt you as no woman has ever been exalted! (*To the valet*) Lead her to the treasury and feed her from my table.

JUDITH: Lord, I may not eat your food, for that would be a sin for me. I did not come to you to desert my God after all, but to serve Him properly. I've brought some food along, and I'll eat some of that.

HOLOFERNES: And when that's gone?

JUDITH: Be certain that my God will accomplish through me what He has planned before I finish this little bit. I have enough for five days, and He will bring His plans to conclusion in five days. I do not know the exact hour as yet, and my Lord will not tell it to me until it has arrived. So give orders that I may go out into the mountains and up to the city without being detained by your men so that I may worship and await His revelation.

HOLOFERNES: You have my permission for that. I've never had the movements of a woman watched. I'll see you in five days then, Judith!

JUDITH (*throws herself at his feet; then goes to the door*) In five days, Holofernes!

MIRZA (*who has long since made clear her horror and disgust with appropriate gestures*) Oh, cursed one, so you've come to betray your people?

JUDITH: Say it loudly! It's good if they all hear that you too believe what I've said!

MIRZA: Tell me yourself, Judith, must I not curse you?

JUDITH: I'm in luck. If you haven't any doubt, then Holofernes surely can't doubt me!

MIRZA: You're crying?

JUDITH: Tears of joy because I've deceived you. I shudder at the power of the lies which my mouth can produce! (*Off*)

ACT V

Evening. The lighted tent of Holofernes. To the rear, a curtain hides the sleeping quarters.
Holofernes. Officers. Valet.

HOLOFERNES (*to one of the Officers*): You've been on reconnaissance? How are things in the city?

OFFICER: It looks as though they'd all buried themselves in it. Those who guard the gates are as if they'd come forth from their graves. I aimed at one, but, before I could even shoot, he dropped to the ground dead.

HOLOFERNES: So it's victory without war. If I were younger, I'd resent that. In those days, I thought I was stealing my life if I didn't win it for myself in daily battle. Whatever was given to me didn't seem like my possession to me.

OFFICER: One sees priests creeping silently and somberly through the narrow streets. Long white garments like the shrouds of our dead. Hollow eyes which try to penetrate the sky. Cramps in their fingers when they fold their hands.

HOLOFERNES: I don't want those priests killed; the despair in their faces is my ally.

OFFICER: When they look up to the sky now, they don't do it to look for their God but to look for a rain cloud. But the sun consumes the thin clouds which promise a quenching drop, and its hot rays fall on their dried-out lips. Then they clench fists, roll their eyes, crush their heads against the wall so that blood and brains spurt.

HOLOFERNES: We've seen that often enough. (*Laughing*) After all, we ourselves have experienced a famine during which a man shyly withdrew when another wanted to kiss him because he was afraid of being bitten in the cheek. Hey, prepare the meal; let's celebrate! (*This is done*) Isn't tomorrow the fifth day?

OFFICER: Yes.

HOLOFERNES: Then it will be decided! If Bethulia surrenders to me as the Hebrew woman said it would, if it comes crawling to me on its own, that stiff-necked city, and places itself at my feet, then. . . .

OFFICER: Holofernes is in doubt?

HOLOFERNES: About everything he cannot command. But if what the woman predicted does occur, if they open up for me without my having to knock with my sword, then. . . .

OFFICER: Then?

HOLOFERNES: Then, we'll acquire a new master. Indeed, I've vowed that the God of Israel, if he does me a favor, will be my God too, and by all those others who are already my gods, by Bel of Babel and by the great god Baal, I'll keep my vow. Here, I'll offer him this cup of wine, to Je . . . , Je . . . (*To the valet*) What did you say His name was?

VALET: Jehovah.

HOLOFERNES: Take pleasure in accepting this offering, Jehovah. It's from a man, and from one at that who needn't make it.

OFFICER: And if Bethulia fails to surrender?

HOLOFERNES: Vow for vow! Then I'll have Jehovah whipped and the city—but I won't already set limits to my rage! That would amount to disciplining lightning. What's the Hebrew woman doing?

OFFICER: Oh, she's beautiful! But she's a prude too!

HOLOFERNES: Did you try her?

(*Officer is embarrassed and silent*)

HOLOFERNES (*wild with anger*): You dared to do that and knew that she pleases me? Take that, you dog! (*He strikes him down*) Take him away, and bring the woman to me. It's a shame that she walks among us Assyrians untouched!—(*The body is taken away*) A woman is a woman, and still, one imagines there is a difference. Of course, a man feel his worth more when embracing a woman than anywhere else. Ha! When, in conflict between their sensual pleasure and chastity, they tremble as they anticipate the man's embrace! When they look as though they wanted to flee, and then, suddenly overcome by their nature, they throw their arms around his neck, when their last bit of independence and self-assurance rises up and spurs them, unable to resist any longer, to cooperate willingly. If then their desire, aroused in every drop of their blood by treacherous kisses, begins to race against the man's, so that they invite where they should be resisting—yes, that is life—then one finds out why the gods took the trouble to create man; there's a satisfaction, an overflowing measure of it! And completely so, if their petty soul had been filled with hatred and cowardly anger just the moment before, if their eyes, now tearful with joy, had closed darkly when the conqueror entered, when the hand which now squeezes his fondly would have been glad to mix poison into his wine but a minute ago! That's a triumph unlike any other, and I've enjoyed it many times. This Judith too—to be sure, her eyes look kind, and her cheeks smile like sunshine; but no one but her God dwells in her heart, and I'd like to drive him out now. When I was a young man and encountered an enemy, I'd sometimes wrestle with him until I had his sword and would then slay him with it instead of drawing my own. That's how I'd like to slay her. She's to dissolve before me because of her own feeling, because of the faithlessness of her senses!

JUDITH (*enters with Mirza*) : You have commanded, noble Lord, and your maid obeys you.

HOLOFERNES: Sit down, Judith, and eat and drink, for you have found grace in my sight.

JUDITH: I shall, my Lord; I shall be glad, for I've never been so honored in my life!

HOLOFERNES: Then, why do you hesitate?

JUDITH (*shudders and points to the fresh blood*) : Lord, I am a woman.

HOLOFERNES: Look closely at this blood; it should flatter your vanity, for it was shed because it was burning for you.

JUDITH: Woe!

HOLOFERNES (*to the valet*) : Bring different rugs. (*To the Officers*) Leave me.

(*The rugs are brought; the Officers off*)

JUDITH (*to herself*) : My hair is standing on end, but still, my God, I thank You for also showing me this terrible man in this way. I can more easily murder the murderer.

HOLOFERNES: Now sit down. You've turned pale! Your breast is heaving. Do I terrify you so?

JUDITH: Lord, you've been kind to me!

HOLOFERNES: Be honest, woman!

JUDITH: Lord, you'd have to despise me if I—

HOLOFERNES: Well?

JUDITH: If I could love you.

HOLOFERNES: Woman, you are very bold indeed! No, forgive me! You are not bold at all. I've never heard such a thing before. Take this golden chain for it.

JUDITH (*embarrassed*) : Lord, I don't understand you.

HOLOFERNES: Woe unto you if you did! The lion looks kindly at the child who boldly pulls on his mane because he does not know lions. But, if the child, grown up and educated, tried to do the same, the lion would tear him to shreds. Sit down with me; let's chat. Tell me what you thought when you first heard that I was threatening your homeland with my army.

JUDITH: I thought nothing.

HOLOFERNES: Woman, one thinks about all sorts of things when one hears about Holofernes.

JUDITH: I thought of the God of my fathers.

HOLOFERNES: And cursed me?

JUDITH: No, I hoped my God would.

HOLOFERNES: Give me the first kiss! (*He kisses her*)

JUDITH (*to herself*) : Oh, why am I a woman?

HOLOFERNES: And when you heard my chariots roll, and my camels, and my clanging swords, what did you think then?

JUDITH: I thought that you were not the only man in the world, and that another would come out of Israel who'd be your equal!

HOLOFERNES: But when you saw that my name alone sufficed to hurl your people in the dust, and that your God forgot to perform his miracles, and that your men wished for women's clothes—

JUDITH: I was ashamed of them and hid my face as soon as I saw a man, and, whenever I wanted to pray, my thoughts rebelled against me and tore each other to shreds and coiled like snakes around the image of my God. Oh, since I've felt that, I shudder at the thought of my own breast; it seems like a cave to me into which the sun shines but which, in spite of that, shelters the worst breed of worms in secret hiding places.

HOLOFERNES (*looks at her from the side*) : How she glows! She reminds me of a ball of fire which I once saw rising in the sky on a dark night. Welcome, pleasure, cooked to a turn in the flames of hatred! Kiss me, Judith! (*She does*) Her lips bore into mine like leeches, and still, they are cold! Drink wine, Judith. Everything we lack is in the wine!

JUDITH (*drinks after Mirza has served her*) : Yes, there is courage in wine, courage!

HOLOFERNES: So you need courage to sit with me at my table, to bear my glance, and to meet my kisses? Poor creature!

JUDITH: Oh you— (*composing herself*) Forgive me. (*She weeps*)

HOLOFERNES: Judith, I can see into your heart. You hate me. Give me your hand, and tell me about your hatred!

JUDITH: My hand? Oh, the scorn which places its axe on the roots of my human nature!

HOLOFERNES: Indeed, this woman is truly desirable!

JUDITH: Leap up, my heart! Don't restrain yourself anymore! (*She draws herself up*) Yes, I do hate you; I curse you, and I have to tell you so! You have to know how much I hate you, how much I curse you, if I am not to go mad! Now kill me!

HOLOFERNES: Kill you? Perhaps tomorrow; but today, we'll go to bed together.

JUDITH (*to herself*) : How relieved I suddenly feel! Now I may do it!

VALET (*enters*) : Lord, a Hebrew waits in front of the tent. He urgently requests that you receive him. Matters of utmost importance—

HOLOFERNES (*rises*) : From the enemy? Bring him in! (*To Judith*) Do you suppose they want to surrender? Then, quickly, tell me the names of your cousins and friends. I want to spare them!

EPHRAIM (*rushes in and falls at his feet*) : Lord, do you guarantee my life to me?

HOLOFERNES: I'll guarantee it.

EPHRAIM: All right! (*Approaches him, quickly draws his sword and begins to attack Holofernes who gets out of his path*)

VALET ' (*enters hastily*) : You scoundrel! I'll show you how to kill men! (*About to kill Ephraim*)

HOLOFERNES: Stop!

EPHRAIM (*About to throw himself on his own sword*) : Judith saw this! Eternal disgrace has befallen me!

HOLOFERNES (*stops him*) : Don't you dare try that a second time. Do you want to make it impossible for me to keep my word? I guaranteed your life; I'll even have to protect you from yourself! Seize him! Didn't my favorite monkey just die? Put him in the monkey's cage and teach him the tricks of his droll predecessor. The man is an oddity! He is the only one who can boast of having tried to attack Holofernes and of having escaped in one piece. I want to show him off at court! (*Valet off with Ephraim; to Judith*) Are there many snakes in Bethulia?

JUDITH: No, but several madmen.

HOLOFERNES: To kill Holofernes; to extinguish the lightning which threatens to consume the world by fire! to throttle germinating immortality; to make a bigmouthed braggard out of someone who's made a promising beginning by depriving him of the end due him—oh, all that may be tempting! That's really interfering with the reins of Destiny! Even I could be lured into doing that if I were not who I am! But to want to do the great deed in a petty way; to weave a web for the lion out of his own generosity first and then attack him as an assassin; to dare to act after buying off danger in a cowardly manner; you must agree, Judith, that amounts to making gods out of dirt; you'll have to be disgusted with that too, even if your best friend were to try this against your worst enemy!

JUDITH: You are great, and others are small. (*Softly*) God of my fathers, protect me against myself lest I have to admire what I abhor! He is a man!

HOLOFERNES (*to the valet*): Prepare my bed! (*Valet off*)
Behold, woman, these arms of mine have been dipped in blood
up to the elbows; every one of my thoughts spawns atrocities
and destruction; my very word is death! The world seems pitiable
to me! I feel that I was born to destroy it so that something
better may take its place. They curse me, but their curse does
not cling to my soul; it merely bats its wings and shakes it off
as though it were nothing. So, I suppose, I'm justified. 'Oh,
Holofernes, you don't know how this feels!' a man groaned
once who was being roasted alive in a red hot oven at my
command. 'I really don't,' I said and lay down next to him.
Don't admire me for that; it was foolish.

JUDITH (*to herself*): Stop! Stop! I'll have to kill him if I am
not to kneel before him!

HOLOFERNES: Strength! Strength is what it is! Let him come
who can hurl me to the ground! I long for him! It is tedious
to be able to honor nothing but oneself! Let him grind me in
a mortar and, if it pleases him, fill in the hole I tore into the
world with the hash he makes of me! I bore further and further
with my sword. If the blood-curdling screams for help fail to
rouse the savior, then none exists. The hurricane rushes through
the world and looks for its brother. But it uproots the oaks
which appear to defy him, topples the towers, and lifts the globe
out of its joints. Only then does it realize that it has no equal
and goes to sleep in disgust. I wonder whether Nebuchadnezzar
is my brother. He's certainly my Lord. Perhaps, some day, he'll
throw my head to the dogs; I hope this food will agree with
them! Perhaps some day I'll feed his entrails to the tigers of
Assyria. Then, yes, then I'll know that I am the measure of
mankind, and, for an eternity, I'll stand before man's dizzied
eyes as an unreachable god girded with horror! Oh that last
moment, the last! I wish it had arrived! 'Come, all of whom I
have hurt!' I'll exclaim, 'you, whom I've crippled, you, whose
wives I tore from your embrace, whose daughters I've snatched
from your side, come, think up tortures for me! Tap my blood
and make me drink it; cut flesh from my loins and give it to
me to eat!' And when they think they've done their worst to
me, and I name something still worse, and ask them in a kindly
manner not to deny me that; when they then stand about in
terrified astonishment and I'm persuading them with a smile
to death and madness, with a smile in spite of all my suffering,
then I shall roar at them: 'Kneel, for I am your god!', and I'll
close my lips and eyes and shall die quietly and in secret.

JUDITH (*trembling*) : And if heaven hurls its lightning at you to shatter you?

HOLOFERNES: Then I'll stretch out my hand as though I myself were commanding it, and its deathly gleam will envelop me in dark majesty.

JUDITH: Monstrous! Terrifying! My feelings and thoughts whirl about like dry leaves. Man, dreadful creature, you are forcing yourself between me and my God. I must pray at once and I can not!

HOLOFERNES: Fall down and worship me!

JUDITH: Ha, now I see clearly once more! You? You are defiant because you have strength. Don't you realize that it has changed and become your enemy?

HOLOFERNES: I'm glad to hear something new.

JUDITH: You think it exists to attack the world, but what would you say if it existed to dominate itself? But you have allowed it to nourish your passion; you are the rider whom his own horses consume.

HOLOFERNES: Yes, yes, strength is destined to suicide, so speaks wisdom which is not strength! To fight against myself, to make my left leg into the bone over which my right stumbles so that it avoids stepping on a near-by ant heap! That fool who fought his own shadow in the desert and cried when night fell, 'Now I'm beaten; now my foe is as large as the world,'—that fool was actually very clever, wasn't he? Oh, show me the fire which extinguishes itself! Can you find it? Then show me the one which feeds on itself. Can't you find that either? Then tell me, does the tree it consumes have the right to condemn the fire?

JUDITH: I don't know whether one can answer you. Where my thoughts used to be there is only void and darkness now. I don't even understand my own heart anymore.

HOLOFERNES: You have the right to laugh at me! One shouldn't try to make a woman understand anything like that.

JUDITH: Learn to respect womankind! A woman stands before you to kill you! And she tells you so!

HOLOFERNES: And she tells me so in order to make it impossible for herself to do the deed! Oh, cowardice which considers itself greatness! But you probably want to do this only because I'm not going to bed with you! To protect myself from you, I need only make you a child!

JUDITH: You don't know Hebrew women! You only know creatures who feel happiest while suffering the deepest humiliation.

HOLOFERNES: Come Judith, I want to know you better! Go on resisting a bit more, I'll tell you myself how much more. One more cup! (*He drinks*) Now stop resisting; that's enough!— (*To the valet*) Go. And anyone who disturbs me tonight will pay for it with his head!

(*He leads Judith off by force*)

JUDITH (*in leaving*) : I have to—I want to—curses on me now and forever if I can't!

VALET (*to Mirza*) : You want to stay here?

MIRZA: I have to wait for my mistress.

VALET: Why aren't you a woman like Judith? Then I could be just as happy as my master.

MIRZA: Why aren't you a man like Holofernes?

VALET: I am who I am so that Holofernes has his comforts. So that the great hero does not have to serve himself his own food nor pour his own wine. So that he has someone who'll put him to bed when he's drunk. But now answer me this: why are there ugly women in this world?

MIRZA: So that a fool can make fun of them.

VALET: That's true, and also so that one can spit in their faces by light if one's had the misfortune to kiss them in the dark. Holofernes once struck down a woman who came to him at an inconvenient time because he didn't think she was pretty enough. He always gets the best. Crawl into a corner, you Hebrew spider, and keep quiet. (*Off*)

MIRZA (*alone*) : Quiet! Quiet indeed! I think some one is being murdered in there. (*She points to the sleeping quarters*) I don't know whether it's Holofernes or Judith! Quiet! Quiet! I once stood by the water and watched a man drown. Fear drove me to leap in after him; fear also kept me back. So I screamed as loudly as I could, and only screamed to keep from hearing his cries. That's the way I'm talking now! Oh Judith, Judith! When you came to Holofernes in a disguise which I could not understand and offered to deliver your people into his hands, I considered you a traitor for a moment. I was wrong about you and felt it right away. Oh, I'd like to be wrong about you now as well! I wish that your half-spoken words, your eyes, and your gestures were deceiving me as they did then! I have no courage; I'm very much afraid; but it is not fear which speaks from me now, it's not fear of failure. A woman is meant to give birth to men, but never is she to kill them!

JUDITH (*rushes in, her hair is streaming loose; she is hardly able to support herself. A second curtain is opened. One sees Holofernes asleep; his sword hangs over the head of his bed)*: It is too bright in here, too bright! Put out the lights, Mirza, they're shameless!

MIRZA (*jubilant*): She lives and he lives!—(*To Judith*) What is the matter with you, Judith? Your cheeks are burning as though your blood were to spurt forth from them! Your eyes look so frightened.

JUDITH: Don't look at me, Virgin! No one is to look at me. (*She totters.*)

MIRZA: Lean on me; you are unsteady on your feet!

JUDITH: What, am I that weak? Leave me alone! I can stand up! Oh, I can do much more than stand up; I can do infinitely more!

MIRZA: Come, let's flee from here.

JUDITH: What? Are you in his pay? You'd tolerate that he dragged me with him, that he made me lie on his shameful bed, that he strangled my soul! You'd tolerate all that? And now, when I want to be paid, recompensed for the destruction I experienced in his arms, now that I want to have vengeance on him for his crude reach into my humanity, now that I want to wash off with his heart's blood the dishonoring kisses which still are fire on my lips, now you don't even blush at the thought of taking me away?

MIRZA: You poor girl, what are you trying to do?

JUDITH: Don't you know, you wretched creature? Your heart doesn't tell you? I am planning murder!—(*When Mirza steps back*) Do I have a choice?—Tell me that, Mirza. I won't choose murder, if I—what am I saying! Not another word, Virgin! The world is spinning around me.

MIRZA: Come.

JUDITH: Never! I'll teach you your duty! Look, Mirza, I'm a woman! Oh, I shouldn't feel that now! Listen to me, and do as I ask. If my strength deserts me, if I should fall in a faint, don't splash me with water. That won't help. Scream into my ear: 'You're a whore!' Then I'll get up quickly, perhaps even take a hold of you and try to strangle you. Don't be frightened then, but call out to me: 'Holofernes made you into a whore, and Holofernes is still alive!' Oh, Mirza, then I'll be a hero, a hero like Holofernes.

MIRZA: Your thoughts grow beyond you!

JUDITH: You don't understand me! But you'll have to, I want

you to understand me. Mirza, you are a virgin. Let me shed a light into the sanctuary of your virgin's soul. A virgin is a foolish creature who even trembles with fear before her own dreams because a dream can mortally wound her, and still, she lives in hopes of not always remaining a virgin. There is no greater moment for a virgin than the one when she stops being a virgin, and every sensation of her blood which she tried to fight, every sigh she choked back enhances the value of the sacrifice she has to make at that moment. She brings all she has—is it too proud a desire to wish to fill with rapture and bliss when giving all one has? Mirza, do you hear me?

MIRZA: How could I help it?

JUDITH: Now think of it in its entire naked horror; imagine it now to the point where shame with hands raised thrusts itself between you and your imagination, the point at which you curse a world in which the most monstrous is possible!

MIRZA: What is this? What am I to imagine?

JUDITH: What are you to imagine? Yourself in the deepest humiliation—the moment when you are poured out—body and soul—to take the place of abused wine and help to conclude one disgusting intoxication with an even more disgusting one— when lust, in going to sleep, borrows as much fire from your own lips as is required to murder what is most sacred within you——when your senses rise up against you like slaves which have been made drunk and no longer know their masters, when you begin to consider your entire life up to that moment, all your thoughts and sensations, nothing but arrogant dreams and see your shame as your true existence!

MIRZA: I am lucky not to be beautiful!

JUDITH: I overlooked that when I came here. But how clearly did I see it when I entered there (*She points to the sleeping quarters*), when my first glance fell on the prepared bed. I threw myself on my knees before the monster and moaned: 'Spare me!' If he had responded to the cry of terror from my soul, I'd never, never—but his answer was to tear my clothes and praise my breasts. I bit into his lips when he kissed me. 'Moderate your passion! You're going too far!' he jeered, laughing, and—oh, my consciouness was about to desert me, my whole body felt like a spasm, when something shiny struck my eye. It was his sword. My fainting thoughts clung to that sword, and, if, in my humiliation, I've lost the right to live, I'll fight to regain that right with that very sword! Pray for me! I'm going to do it now!

(She rushes into the sleeping quarters and takes down the sword)

MIRZA *(on her knees)* : Rouse him, oh God!

JUDITH *(kneels)* : Oh Mirza, what are you praying?

MIRZA *(rises)* : Thank God, she can't do it!

JUDITH: It's true, is it not, Mirza, sleep is God Himself embracing tired men? He who sleeps must be safe. *(She rises and looks at Holofernes)* And he sleeps so peacefully; he does not suspect that murder is raising his own sword against him. He sleeps peacefully—ha! cowardly woman, what was to stir your abhorrence rouses your sympathy instead, does it? That peaceful sleep, after such an hour, is it not the worst sacrilege of all? Am I a worm that he may crush me with his feet and then go to sleep so peacefully as though nothing had happened? I am no worm! *(She draws the sword from its sheath)* He is smiling. I know that smile of hell! He smiled that way when he pulled me down, when he—kill him, Judith! He's dishonoring you a second time; his dream is nothing but a cur's reenactment of your shame. Now he stirs. Will you hesitate until his lust is hungry again and awakens him, until he seizes you once more and—

(She cuts off Holofernes' head)

You see, Mirza, there's his head! Ha, Holofernes, do you respect me now?

MIRZA *(fainting)* : Hold me.

JUDITH *(convulsed with shudders)* : She is fainting—is my deed so monstrous that it makes the blood stop in her veins and throws her to the ground as though she were dead? *(Violently)* Come to, you fool; your fainting is like an accusation of me and I won't have that!

MIRZA *(coming to)* : Cover it with a cloth!

JUDITH: Be strong, Mirza, I beg you, be strong! Each one of your shudders costs me a part of myself. This dizzy swaying away from me, this cruel averting of your eyes, this paleness of your face could persuade me that I have done something inhuman, and then I'd have to— *(She reaches for the sword)*

(Mirza embraces her)

JUDITH: Rejoice, my heart! Mirza can still embrace me! But, woe unto me, she only flees to me because she can't bear to look at the dead man, because she is afraid to faint again! Or will it make you faint again to embrace me? *(Pushes her away)*

MIRZA: You're hurting me! And yourself even more!

JUDITH (*gently takes her hand*) : It's true, isn't it, Mirza, if it were a monstrous deed, if I'd really committed an inhuman crime, you would not let me feel it; and if I were to accuse and condemn myself, you'd say to me in a kind way: you're not being just with yourself; it was a heroic deed!

(*Mirza is silent*)

JUDITH: Ha, don't think that I am standing before you as a beggar, that I've already condemned myself and hope for your plea for mercy. It was a heroic deed, for that one over there was Holofernes, and I, I am a creature like you! It is more than a heroic deed. I'd like to see the hero whose greatest feat cost him half as much as mine cost me!

MIRZA: You spoke of vengeance. I have one question. Why did you come to this pagan camp with all the splendor of your beauty? Had you never entered it, you'd have had nothing to avenge!

JUDITH: Why I came? The suffering of my people drove me here with whips, the threat of famine, the thought of the mother who opened her veins to give her child to drink before it died of thirst! Now I'm reconciled with myself again! I'd forgotten all that because I was thinking about myself!

MIRZA: You had forgotten it! So it wasn't that which drove you to dip your hand in blood!

JUDITH (*slowly, defeated*) : No, no, you're right—it wasn't that—nothing drove me but the thought of myself. Oh, this is madness! My people is saved, but if a stone had shattered Holofernes—they'd owe that stone more gratitude than they owe me now! Gratitude? Who wants that? But now, I have to carry my deed alone, and its weight crushes me!

MIRZA: Holofernes embraced you. What, if you bear his child? What will you tell this child when he asks you about his father?

JUDITH: Oh, Mirza, I must die, and I want to die! I'll run through the sleeping camp; I'll hold up the head of Holofernes; I'll shout that I've killed him, so that thousands of men will rise up and tear me to shreds. (*Wants to go*)

MIRZA (*calmly*) : Then they'll tear me to shreds too.

JUDITH (stops) : What am I to do? My brain is dissolving in smoke; my heart is like a mortal wound. And still, I can't think of anything but myself! I wish it were not so! I feel like an eye that's directed inward. And, as I look more and more sharply at myself, I become smaller, smaller and smaller, smaller still; I'll have to stop, or I'll disappear completely.

MIRZA (*listening*) : Oh God, someone's coming!

JUDITH (*confused*) : Keep calm! Keep calm! No one can come. I've wounded the heart of the world (*Laughing*), and I've wounded it deeply. The world will probably stop! What do you suppose God will say about it when He looks down tomorrow morning and sees that the sun can't go on, and that the stars are paralyzed? Do you suppose He'll punish me? Oh no, after all, I am the only one who's still alive; Where would new life come from? How could He kill me?

MIRZA: Judith!

JUDITH: Don't say that! My name hurts me!

MIRZA: Judith!

JUDITH (*annoyed*) : Let me sleep now. Dreams are dreams! I could cry now; isn't that ridiculous? If I only had someone to tell me why?

MIRZA: She's finished! Judith you are a child!

JUDITH: Indeed I am, thank God! Just think, I'd forgotten that; I had really played myself into reasoning, like a prison it was, and the door had slammed shut behind me, dreadfully, impenetrably, like an iron gate! (*Laughing*) It's true, isn't it; I won't be old tomorrow, nor even day after tomorrow! Come, let's play another game, but let's choose a better one. I've just played a wicked woman who's killed a man! Ugh! Now tell me, what shall I act out now?

MIRZA (*turned away*) : My God! She's going mad!

JUDITH: Tell me what I am to be! Quickly now! Otherwise I'll turn into what I was before.

MIRZA (*points to Holofernes*) : Look!

JUDITH: Did you think I had forgotten that? Oh no! Not at all! I'm just begging for madness, but there's just a little grayness inside me now and then; there's no blackout. There are thousands of burrows in my head, but they are all too small for my big fat brain; it tries in vain to crawl in.

MIRZA (*most frightened*) : It will soon be morning; they'll torture both of us to death if they find us here. They'll tear us limb from limb!

JUDITH: Do you really believe that one can die? I know they all believe it, and that we're supposed to believe it. I used to believe it too, but now death seems such a monstrous thing to me, an impossibility! To die! ha! What gnaws at my insides now will always gnaw at me, it's not like a toothache or a fever, it's already part of me and suffices for ever. Oh, one learns something from being in pain. (*She points to Holofernes*) He isn't dead either! Who knows whether it isn't he who tells me all that, whether he isn't getting his vengeance on me by acquainting my shuddering spirit with the secret of his immortality!

MIRZA: Judith, take pity, and come now!

JUDITH: Yes, yes, I beg you Mirza, always tell me what to do; I'm afraid of doing anything on my own now.

MIRZA: Follow me then.

JUDITH: Ah, but you mustn't forget the most important thing! Put the head in this sack; I won't leave it behind! You won't? Then I won't take one step! (*Mirza picks it up, shuddering*) Look, the head is mine! I'll have to take it along, so they'll believe me in Bethulia when I tell them that I—oh woe! Woe! They'll laud and praise me when I tell them about it, and woe again! I feel that I had thought of that before!

MIRZA (*about to leave*) : Now?

JUDITH: I have an idea! Listen, Mirza, I'll tell them, you did it.

MIRZA: I?

JUDITH: Yes, Mirza! I'll say that I'd lost my nerve at the moment of decision, but that the spirit of the Lord had come over you, and that you have saved your people from its greatest enemy! Then they'll despise me as a tool rejected by the Lord, and you'll have the praise and paeans of Israel!

MIRZA: Never!

JUDITH: Oh, you're right! It was cowardice on my part. Their cries of jubilation, their clashing cymbals and beating drums will crush me, and then I'll have my reward! Let's go (*Both off*)

***

The city of Bethulia, as in Act III. Public square with a view of the gate. Guards at the gate. Many people, lying and standing in all kinds of groups.

Two priests, surrounded by a group of women, mothers, etc.

A WOMAN: Did you lie to us when you told us that our God is almighty? Is He like a human being that He can not keep his promises?

PRIESTS: He is almighty. But you yourselves have tied His hands. He may only help you as you deserve to be helped!

WOMAN: Woe! woe! What will become of us?

PRIESTS: Look behind you; then you'll know what's ahead!

A MOTHER: Can a mother fall so deeply into sin that her innocent child must die of thirst? (*Holds up her child*)

PRIEST: Vengeance has no limits, for sin has none.

MOTHER: I tell you, oh Priest, a mother can not fall that deeply into sin! If the Lord is enraged, He can let the child suffocate while he is still in her womb; once he's born, he should live. We give birth so that we'll have our self doubly, that we may love it in our child, in whom it smiles at us in purity and holiness, even if we must despise the self within us.

PRIEST: You flatter yourself. God allows you to give birth so that He can chastise you in your flesh and blood and can pursue you even beyond your grave.

SECOND PRIEST (*to the first*): Are there not enough people despairing in our city?

PRIEST: Do you want to be idle when you should sow? Plant your root now while the ground is soft!

MOTHER: My child must not suffer for me. Take him! I shall lock myself in my room, and recall all my sins, and torture myself doubly for each one; I'll torture myself until I die or until God Himself calls down from heaven: 'Stop!'

SECOND PRIEST: Keep your child, and take care of him. That is the will of the Lord, your God!

THE MOTHER (*presses him to her breast*): Yes; I shall look at him until he turns pale, until his whimper dies within him, and his breath stops! I shall not avert my glance from him, not even if his suffering makes his childish eyes clever before they should be, and they terrify me like a staring abyss of wretchedness! I shall do it in order to do more penance than anyone else! But what, if my child becomes still more clever, looks upward and clenches his hands into fists?

PRIEST: Then you must fold them for him! And then you will realize amid shudders that even a child can rebel against God!

THE MOTHER: The staff of Moses hit a rock, and a cool spring gushed forth. That was a rock! (*She beats her breast*) Accursed breast, what are you? From the inside, the most passionate love urges; from the outside, hot and innocent lips press you! But you won't give a drop! Oh, give, give! Suck all my veins dry, but give one more drink to my little one!

SECOND PRIEST (*to others*): Doesn't that touch you?

PRIEST: It does. But, in being touched, I always see the temptation to be untrue to myself and therefore suppress this emotion.

In your case, your manliness is dissolved in tears; you can catch it all in a handkerchief and water a violet with it.

SECOND PRIEST: Tears of which one is unaware are allowed.

ANOTHER WOMAN (*pointing to the Mother*): Have you no consolation for her?

PRIEST (*coldly*): No!

THE WOMAN: Then your God is nowhere but on your lips!

PRIEST: This statement alone makes Bethulia deserve to fall into the hands of Holofernes! I place the burden of guilt for the destruction of the city on your soul! You ask why she has to suffer. Because you are her sister! (*They pass*)

(*Two citizens who have watched the previous scene*)

FIRST CITIZEN: I feel that woman's suffering more deeply than I do my own. Oh, it is terrible!

SECOND: Things are not as terrible as yet as they are going to be! They will be most terrible when it occurs to this mother that she can eat her child! (*He puts his hand to his forehead*) I fear such a thing has already occurred to my wife!

FIRST: You are mad!

SECOND: I fled from the house so that I would not have to beat her to death! No, I shouldn't lie! I ran away because I shuddered at the inhuman meal she seemed to desire, and because I was afraid that I might eat it with her! Our little son was dying. She had thrown herself to the floor with great lamentation. Suddenly, she rose and said softly, ever so softly: 'Is it actually a misfortune that the boy is dying?' Then she bent over him and murmured as though annoyed: 'There's still life in him!' It became dreadfully clear to me; she now saw her child as nothing but a piece of meat!

FIRST: I could go and kill your wife even though she is my sister.

SECOND: You'd be either too early or too late. If she did not take her own life before she ate, she surely killed herself when she had eaten!

A THIRD CITIZEN (*joins them*): Perhaps we'll still be saved after all. Today is the day on which Judith is going to return.

SECOND: Saved after all, now! Now? God! God! I recant all my prayers. That you might hear them now, when it is too late, that is an idea which had not occurred to me as yet and which I can not bear! I shall glorify and praise You, Lord, if You will prove Your infinity in the ever-growing suffering, if You can drive my petrified spirit beyond its endurance, if You can show me an atrocity which will make me forget and even laugh at the atrocities I have already seen. But I shall curse You if You now, this late, come between me and my grave, if I must bury my wife and child and cover them with earth instead of covering them with the clay and dust of my own body! (*They pass*)

MIRZA (*before the gate*) : Open up! Open up!

GUARDS: Who's there?

MIRZA: It's Judith. Judith, with the head of Holofernes.

GUARDS (*call to the city as they open the gates*) : Hear this! Hear this! Judith is back!

> (*The people gather. Elders and Priests come. Judith and Mirza enter through the gate*)

MIRZA (*throws the head down*) : Do you know him?

PEOPLE: We don't know him!

ACHIOR (*joins them and falls on his knees*) : You are great, God of Israel, and there is no God but You! (*He rises*) That is the head of Holofernes! (*He takes Judith's hand*) And that is the hand into which he was given? Woman, my head spins when I look at you!

THE ELDERS: Judith has freed her people! Praised be her name!

PEOPLE (*gather around Judith*) : Blessed be Judith!

JUDITH: Yes, I have killed the first and last man of the earth so that you (*To one*) can graze your sheep in peace, you (*To a second*) can plant your cabbage, and you (*To a third*) can engage in your work and father children who resemble you.

VOICES FROM THE PEOPLE: Let's go to the camp! Now they have no leader!

ACHIOR: Wait a while. They don't know as yet what has happened during the night. Wait until they themselves give us the signal to attack. When their cries are heard, then let us attack!

JUDITH: You owe me a debt of gratitude which you can not repay with the firstlings of your flocks and the first fruit from your gardens! I felt impelled to do the deed; it is up to you to justify it. Become holy and pure; then I can justify it!

> (*Wild, confused cries become audible*)

ACHIOR: Listen! Now is the time!

A PRIEST (*points to the head*) Put it on a spear and carry it as a banner.

JUDITH (*steps before the head*) : This head must be buried at once.

GUARDS (*call down from the wall*) The guards at the well are fleeing in wild disorder. One of the officers bars their path—they raise their swords against him! One of ours is running towards them. It's Ephraim! They don't even see him!

EPHRAIM (*before the gate*) Open up! Open up!

(*The gate is opened. Ephraim rushes in; the gate remains open; one sees Assyrians passing in flight*)

EPHRAIM: They could have put me on a spit and roasted me alive! I've escaped all that! Now that Holofernes has lost his head, so have they all! Come along, come! Any one who's still afraid is a fool!

ACHIOR: Let's go!

(*They storm through the gate. Voices are heard: In the name of Judith!*)

JUDITH (*turns away in disgust*) : That's butcher's courage!

(*Priests and Elders form a circle around her*)

ONE OF THE ELDERS: You have erased the names of our heroes and put yours in their place!

FIRST PRIEST: You have done much for the people and for our religion. From now on, I need no longer point to the dark past if I want to show how great the Lord, our God is!

PRIESTS AND ELDERS: Demand your reward.

JUDITH: Are you making fun of me? (*To the Elders*) If it was not my sacred duty, if I didn't have to do it, isn't it an act of arrogance and sacrilege? (*To the priests*) When the sacrifice falls on the altar and breathes its last, do you torture it by asking what price it sets on its blood and life? (*After a pause, as though seized by a sudden thought*) And still, I shall demand my reward! Promise me first that you'll not refuse my demand!

ELDERS AND PRIESTS: We promise it! In the name of all of Israel!

JUDITH: You are to kill me if I should desire it!

ALL (*horrified*) : Kill you?

JUDITH: Yes, and I have your promise.

ALL (*shuddering*) : You have our promise!

MIRZA (*takes Judith by the arm and leads her to the head of the circle*) : Judith! Judith!

JUDITH: I will not bear the son of Holofernes! Pray to God that my womb be barren. Perhaps he will have mercy on me!

PART TWO

Herod and Mariamne

Introduction to
Herod and Mariamne

SUMMARY OF HEBBEL'S SOURCE:
JOSEPHUS FLAVIUS, *JEWISH ANTIQUITIES*

Herod, an Idumean (half-Jew), made king of Judea by Marcus Flavius in recognition of large payments, married Mariamne, the daughter of Alexander and Alexandra, granddaughter of Hyrcanus, ex-high priest, and sister of Aristobolus. Her family was of Maccabean descent, numbering Judith, the assassin of Holofernes, and Judas Maccabeus, restorer of monotheistic worship in Jewish temples, among its ancestry. Because of its tradition, the family was highly respected among the Jewish people.

Highly impatient with old-fashioned Jewish tradition, the half-pagan Herod wanted to make the Jews more "progressive" and himself more powerful. The marriage, on the other hand, may be regarded as a concession to the Jews although love certainly entered in for Herod, and, it seems, for Mariamne as well.

The details concerning young Herod (either fifteen or twenty-five years of age) before the Synedrion (Sanhedrin), the assembly, are as follows: Herod had apprehended a Syrian brigand named Hezekiah and had put him to death without benefit of the judgement of the assembly. When called to account by that body, he appeared with his bodyguard and intimidated the elders. In spite of Sameas' warning, Hyrcanus, whose granddaughter later became Herod's wife, helped him flee.

When Herod had become king, he made Ananelus high priest. His mother-in-law, Alexandra, felt that her family had been slighted and complained to Cleopatra about it and also sent Antonius, who had a deserved reputation as a libertine, pictures of her children, Aristobolus and Mariamne, to arouse his interest in them. Antonius asked Herod to send Aristobolus to him, but Herod knew Antonius too well and made the sixteen-year-old Aristobolus high priest so that he could not leave the country. Since Mariamne's brother was a very handsome youth and very popular among the Jews, however, Herod soon came to consider his own position threatened and had Aristobolus killed. Before the assassination, Alexandra, sensing danger, had written to Cleopatra, who had invited her to flee to Egypt with her son. This attempted flight had been foiled when Herod, informed of her plans, had come to the boat and found the mother and the son hidden in coffins. After the death of Aristobolus, Alexandra wrote to Cleopatra, whose intercession with Antonius on Alexandra's behalf resulted in Herod's summons to the Roman to defend and explain his actions. Herod soothed Antonius with great tribute payments and achieved his support. Before his departure, he had asked Joseph, his uncle and brother-in-law, to kill Mariamne if he failed to return. Mariamne learned of this when Joseph told her about it as a proof of Herod's great love for her. Herod's return was marked by a temporary coolness between man and wife, Mariamne's revelation of what Joseph had told her, and Joseph's execution without a hearing.

When Herod went to Arabia to collect tribute for Cleopatra, she and Antonius were preparing to fight against Octavian at Actium (31 B.C.). Before he went on the mission, Herod put Sohemus in charge and commanded the latter to kill Mariamne in case he did not return. Sohemus, fearing for his position with Herod if the king did return, told Mariamne about it. Some time after Herod's return, his sister Salome concocted a tale about Mariamne's desire to poison Herod. Herod, immediately certain that this could only be the result of Sohemus' indiscretion concerning Herod's command, had him executed. Mariamne was given a hearing before Herod's staunchest supporters, who realized that the death verdict was expected and sought by Herod. Alexandra, prompted by her own opportunism, publicly reproached her daughter, who remained composed and went to her death with noble courage.

After her execution, Herod did mourn for Mariamne by

lamenting, by ordering the servants to call her as though she were still alive, and, finally, by becoming very ill. When he learned that Alexandra was plotting against him, he also had her slain.

Herod died in 4 B.C.

In constructing this drama, Hebbel skillfully limited his presentation on stage to the basic problem in the relationship of Herod and Mariamne, but, without overwhelming us with historical detail and names, managed to work all the historical background into narrated exposition. We are totally enabled to understand Herod in the light of his personality and his times while Herod mirrors the times for us through his personality. Mariamne is a credible, beautiful human being who reflects her family tradition without losing her personality and individuality. The secondary characters, even those with the smallest function, act as foils for the main characters but also as reflections of the period of history, which we need to understand in order to realize that this drama of two human beings has a statement to make about their time and about all times and all human beings as well. Again, Hebbel's main themes are individuation and the change which is the only constant factor in history.

In his critique of Massinger's *Lodovico*, Hebbel retells the story of Herod and Mariamne as he knows it from Josephus. The essay is written in 1849, the year of Hebbel's play, and, Hebbel states, certain points are only obscurely implied by Josephus and not forged into the whole. The material of this story, he states, has already

been raised so far beyond its province [history] and requires a talent which knows how to trace its special events and actions, which remain incredible and improbable in spite of any documentation of their accuracy, from the universal conditions of their world, people and time, a talent capable of developing Herod's fever from the atmosphere which he inhaled, and of developing this atmosphere from the steaming, vulcanic ground on which he stood.

In characterizing Herod, we again must consider Hebbel's own statement in the same essay:

Herod left the world as a bloodspurted monster . . . but did not enter the world as a monster. As a young man, he appears great and noble, equipped with all the splendid attributes which a man and hero possesses, and he stays this way for a long time. . . . Whoever . . . compares [Herod's] beginning and end will doubtless say to himself: This is the material for a shattering tragedy of the highest rank, one which depicts human nature in its dependency on the powers of fate, one which does not describe a circle within a circle, but rather the circle itself which comprehends everything else. If he is then also possessed of some artistic sensitivity, he will add immediately: only that man will raise this treasure who is capable of deriving this end from that beginning with convincing necessity.

Herod individuates in his attempt to rule his kingdom and his household solely according to his personal sense of values and order. He is not part of the Jewish world of Judea since he is a pagan and a self-made man, especially when he compares his ancestry (lacking tradition and dynasty because his father was the first ruler of the family) with that of the Maccabeans. At the same time, he is embarrassed about and impatient with the traditionalism of the Jews, their adherence to what he, as an outsider and upstart, considers antiquated laws, and openly flaunts his power to disregard or disobey such laws; examples are: his youthful victory over the Synedrion (Sanhedrin); his disregard for Sameas' warning not to bury a suicide; his embarrassed amusement when Joab reports about the taunts he received in Antonius' camp when he refused to eat and drink there; his own report concerning the feasting with Antonius, in which he had engaged without dietary scruples; his comparison of Jewry with the Dead Sea. In his home life, Herod's individuation is shown in the demand he makes of Mariamne that she commit suicide if he should not return; his inability to understand her objection to such a demand; his order to Joseph and his repetition of it to Sohemus. He demands the highest, most unselfish love from his wife and yet does not trust her, treats her like an object, a possession of which he can dispose as he sees fit. Actually, Herod is totally unscrupulous and interested only in his own success and well-being, so much so that he has to imperil his wife whenever he gambles his own life and position to further his political ambitions; but Hebbel somehow succeeds in making him human:

> Herod stands all alone, and it is just that which makes his excessive love, his passionate clutching of the only person sincerely devoted to him so understandable and so natural.[1]

Mariamne herself points out that Herod knows how to justify anything, even the murder of her brother. When he explains why he had to place Mariamne under the sword of Joseph, there is an obvious sincerity in his statement that he knew that he would risk his utmost to save Mariamne's life; Herod's explanation that he won the favor of Octavianus by neither lying nor groveling but by the candid admission of his friendship for Antonius and his offer to become the friend of Octavianus forces us to admire his daring and optimism as well as his insight into his adversary's personality and his political success. While the hearing he provides for Mariamne is a travesty on justice, even it is made tolerable by the evident sincerity of his admission that he can not bear the torture of his jealous uncertainty any longer. We also tend to sympathize with him when he experiences the shock of Titus' revelation after which he states that he would gladly bury himself with his own hands if this would bring Mariamne back to him. And yet, it is at the end of this speech, that Herod resolves to be inhuman and monstrous. He decides that henceforth his possessions, chiefly his crown, will receive the attention, devotion and energy he had formerly devoted to Mariamne. To hold on, to stop any competitor, including the newly born king in Bethlehem, he will become a monster. As a start, he will have all the infants in Bethlehem killed.

Herod, who was amused at the traditionalism of the Jews and thought that it kept them backward, living in the past, will fight the dawning new era, in which there is no place for him, with all his energy. Instead of growing more humane through understanding of Mariamne's death, he rejects this last opportunity for introspection and improvement. The new era, Christianity, will stress humaneness as did the Jewish tradition. Therefore, Herod's rejection of it, his sullenness and defiance before the new, mark the path to his destruction but will not stop the movement of time, will not preserve him and his way of life.

---

1. Hebbel, *Lodovico*

This is not stated in the drama, but it is clearly present. Herod, who feels himself ahead of his time, is, in reality, already a reactionary and must perish so that the harmonious new and better world can come into being. The survival of Christ during the slaughter of the infants is known to the reader or spectator and is also implied by Joab's remark at the end that Moses had been saved in spite of Pharaoh.

Although Mariamne is a typical Hebbel heroine, she is doubtless also his most successful one. She is all woman, but combines her femininity with a strong consciousness of her human dignity and value. She has high ethics and morals and deeply loves the man whom she has not even chosen for herself. The ideals of personal and religious integrity have been strongly instilled in her through her Maccabean heritage, but, as a wife, she wishes to put her husband even before these ideals, just as she would like him to come to her not as her king but as her husband. Her consciousness of the dilemma of being unable to reconcile the Maccabean tradition and family with being Herod's wife begins with the murder of her brother, Aristobolus, at the command of Herod. And yet, while she can not deny Herod's guilt in this, she retains the objectivity to see that her mother's machinations had forced Herod to fear for his position and had thus led him to this crime. This does not mean that she forgets what Herod has done; but she does continue to love Herod. When he asks her to express her opinion of the woman who committed suicide after her husband had died, she all but states that she herself might do the same but emphasizes that such an action must be voluntary, in fact instinctive, on the part of the widow if it is to be meaningful. She realizes how much Herod can dominate her because of his masculine virtue, but she never tells him so. She does vow to end her life if Herod should not return from Antonius, but she does it only after Herod has left, and does it in part at least to indicate her human independence by protesting against her mother's demands.

Mariamne is deeply hurt when she learns from Joseph that Herod had ordered him to kill her because this revelation shows her Herod's lack of trust in her and her love, and must therefore also destroy her confidence in him. She tells Herod this, but their communication does not suffice for him to learn the lesson. She had hoped that he had understood and waits to see how Herod will use his second chance to prove his love and trust when he is sent to Arabia. Herod again misunderstands her because he fails to see her as a fine human being, and merely regards her as his prize possession. He misinterprets her joy at the opportunity for Herod to right his wrong, for he thinks that she can not wait for his death in her eagerness to be free of him. When Mariamne learns that Herod has left orders with Sohemus that she be killed if the king fails to return, she first wants to take her own life. What stops her is the desire to die in such a way as to prove that she does love Herod. For this reason, she decides to show herself to Herod as he sees her and to force him to put her to death. Only after her death is he to learn the truth. She orders the feast at which she dances; when Herod returns, he thinks that she is dancing to celebrate his death. During the trial, Mariamne retains her composure and does not explain herself at all until she speaks to Titus, who has been her most severe critic.

Mariamne's decision to die at the hands of Herod on her terms marks her return to the noble tradition of the Maccabeans as liberators of human and religious dignity. Her opening remarks at her trial make this fact clear. She states that she is on trial before her ancestors and especially apostrophizes Judas Maccabeus with the promise: "you'll be satisfied with me!" So her death must be seen as her return to the tradition from which she tried to remove herself in order to be a good wife to Herod. She had found it difficult to be a good wife with the conflict between her high human values and Herod's political expediencies, but she tried to let her love dominate over her Maccabean world. There seems to be no difficulty in seeing that she could protest against her mother's political machinations and still be a good Maccabean, for her mother is too petty to represent that family.

If Mariamne's individuation was her attempt to break with the Maccabean world and to live only for Herod, then this breach is healed when she decides to have Herod find her guilty of death and execute her. Since she dies with this awareness, which she made clear at her trial, the totality and harmony of the world is restored. Mariamne dies at peace with herself, averring human dignity.

Hebbel's statement that the cause of the dissonance can not be explained by the outcome of the drama is applicable here just as it is in *Judith*. The cause of the dissonance lies in the nature of the woman who falls in love with a man whom she should not love. Mariamne experienced a conflict similar to Judith's, who had found herself beginning to fall in love with the man she had set out to kill.

Herod and Mariamne

DRAMATIS PERSONAE

KING HEROD
MARIAMNE, *his wife*
ALEXANDRA, *her mother*
SALOME, *the king's sister*
SOHEMUS, *governor of Galilee*
JOSEPH, *viceroy in Herod's absence*
SAMEAS, *a Pharisee*
TITUS, *a Roman captain*
JOAB, *a messenger*
JUDAS, *a Jewish captain*
ARTAXERXES, *a servant*
MOSES, *a servant*
JEHU, *a servant*
OTHER SERVANTS
SILO, *a citizen*
SERUBABEL, *a Galilean*
PHILO, *Serubabel's son*
A ROMAN MESSENGER
AARON, *a judge*
FIVE OTHER JUDGES
THREE KINGS FROM THE EAST, *later called the Three Wise Men
     by the Christian Church*

THE PLACE: *Jerusalem*
THE TIME: *Around the birth of Christ*

ACT I

Zion Castle. Large audience hall. Joab. Sameas. Serubabel and
his son. Titus. Judas and many others.
Herod enters.

SCENE I

JOAB (*approaches the king*) : I have returned!
HEROD: I'll see you later.
The most important first!
JOAB (*stepping back, to himself*) :   The most important!
I should have thought that would be finding out
Whether our head is still secure or not!
HEROD (*signals Judas*) : How are things at the fire now?
JUDAS: The fire?
Then you already know what I report?
HEROD: Its outbreak was at midnight. I was first
To see it and to summon thence the guard.
I think I was the one who wakened you!
JUDAS: It is put out! (*To himself*) It is the truth then
That he steals through the streets in masked disguise
While others sleep! Then we must guard our tongue
Lest ever it confront his listening ear.
HEROD: When all was up in flames, I did espy
A young girl through the window of a house.
She seemed to be quite stricken. Was she saved?
JUDAS: She did not want our help.
HEROD: Not want?
JUDAS: By God,
How she resisted those who tried to save her
By force. How she did beat at them with hands

And feet! And how she gripped the very bed
On which she sat screaming the while that she
Had been about to kill herself that moment,
And now, conveniently, death came by chance.
    HEROD: She probably was mad!
    JUDAS: It's possible
That in her grief she had indeed gone mad.
Her husband had just died the previous moment.
His corpse, still warm, was lying by her side.
    HEROD (*to himself*): I shall recount this tale to Mariamne
And closely watch how she reacts! (*Aloud*) This woman,
I trust, was childless. But, if she had a child,
I shall provide for him. Let her be
Buried in opulence and noble splendor.
She may have been the queen of womankind.
    SAMEAS (*approaches Herod*): Be buried? But this cannot be
        allowed!
At very least, not in Jerusalem!
For it is written—
    HEROD: Do I not know you?
    SAMEAS: You had the chance to meet me at one time;
I was the tongue of the Synedrion
When it was silenced by you!
    HEROD: Sameas,
I hope you know me too! You did pursue
Me harshly in my youth and would have liked
To make a present to the hangman of
This head; as man and king, I have forgotten
What you once did; your head is still attached!
    SAMEAS: If I am not to use it for the reason
That you did not remove it, take it now.
Disuse would be far worse than losing it!
    HEROD: Why did you come? I've never seen you here
Within these walls before.
    SAMEAS: For just that reason
You see me here today. You thought, perhaps,
That I had fear of you. I fear you not,
Not even now, when many a man has learned
This fear, who until now, I mean until
The death of Aristobolus, had none.
And now that opportunity has come
For me to show my gratitude to you

I seize it. And I warn you seriously
Not to commit an act the Lord has damned.
The bones of such a woman are accursed.
She did resist the rescue like a heathen,
That is as though she'd taken her own life.
And since—

HEROD: Some other time! (*To Serubabel*) From
Galilee!

You're Serubabel who did—welcome, friend!
Your own fault that I see you only now!

SERUBABEL: Your recognition honors me, oh King!
(*Points to his mouth*) Of course, these two big teeth of mine
do help,
Which make me look the cousin of a boar!—

HEROD: I should forget this face of mine before
The face of any man who served me well!
While I pursued the robbers in your province,
You were my shrewdest spy. What do you bring?

SERUBABEL (*signals his son*) : Not very much! I bring Philo,
my son,
You need good soldiers. I have need of none,
And this one is a Roman, who was, quite
By accident, born of a Hebrew mother.

HEROD: I always get good gifts from Galilee!
Wait, I shall have you called. (*Serubabel and his son step back*)

TITUS: Deception, vile,
Which I discovered forces me—

HEROD: Reveal it!

TITUS: The mute do speak!

HEROD: Explain!

TITUS: Your very footman
Who stood guard for you with one of my
Centurions last night, before your room—

HEROD (*to himself*) : Whom Alexandra, mother of my wife,
Brought to my service—

TITUS: Is by no means mute
As all the world seems to believe he is;
He did speak in a dream; in fact, he cursed!

HEROD: While in a dream?

TITUS: He stood there, fast asleep,
And my centurion did not waken him.
He did not think that was his obligation

Since that one is no soldier like himself.
But closely watch he did, to catch him if
He fell, lest he disturb you in your room,
For it was early, and you were asleep.
As my man watches, this mute suddenly
Begins to murmur, uttering your name,
And to it adds the most abhorrent curse.

    HEROD: It's certain? Your centurion does not err?

    TITUS: Then he himself would have been sound asleep,
And that would be an omen far, far worse
For the eternal city than the lightning
Which struck the she-wolf on the Capitol!

    HEROD: I thank you then! And now— (*sends all but Joab away*)
                                That's how it is!

Betrayed in my own house with open scorn
Among the rabble of the Pharisees!
They're bolder now, because I cannot punish,
Lest I should make a martyr of a fool;
There is some love for me in Galilee;
No, it is really selfish; they depend
On me, the bugbear with the unsheathed sword
Who frightens from afar their vulgar mob,
And—this man surely brings bad news to me;
His haste to state his message was too great.
For even that one, though he is my servant,
Enjoys upsetting me if he but knows
That I must act, as though I did not notice!
(*to Joab*) What's new in Alexandria?

    JOAB: I saw
Antonius!

    HEROD: A strange beginning, this!
You saw him then? But I am used to this!
All men receive my messengers at once!
Indeed, you are the very first to see
Necessity to mention such success!

    JOAB: They made it hard enough for me! Refused
Me stubbornly!

    HEROD (*to himself*):   Octavian and he
Must still be better friends than I had thought!
(*Aloud*) That proves to me your choice of hour was poor!

    JOAB: Indeed, I chose each of the twenty-four
Of which the day consists; no matter how

They acted, I did not withdraw, not even
When I was offered food by soldiers who,
When I refused it, jeered at me and said:
He only eats from what the cat has tasted
And what the dog has chewed with his own mouth!
At last, success—
   HEROD: Which for a brighter man
Would have been instant—
   JOAB: He received me then.
But it was night, and first I had to think
He'd had me called in order to continue
The jeering which the soldiers had begun;
For, when I entered there, what did I find?
A group of topers stretching out on couches.
But then he filled a cup for me himself
And cried: Here, drink this to my health!
And when, politely, I refused to drink,
He said: Were it my aim to kill this man,
I'd merely need to call him to my table
For eight successive days and place on it
The tribute paid to me by earth and sea;
This one would idly sit and starve himself
And swear in death he felt no hunger pangs.
   HEROD: Indeed they know us well! But that must change!
What Moses, if he was no fool, commanded
Only to keep the people from return
To idol worship is obeyed today
As though it had a purpose of its own!
Thus does the healthy man demand the drug
Which, once in sickness, brought about his cure
As though the drug gave nourishment as well!
That should—go on!
   JOAB: But I soon understood
That I had been in error, for, indeed,
While drinking, he performed official acts:
Appointed magistrates, and then arranged
For sacrifice to Zeus; he questioned augurs;
He spoke with messengers as they arrived,
Not just with me. It really looked quite strange;
A slave stood there, behind him, listening hard,
With slate and stylus ready for dictation
And with ridiculous sobriety

Wrote down what issued from his drunken lips.
I later heard he reads this tablet over
On the next morning, hangover and all,
And so exactly keeps with what it says
That he, they say he vowed this recently,
Would even wring his neck himself if ever
In his intoxication he had given
Away the world he owns and, doing so,
Deprived himself of any place thereon.
Whether he zigzags when he walks by day—
He does while looking for his bed at night!—
Makes little diff'rence in my estimation.

HEROD: Octavian, you conquer; there just remains
The question: now or later? Well?

JOAB: At last,
When my turn came, and I gave him the letter,
Which I had for him, then what did he do?
He threw it scornfully in the direction
Of his scribe instead of op'ning it.
His steward then was told to bring to him
A picture which was placed before me
To tell how good a likeness it presented.

HEROD: The picture was—
                    Of Aristobolus,
Of that high priest who drowned so rapidly;
From Alexandra, mother of your wife,
Who writes to him, it had come long ago.
But greedily, he looked upon it as if
He'd never had it in his hand before.
I stood confused and silent. Then he said
As he examined it: The lamps in here
Seem very dull! And, picking up your letter,
Set it aflame and let it turn to ash
Before the picture like an empty sheet.

HEROD: That's bold even for him! But—he was drunk!

JOAB: I cried: What are you doing there? You have
Not even read the letter! And he replied:
I want to speak with Herod. I intend that.
He stands accused before me of a crime!
And then I had to tell about the high priest
And how he died. And, when I told him that
A dizzy spell had seized the bathing priest,

He interrupted me: 'Had seized' is right,
That dizzy spell had fists, that is a fact!
And then I heard, forgive that I report it,
That Rome does not believe that the young priest
Did drown. Instead, they do accuse you there
Of having caused your chamberlains to see
That he be choked while in the river bath.
    HEROD: You, Alexandra, do I thank!
    JOAB: He signaled
For me to go. I did. But then he called
Me back again and said: You still owe me
The answer to the question I put first.
Therefore, I shall repeat it. Does this picture
Resemble him who died? I had to nod.
He asked: Does Mariamne look like him
Who was her brother and met dreadful death?
Does every woman hate her lovely face?
    HEROD: And you?
    JOAB: First hear what all the others said,
For they had risen then and stood around
The picture with me. Laughingly they cried
While with Antonius they traded smirks:
Say yes if e'er the dead man gave you gifts.
Then you'll see him avenged, you may be sure!
I said, however, that I could not know,
For never had I had the chance to see
The queen without her veil. And that's the truth!
    HEROD (*to himself*): Ha, Mariamne! But—I laugh at this,
For I know how to guard against this case
For sure, no matter how it comes about!
(*To Joab*) And what are you to tell me from his lips?
    JOAB: Nothing at all! If there were any message,
There'd be no need to tell all this detail.
But, in this case, it seemed important.
    HEROD: Fine!
You'll go to Alexandria with me
At once. So do not leave the castle now.
    JOAB: Nor shall I talk within your castle walls.
    HEROD: I know. For who likes death upon the cross,
Now, of all times, when figs are ripening?
The mute is to be throttled. Should he ask
Why, then tell him for his ability

To ask. (*To himself*) At last I know from whom that snake
So often learned what I—that wicked woman!
(*To Joab*) Attend to it. I'll have to see the head!
I want to send it to my moth'r in law.
(*To himself*) Apparently, she needs a warning sign.
    JOAB: At once!
    HEROD: And then, the youth from Galilee,
The son of Serubabel, takes his place.
I want to see him too before we leave. (*Joab off*)

SCENE II

    HEROD (*alone*) : So this is it! Again, I almost said,
But I can see no end. I'm like the man
Of legend whom the lion seized in front,
The tiger, from behind, while birds of prey
Were menacing above with beaks and claws,
The while his feet stood in a clump of snakes.
All right. I shall resist each enemy
And each sword too, as well as possible.
Let that, henceforth, be rule and law for me.
I shall not be concerned how long I last
As long as I assert myself until
The end, and lose no thing I called my own.
Then let this end approach whene'er it will.

SCENE III

    A SERVANT (*enters*) : The Queen!
(*Mariamne follows him*)
    HEROD (*goes toward her*) :   You have anticipated me!
        I wished—
    MARIAMNE: Surely, you would not come yourself
So I could thank you for the splendid pearls?
I did refuse you twice. To try once more,
To see if I had changed my mind, would be
Too much, I'm sure, for any man and thus
Too much indeed for any king. No, Sire,
I know my duty, and, since you
Have daily given splendid gifts to me
Since, suddenly, my lively brother died
As though you're courting me again, I've come

At last to show my gratitude to you.
    HEROD: I see it!
    MARIAMNE: 'Tis true, I do not know for sure
What you intend for me. Into the deep,
You send the diver, and, if there is none
Who would disturb Leviathanian calm
For shiny payment, then you open up
Your prison's gates and simply say you'll give
That robber back the head he was to forfeit
Who'll fish for pearls for you to give to me.
    HEROD: And this seems wrong to you? You know I freed
A murderer, already crucified,
When there was opportunity to save
A child from fire, and I said to him: If
You restore him to his mother, I
Shall say you've paid your debt with your own death.
He did rush in—
    MARIAMNE: And did he come back out?
    HEROD: It was too late. But still, my word I would
Have kept and sent him in a uniform
To Rome, where there is need for tigers now.
One should be usurer with everything,
Why not with life that's lost its usefulness?
There may be cases where it might have use!
    MARIAMNE *(to herself)* : Oh, that his hands were not so stained
        with blood!
I shall say nothing, for, whate'er he's done,
He speaks of it, as though it were for good.
How horrid, if he were to force me now
To see my brother's murder in this light
As necessary, good, inevitable!
    HEROD: You do not speak?
    MARIAMNE: Perhaps I am to speak
Of pearls, that's what the subject was 'til now.
We spoke of pearls which are so pure and white
That they don't lose their lustrous purity,
Even when held by bloodstained hands. You gave
Me quite a few.
    HEROD: Does that distress you?
    MARIAMNE: Not me!
You cannot hope to pay off thus the guilt
Acquired, and, it seems to me, I have

A perfect right as wife and queen to own
Jewels and pearls. Indeed, like Egypt's queen,
I may state of the precious gem I hold:
It is my servant whom I shall forgive
For badly representing stars to me
Since, doing so, it does outshine the flow'r.
But then, you have a sister, Salome—

    HEROD: And she—

    MARIAMNE: Well, if she is to murder me,
Then just go on, plunder the sea for me.
If not—then let the diver have a rest.
My debt to her is great enough! You look
At me with doubt? It's true! It's true! When I
Lay at death's door last year, your sister kissed me.
It was the first, indeed the only time!
I thought immediately: That's your reward
For passing on to death. And I was right!
But I deceived her then, for I got well.
So now I have her kiss to no avail,
And she has not forgotten. I feared she might
Remember this if I should call on her
And wore around my neck those splendid pearls
With which you last displayed your love for me!

    HEROD (*to himself*): Now all I need is that my own left hand
Decide to turn against my right!

    MARIAMNE: I should,
At very least, refuse her welcome-drink!
And if, instead of spicy wine, she were
To offer guileless water, in crystal glass,
I should not even touch that! To be sure,
That would mean nothing! It would be natural
Indeed; for even water could not have
The meaning for me which it used to have:
A gentle element to nourish plants,
Refreshing me and all the world. It now
Infuses me with shudders, fills with dread,
Because my brother was consumed by it.
I keep rememb'ring life dwells in the drop,
But, in the wave, does bitter death reside!
For you it must be even worse!

    HEROD: Why's that?

    MARIAMNE: Because a river slanders your good name,

A river which presumes to burden you
With its cruel treachery. But do not fear,
I contradict it!
    HEROD: You do?
    MARIAMNE: I can!
How could one reconcile the two: to love
The sister and to kill the brother?
    HEROD: Perhaps
One could, if such a brother planned one's death,
And if one only could survive this way:
Opposing, no, anticipating him!
We only speak of possibilities!
If he, himself naive, allowed himself
To be a weapon in th' opponents' hands,
A deadly weapon which must kill for sure
Unless one breaks it first, before it's used.
We only speak of possibilities!
Suppose, this weapon menaces not just
An individual's but a nation's head,
And one the nation needs so urgently
As any rump could ever need its head.
We only speak of possibilities!
If this were so, the sister, out of love
She owes her husband as his wife, out of
Duty as her people's daughter, and
Then out of both as queen, would have to say:
I cannot cast reproach for what occurred!
(*He takes her hand*) And, even if a Ruth could not grasp this,
How could she, she who had to glean the fields?
The Maccabean woman understands!
You could not bear my kiss in Jericho;
You will permit it in Jerusalem!
(*Kisses her*) And if the kiss still causes you regret,
Then hear what's sure to reconcile your heart.
I snatched this kiss to take my leave from you,
And this leave-taking might well be our last!
    MARIAMNE: Our last?
    HEROD: Antonius has summoned me.
Whether I shall return, I do not know!
    MARIAMNE: You do not know?
    HEROD: Because I do not know
How harshly my—your mother spoke of me.

MARIAMNE (*wants to speak*)

HEROD: No matter! I shall hear. But I must know
This from your lips. You must tell me:
Should I defend myself and in what way—

MARIAMNE: Should you—

HEROD: Oh, Mariamne, do not ask.
You know the spell by which I'm bound to you.
You know that ev'ry day has strengthened it,
So you must feel that I now can not fight
Just for myself unless you do assure
Me that your heart still beats for me with love!
Is your love fire, or has it turned to ice?
Then I shall know whether Antonius
Will call me brother or, instead of that,
Condemn me to his dungeon, there to die
As did Jugurtha, whom he starved to death.
You do not speak? Speak, Love. I realize
That this confession ill becomes a king.
He should not be subjected to the fate
Of ordinary men, should not be bound
Within to anyone except himself;
He only should be slave to God, the Lord.
This is not so for me. When you, last year,
Were at death's door, I did consider then
Killing myself, so that I would not live
To see you die, and—since you know this now—
You should know too that I, when my turn comes,
When I'm about to die, I might well do
What you expect of Salome; I could
Give you a deadly drink—poison in wine—
So that I could be sure of you in death

MARIAMNE: If you did that, you surely would get well!

HEROD: Oh no, my love, For I should share it with you.
But tell me now, could you forgive me for
Such proof as this of my excessive love?

MARIAMNE: If, after drinking such a deadly drink
I had in me the strength for one last word,
Then I should curse you with my final breath!
(*To herself*) I'd do that all the sooner surely, since
I know, if death would summon you from me
I'd seize the sword and take my life from grief!
One has to will such death; it can't be forced!

HEROD: In this night's fire, there was a wife who chose

To perish with the man she loved. They tried
To save her; she resisted; you despise
This woman's act, don't you?
MARIAMNE: Who tells you that?
She was not sacrificed by anyone;
She sacrificed herself, which proves: to her
The dead man meant more than the world and life.
HEROD: And you? And I?
MARIAMNE: If you may tell yourself
That you made up for all the world to me,
Then what should keep me in it when you die?
HEROD: The world! There's many a king within the world;
And none among them would refuse to share
His throne with you. There's none who would not leave
His bride for you or send his wife away
Though't were the first day of his honeymoon.
MARIAMNE: Is Cleopatra dead that you speak thus?
HEROD: You are so beautiful that all who see
You must believe in immortality
With which the Pharisees flatter themselves,
Since none can grasp that beauty such as yours
Can fade away; your beauty's such that I'd
Not be astonished if the mountain mines
Were suddenly producing nobler ore
Than gold and silver, metal they had saved
For you to complement your beauty. Yes,
So lovely—And then know that you'll die
Right after one who did in death precede,
You'll die for love to hasten after him,
So that, within the sphere where one both is
And is not, that's what I would imagine,
You'll fuse, one last breath, with another's last—
That would be worth committing suicide,
That would indeed be finding bliss beyond
The grave and all the terrors it contains.
Oh Mariamne, may I hope, or should
I dread—Antonius asked concerning you!
MARIAMNE: For deeds, there's no certificate of debt,
And much less still for pain and sacrifice
Such as despair might cause, I feel it's so,
But love could never make demand of them!
HEROD: Farewell!
MARIAMNE: Farewell! I know you will return!

Your life (*she points to heaven*) is in His hands.
HEROD: So little fear?
MARIAMNE: So great my confidence!
HEROD: But love would fear!
It even trembles in a hero's heart!
MARIAMNE: My love does not!
HEROD: It's you who tremble not!
MARIAMNE: It's my turn now! Have you no confidence
Since you did cause my brother's—woe to me
And woe to you!
HEROD: You did withhold your word,
A simple word, and I had hoped that you
Would swear to me. In what shall I trust now?
MARIAMNE: And if I were to swear, what would ensure
That I would keep my oath? Only myself,
My person, as you know me. So it seems,
You should begin with hope and confidence
In me, which, in the end, you still would need.
Go then! I can't say otherwise today! (*off*)

SCENE IV

HEROD: Not this day? But the next? Or later still?
She wants to do me good after my death!
Speaks thus a wife? 'Tis true, she often did
Distort her face to ugliness, when I
Had told her she was beautiful. I know
Too that she cannot weep, has cramps instead
When others cry. I also know that she
Had quarreled with her brother just before
He bathed and met his death, and then she had
Pretended that he could not reconcile
Her. Yes, what's more, after his death, she did
Receive a present he had sent to her
Which he had bought while going to the bath.
And still, is this the way a wife would speak
To one she loves, or should love, when he is—
She does not come again, as she did once;
She's left no scarf for which she could—she cares not
That I, with this impression—so be it!
To Alexandria—the grave—all right!
But one thing first! May earth and heaven hear:

You did not swear; I swear this oath to you.
You too will die, and by the sword. So, if
Antonius deserts me for your sake—
Which for your mother's he would never do—
He still will be deceived. Although there's doubt
That what I wear in death will follow me
Into the grave, since any thief can steal
It from me, you shall follow me in death!
That's certain now! If I do not return,
Then you will die! I shall leave this command.
Command! That word brings up an evil point:
What will ensure that I shall be obeyed
If no one needs to fear me anymore?
I'll need a man, I think, who trembles at
Her sight!

SCENE V

SERVANT: Your broth'r-in-law!
HEROD: He's welcome now!
He is my man! My sword I'll give to him
And then incite him, in his cowardice,
To have the courage needed for its use.
JOSEPH (*enters*): I hear you'll leave for Alexandria
Quite soon. I've come to say farewell.
HEROD: Farewell! Perhaps, we'll never meet again.
JOSEPH: We'll never meet again?
HEROD: It could be so!
JOSEPH: I've never seen you thus!
HEROD: Let that confirm
I've never faced a problem such as this.
JOSEPH: If you lose courage—
HEROD: I shall not do that,
For I shall bear whatever comes; but I
Have lost the hope that things will turn out well.
JOSEPH: And now I wish I had been blind so that
I never could have learned the secret plans
Of Alexandra!
HEROD: I am sure that's true!
JOSEPH: Had I not learned that to Antonius
She'd sent the face of Aristobolus,
Painted in secret, and had I not learned

About her messenger to Egypt's queen,
And if I only had not stopped her in
The harbor, where I'd found her with her son;
They'd hidden in a coffin, were in flight
When I did stop them there—

HEROD: Then she'd have
No cause to thank you. Calmly, you could gaze
Upon her daughter sitting on the throne,
Which she, the fearless Maccabean queen,
Will surely seize if I do not return
Unless another sits upon it first.

JOSEPH: That is not what I meant. I meant that much
Would not have been then.

HEROD: Much indeed. You're right!
But many other things would have occurred.
No matter now.—You mentioned many things;
There's one you still forgot.

JOSEPH: Which do you mean?

HEROD: You too were in the bath when—

JOSEPH: That is true!

HEROD: You struggled with him?

JOSEPH: Yes, initially.

HEROD: Well then!

JOSEPH: 'Twas not in my arms that the spell
Of dizziness o'ercame him. If it had,
I should have saved him, or he would have drowned,
Pulling me down with him to share his fate.

HEROD: I do not doubt your word. But you will know
That no one who was there speaks diff'rently,
And since misfortune has it thus that you
Not only went with him but also did engage
In struggle there with him—

JOSEPH: Why do you stop?

HEROD: Dear Joseph, you and I, we both must face
Harsh accusations!

JOSEPH: I?

HEROD: You are not just
My broth'r-in-law; you are my trusted friend.

JOSEPH: I like to think so!

HEROD: Would you'd never been!
If I, like Saul, had thrown a spear at you,
You'd have the proof you'd need, of fatal wounds.

'Twere better for you if this slander had
Found no believing ear, and you would not
Face death, decapitation, for a crime
You never did commit.

JOSEPH: Do I face death?

HEROD: That is your fate if I do not return
And Mariamne—

JOSEPH: But I am innocent!

HEROD: What good is that? Appearances convict!
And even if you were believed, are not
The many, many things you did for me,
In Alexandra's judgement, crimes you did
Commit against her? Don't you know she'll think:
Had he, that time, allowed me to escape,
Then my dead son would be alive today?

JOSEPH: True! True!

HEROD: Quite justly, can she now demand
Your life as payment for another which,
Through your responsibility, was lost,
And will she not obtain it through her daughter?

JOSEPH: Oh Salome, that was because I went
To have my portrait done! Each year she asks
Me for a new one!

HEROD: Yes, I know her love!

JOSEPH: 'Twere better she loved me less! Would I have seen
Of Aristobolus the portrait there
If I—well, now she'll soon receive my last
Portrait; it will have no head!

HEROD: Joseph,
One must defend one's head!

JOSEPH: But if you say
That yours is lost?

HEROD: I'm not convinced it is,
And I shall try to save it in the end
By placing it, by my free choice, inside
The lion's mouth!

JOSEPH: That worked for you before!
That time when Pharisees—

HEROD: It's much worse now!
No matter though what happens in my case,
You must henceforth be master of your fate;
You always were a man; now be a king!

I'll place the purple robe about you now
And give to you the scepter and the sword.
Keep these, and give them back only to me!
JOSEPH: Am I to think that—
HEROD: To ensure that you
Will keep the throne and, with it, your own life,
Kill Mariamne when you get the news
That I have died.
JOSEPH: Kill Mariamne—I?
HEROD: She is the last tie Alexandra has
That binds her with the people since her son
Has died. She is the helmet-plume which will
Be worn by the rebellion which will rise
Against you when—
JOSEPH: But—Mariamne—kill!
HEROD: You wonder—Joseph, I shall not pretend!
What I advise is best for you. Need I
Say more? True, it's not only for your sake
Alone—In honesty, I can not bear
The thought that to another she would give—
That would hurt more than—She is proud, of course,
But after my death—An Antonius—
And then, above all, such a moth'r-in-law
Ready to rouse the dead against the dead—
My meaning you must grasp!
JOSEPH: But—
HEROD: Hear me out!
She gave me hope that she would take her life
Herself if I—now, such a debt one may
Seek help collecting, eh?—One even might
Use force—What's your opinion?
JOSEPH: Perhaps so!
HEROD: Then promise me that you will kill her if
She does not kill herself. Do not make haste,
But don't delay too long! Just go to her
As soon as you have heard my messenger—
For I shall send one—when you know I've died,
Tell her and see if she will take a sword
Or what she does. Now will you promise?
JOSEPH: Yes!
HEROD: I shall not ask you for your oath, for none
Was ever forced to vow to crush a snake

Which threatened him with death. One does that quite
By instinct to survive, it's rational,
Since one could sooner and with lesser peril
Stop taking food and drink than save the snake.
    JOSEPH (*gestures*)
    HEROD: I know you well, and I shall surely tell
Antonius that you're the only man
Whom he can trust; you will prove this a fact
By showing that a relative by blood
Is not too sacred to be sacrificed
In order to put down rebellious mobs.
For this will be the point of view from which
You must explain your deed to him. It will
Be followed by a riot; you will say
That rioting began before your act
And that it ceased because of what you did.
The populace will surely shudder then
To see your bloodstained sword; and some are sure
To say: I did not fully know this man!
And now—
    JOSEPH: We'll meet again another day.
I know for certain that you will return.
    HEROD: It's not impossible, so one more thing!—
(*Long pause*)
I now have sworn an oath concerning you!
(*Writes and seals*)
It's here. Receive this sealed instruction then;
You see it's destination—
    JOSEPH: The hangman!
    HEROD: I'll keep the promise I made in that note
If you should ever try to tell a tale
About a king who—
    JOSEPH: Then you can command
That I deliver it to him in person. (*Off*)

SCENE VI

    HEROD (*alone*) : The sword will now hang over her. That's spur
For me to do and bear what I have never had
To do and bear, and to be solaced if
It proves in vain. And now to go! (*Off*)

ACT II
Zion Castle. Alexandra's suite.

SCENE I
(Alexandra and Sameas)

ALEXANDRA: You know it now!
SAMEAS: 'Tis no surprise to me!
No, nothing Herod does surprises me!
The youth who challenged the Synedrion
Who did confront his judge with open sword
To warn that, as the executioner,
He could not execute himself—can now,
In manhood—Ha! I still can see that scene
When he stood face to face with the high priest,
Leaned on the column, and around him stood
The soldiers in his pay who, hunting thieves,
Had turned themselves into a robber's band.
How he surveyed us, counting all our heads,
As though before him grew a bed of weeds
And he considered how to clean it up.
ALEXANDRA: Indeed that was a moment in his life
Which he may still recall with glowing pride!
A crazy youth of barely twenty years
Called to account by the Synedrion
When, sacrilegiously exuberant,
He broke the law when he did execute
Before the verdict was pronounced by you.
The dead man's widow comes to curse. Inside
Sit all the gray heads of Jerusalem.
But since he does not come in sackcloth nor
Strews ashes on his head, you are turned weak,
Don't even think that you should punish him,
Don't even think that you should threaten him;
So you say nothing, and he laughs and leaves!
SAMEAS: I spoke!
ALEXANDRA: Too late!
SAMEAS: And if I earlier
Had said my piece, it would have been too soon.
I did not speak out of respect for the
High priest. His should have been the first word; mine,
The last. For he was oldest; youngest, I.

ALEXANDRA: At any rate, if you had shown him then
The simple courage duty can instill,
No greater courage would be needed now!
But now, do try to—no, another way
Remains for you. If you refuse to fight
Against him, and, indeed, it would be very
Foolish; I'd advise against it; you
Must simply enter into battle against
The lion or the tiger he commands!
    SAMEAS: What do you mean?
    ALEXANDRA: You know the fighting games
The Romans play?
    SAMEAS: Thank God, I do not!
I think I'm fortunate to know no more
About the pagans than what Moses told;
And, every time a Roman soldier comes
Across my path, I quickly close my eyes
And bless my dear departed father's name
For never teaching me their Roman tongue.
    ALEXANDRA: Then you have no idea that they import
To Rome wild beasts from Africa? I mean
Hundreds of them!
    SAMEAS: Indeed, I do not know!
    ALEXANDRA: That there they drive them in a stone arena,
And then force slaves to meet them face to face;
They have to battle with them to the death
The while the Romans sit on their high seats
Surrounding them and crying out with joy
When mortal wounds begin to open up,
And when the red blood spurts upon the sand?
    SAMEAS: My wildest dream has shown me no such scene,
But I am glad, my soul is overjoyed
If they do that. I'm sure, it suits them well!
(*With hands raised*) Lord, Thou art great! Though to the pagan
    Thou
Hast granted life, Thou dost exact from him
A dreadful tribute which does befit him well:
Thy punishment on him is how he lives!
I'd like to see those games!
    ALEXANDRA: Your wish will be
Fulfilled as soon as Herod does return;
He plans to introduce them!

SAMEAS: Never here!
ALEXANDRA: He will, I say! Why not? For, after all,
We have a good supply of lions here!
The herdsman will be glad if it's decreased,
For he will keep more of his herd alive.
    SAMEAS: Aside from other things, where would he find
The men to fight? For here we have no slaves
Who are obliged to him on pain of death.
    ALEXANDRA: The first—I see this minute!
SAMEAS: What?
ALEXANDRA: Of course!
Perhaps you will grimace, as you do now,
Or even clench your fists and roll your eyes
And grit your teeth if you're alive on that
Great day when he, solemn as Solomon,
Does dedicate the pagan theater
As though it were the temple of our God!
This won't escape him, and, as your reward,
He'll make a sign for you to enter the
Arena then to show the people what
A man you are when you confront the lion,
The lion they have starved for many days.
For, since we lack the slaves, then simply let
The criminals deserving death replace
Them. And who would deserve to die as much
As one who openly defies the king?
    SAMEAS: He could—
ALEXANDRA: Don't doubt! It would be bad if he
Would lose his head too soon, for, with this man,
Some plans would perish which Pompey himself,
Audacious heathen, he who dared to walk
Into the temple's holiest of holies,
Perhaps—
    SAMEAS *(losing control)*: Antonius, if you catch him,
I shall not curse your name for one whole year!
And if you don't, well then—we are prepared!
    ALEXANDRA: He thinks, if we were not supposed to mix
With other peoples, then God would have placed
All of the earth into our hands alone.
    SAMEAS: He does?
ALEXANDRA: But since this is not so at all,
He sees the need to sever now the dams

Which separate us from the world as though
We were a static lake far from the sea.
And this would happen if we merely would
Adapt ourselves to change and learn their ways.
    SAMEAS: Their ways— (*Toward heaven*) oh Lord! If I am not
        to rage,
Then let me see, oh God, how he will die!
Show me the death which does deprive of all
Its horror ev'ry other death. Proclaim
To me that it is Herod's own, his death!
    ALEXANDRA: Why not be his assassin?
    SAMEAS: If I fail,
I'll kill myself. I swear! If I can not
Prevent such horror, I shall punish my
Impotence with suicide (*Gestures toward his heart*) before
The first day breaks which he would stain!
That is a vow which forces me to do
A wicked deed if I'm incapable
Of heroism. Has ever man sworn more?
    ALEXANDRA: Good. But don't forget, if your arm lacks
The strength to overthrow the enemy,
You must not spurn another helping arm.
    SAMEAS: This other arm?
    ALEXANDRA: Is easily involved.
    SAMEAS: Make yourself clear.
    ALEXANDRA: To whom does Herod owe
His kingship?
    SAMEAS: To Antonius! Whom else?
    ALEXANDRA: Why did he crown him then?
    SAMEAS: He liked him, or
Because we did not like him. Could there be
A better reason for a pagan's mind.
    ALEXANDRA: Go on. What keeps him firmly on the throne?
    SAMEAS: It's not the people's blessing. Its curse, perhaps?
Who is to say?
    ALEXANDRA: I! Nothing but the trick
Of sending every year the tribute, which
The Romans levy here, before it's due
And even doubling it of his free will
Whenever they're engaged in a new war.
The Roman only wants our gold, that's all.
He let's us keep our faith and our own God,

Would even join us in our worship of Him,
Assigning Him a space near Jupiter
And Ops and Isis on the Capitol
If He, like them, were also made of stone.

SAMEAS: If this is so, and, sad to say, it is,
What hope can one place in Antonius?
We must admit that Herod does not fail
In this one point. Just now—I saw him leave!
One of his mules collapsed with broken back
Even before it reached the city gate!
For ev'ry drop of blood that's in his veins
He offers up to him an ounce of gold:
Do you think he'd refuse it for your sake?

ALEXANDRA: Indeed not, if I were to plead my case!
But Cleopatra is my advocate,
And Mariamne also I may hope.
Surprised? But understand, it's not in person;
She herself might well oppose my case;
It is her picture, and not even hers,
Another's which is very like her own.
For as the jungle hides the lion and
Its enemy, the tiger, side by side,
So, in this Roman heart, must nest, I'm sure,
Th'entire wormlike species of the passions,
And each must seek to dominate the rest.
If Herod should trust in the first, I trust
The second, and I do believe that it
Will bring Antonius to my side.

SAMEAS: You're—

ALEXANDRA: No Hyrcanus, but his daughter, yes!
But, lest you misinterpret what I did:
I am not Mariamne! Even if
Antonius were to destroy the man
Whose wife she is to clear a path to her,
To make her own decision she is free
And may decide to keep the widow's veil.
But I am sure of this: that he has laid
His hand upon the sword but has not drawn
Because of one consideration, for
The Romans deem the lucky soldier Herod
To be the ring of solid iron which
Preserves the unity within our land.

If you can prove the opposite to him,
Disturb the tired peace, rebellion rouse,
He'll draw.
    SAMEAS: I'll prove it easily to him!
In thought, the people has already slain
The man. They say—
    ALEXANDRA: Then put your seal on it,
And quickly open up his testament.
You know its contents now; the fighting games
Come first. And, if each man believes that, by
The death of Herod, he has been deprived
Of crucifixion or a hundred blows,
Then each believes the thing he may believe.
For what's ahead for Israel is such
That many hearts will wish in deep despair
That the Red Sea had swallowed up that day
All Israel, all the twelve sacred tribes,
And Moses, him before the other men.
    SAMEAS: I'm going now! And ere it's noon—
    ALEXANDRA: I know
What you can do, when, in your sackcloth, you
Go through the streets and cry out 'woe to all.'
You'll be like Jonas, your old ancestor.
Besides, quite useful it might prove to be
To pay a call upon the fisherman
And join that cousin then in eating up
What he enjoys because it was not bought.
    SAMEAS: It will be proved that we, the Pharisees,
Are not forgetful of the shame we have
Although you seem to think so. Hear this then
Which only through our deeds you were to learn:
We've plotted, long before today, against
Him, have undermined all of Judea;
And, in Jerusalem, so you may see
How firmly we can count on all our men,
There even is a blind man in our group.
    ALEXANDRA: What good is he?
    SAMEAS: No good! He knows it too.
But he's so filled with hate and burning rage
That he must share with us in planning this,
And he would rather die than carry on
His life in this world if our plot does fail.

I deem that a good omen on our side! (*Off*)

SCENE II

    ALEXANDRA (*alone*) : In thought, the people has already slain
The man. I know! I know! Thus I can see
How much they wish that he would not return!
How fortunate that swarms of locusts rose
As he was leaving, for that can be thought
An omen that this wish was not in vain.
It's also possible that even now
Without his head—not that! Say what you think;
The Pharisee's not listening at the door!
Antonius is what he is, of course,
But he's a Roman too, and they don't judge
With undue speed although they execute quite fast.
He may be captured now, although not kept
In prison. If one used that, it might
Lead further. That is why it would be good
If there were a rebellion now although
I know what it would mean and also know
What the results might be if he would still
Return here. If! And it could happen still,
Consider that! When he departed, he
Sent you a severed head as parting gift,
Which shows you—stop speaking like your father!
It shows me that he's quick, as tyrants are,
And also that he'd like to frighten me.
The first I've always known, and, in his wish,
He shan't succeed! If it came to the worst,
If all my efforts failed, and, if, despite
The passion he bears Mariamne—which
Grows, not cools, and thus protects me well
If it's her will—if he still dared the worst,
What would it mean? I'd risk it all to have
Revenge. And I'd have my revenge in death,
Revenge on him who'd do it, and on her
Who'd let it pass. Our people here never
Would countenance it, nor would Rome look on.
As for myself, in this most bloody case,
I'd fit among my ancestors quite well.
For, after all, most of my ancestors,

The mothers of my tribe, the fathers too,
Did have to leave the world without their heads
Because they had refused to bow them down.
Their lot would then be mine; that would be all.

SCENE III

(*Mariamne enters*)
    ALEXANDRA (*to herself*) : She comes. Now, if she could be drawn
        from him
And then be moved to follow me to Rome.
Then—but she both loves and hates him now!
My last attempt? I dare it? I must try!
(*Hurries toward Mariamne*) You look for solace where it can
        be found!
Come to my heart.
    MARIAMNE: Solace?
    ALEXANDRA: You have no need?
Then I've misjudged you! But I had good grounds
To deem you diff'rent from the way you are.
You had been slandered to me!
    MARIAMNE: I? To you?
    ALEXANDRA: I heard about embraces, kisses too,
Which, when the murder was committed, your
Brother-killing husband—Forgive, I should
Not have believed it.
    MARIAMNE: Not?
    ALEXANDRA: No, I should not!
For many reasons. Could you coldly refuse
Your brother's bloody shade his sister's gift
Of vengeance which you could grant to the dead,
Not by the sword of Judith, nor Rahab's nail,
But solely by the turning of your mouth
And by the silent crossing of your arms?
The murderer himself would not have dared
To come to you, for you look like the dead
Man; you would have looked just like the corpse
Of Aristobolus with rouge; and he,
With shudders, would have turned and gone away.
    MARIAMNE: He didn't do the one, nor I, the other.
    ALEXANDRA: Then be—But no! Perhaps you had a doubt

Remain about his guilt. Do you want proof?
  MARIAMNE: I do not need it!
  ALEXANDRA: Not need—
  MARIAMNE: It's meaningless!
  ALEXANDRA: Then—But I shall withhold the curse as yet;
Another curse already shattered you!
You are still captive in the chains of love,
A love which never brought you honor—
  MARIAMNE: I thought
It did; I thought I had not chosen him
My husband, rather yielded to my lot
Which you and Hyrcanus did shrewdly choose
For me, your only daughter and his grandchild.
  ALEXANDRA: Not I, my coward father wanted it.
  MARIAMNE: Then did he do what you disliked?
  ALEXANDRA: Not that!
If I had wanted to, we could have fled;
In Egypt was asylum for us both.
I only say that he suggested this,
The first high priest, who lacked all courage,
And I objected mainly to my feeling of
Aversion when he first began to speak.
But I said yes; the coward's trade seemed good!
I quickly gave the pearl of Zion for
Edom's sword when he pressed me for action.
But, if the snake which bit th' Egyptian queen
At that time had a viper been, or if
Antonius had come to this land with
His expedition at that very time,
I should have answered no! But I said yes.
  MARIAMNE: Still—
  ALEXANDRA: I did expect of you that you
Would not make wasteful use of our great price,
And that, for Herod, you—
  MARIAMNE: Oh, I know that.
Before each kiss, I was to bargain with him
So he would take a head that you disliked.
And, when, at last, his was the only head
That dared defy you, then I was supposed
To urge his suicide and, if that failed,
I should repeat, you thought, some silent night
With catlike stealth, the deed which Judith did.

That would have made my mother proud of me!
    ALEXANDRA: More proud, indeed, than now, I must admit.
    MARIAMNE: But I preferred to be a wife to him
To whom you led me and, because of him,
Forget my Maccabean origin,
As he forgot for me that he was king.
    ALEXANDRA: In Jericho, you did recall it once,
For there, at least, you were the first to voice
An accusation; I delayed to test
You first. Was it not so?
    MARIAMNE: In Jericho
The dreadful happening confused me so;
Too fast: from table to the bath, from bath
To grave, my brother! I was dizzy then!
But that I, stubborn and suspicious both,
Refused admission to my husband-king,
I do regret this, and my sole excuse
Is that I felt a burning fever then.
    ALEXANDRA: A burning fever!
    MARIAMNE (*half to herself*):   But I'd not have done it
If he had not appeared in mourning clothes!
Yes, in red, dark red, I could have seen him!
    ALEXANDRA: He found those quickly, surely had supplied
Himself ahead of time, as one who kills
Might draw a drink of water and then kill—
    MARIAMNE: Mother, do not forget!
    ALEXANDRA: What? That you are
The killer's wife? You've just become his wife!
And will be his only while you so wish;
Who knows? Perhaps you are not even now.
The sister of my son, you always were
And will remain, will stay his sister still
When you cry out—you seem inclined to this—
Into his grave: You got what you deserved!
    MARIAMNE: I know I owe respect to you and want
To give it, so I ask you please to stop,
Or else I might—
    ALEXANDRA: Might do what?
    MARIAMNE: Ask myself
On whom to place the blame for this, on him
Who did it since he had no choice, or her
Who forced him? Let the dead rest in their graves!

ALEXANDRA: Thus speak to one who did not give him birth!
I carried him within me, therefore must
Avenge him now when I can not arouse
Him anymore to take his vengeance!
    MARIAMNE: Do
Avenge! But have your vengeance on yourself!
You know quite well the high priest was the one
Dizzied by populous rejoicing mobs,
And not the youthful Aristobolus,
Who caused the ominous occurrences.
Who drove the young man, tell me that, I beg
Out of complacency in which he lived?
He did not lack the coats of many colors
To merit second looks from pretty girls,
And more he did not need to live in bliss.
What good was Aaron's priestly robe for him,
Which quite superfluously, you placed on him?
He had no other thought while wearing it
Than this: How do I look? but others thought
That, from the moment when he put it on,
He was the second head of Israel,
And soon you did delude him that he thought
That he alone was first and only head!
    ALEXANDRA: You slander him and me.
    MARIAMNE: That is not true.
If this young man, the purpose of whose birth
Did seem: to show the world a happy man,
If he so quickly met a dire end, and
If the man who makes a woman out of
Every man when he but draws his sword,
If he—I know not that he did, but I
Fear it—then love of pow'r, ambition are
To blame, not his ambition, nor the king's.
I wish not to accuse you, it's not right;
I do not ask to see a rueful tear
From you who sent a ghost to us,
A bloody ghost, into our marriage bed,
Although we'll never be alone again,
And the dead man does so disturb my mind
That I am silent when there's need to speak,
And that I speak when silence is required.
I do not even wish to throttle now

Your thirst for vengeance, nor ask: do you
Avenge your plans or Aristobolus?
Do what you will, go on or stop, but know
That, if you aim at Herod, you will surely
Strike at Mariamne; I now take
The vow I did withhold when, parting, he
Demanded it of me; I too shall die
When Herod dies. Now act, and say no more.

    ALEXANDRA: Then die! At once! For—

    MARIAMNE: Yes, I understand!
That's why I needed solace, isn't it?
Oh no! You're wrong; it does not frighten me
That, with its mouth, the rabble, which only bears
The chosen few because they too are mortal men,
Has murdered him already. After all,
What can a slave do when his king goes by
In splendor and magnificence but think
Within him: he must die like me? I don't
Begrudge him that, and, if, next to the throne,
He moves a battlefield with many graves,
I praise it, for it stifles envy's sting.
But my heart tells me this: Herod does live
And will live on. Death casts a shadow which
I know would strike my heart.

SCENE IV

    A SERVANT: The viceroy comes.

    ALEXANDRA: I'm sure he's armed as always when he comes
To see us ever since he failed in the
Attempts to win us with his flattery.
He seemed to try that out the first few times;
You know that Salome just raged, poor thing,
Consumed with jealousy.

    MARIAMNE: She still is that!
For, smilingly, in intimate tones, I tell
Him all the worst when she is there to hear.
And, since she never tires of spying on me,
I do not tire of finding punishment
To fit her folly.

    JOSEPH (*enters*)

    ALEXANDRA (*pointing to Joseph's weapons*): There, you see?

MARIAMNE: Let him.
His wife demands it, so that she can dream
That she is married to a warlike man.
  ALEXANDRA (*to Joseph*) : I am still here.
  JOSEPH: A strange reception this!
  ALEXANDRA: My son is still here too. As once before,
He's hidden in a dead man's box. Go chase
Him out of it, and I shall pardon you
For doing it before without command.
But this time, do not seek the box upon
A ship that's bound for Egypt; rather seek
It here, within our graveyard's innards now.
  JOSEPH: I'm not the man who can wake up the dead.
  ALEXANDRA (*with scorn for Mariamne*) : True, I suppose. Or
        else, you would have joined
Your lord, in case his kneeling and his pleas
Do not protect him from the lictor's axe.
  MARIAMNE: He kneels and pleads?
  JOSEPH: And I can show you how!
'I stand accused of this, I do admit,
But not of that, I'll add it here and now
So that you know it all'—that's what he'll do
  ALEXANDRA: You boast for him?
  JOSEPH: That's what he did before!
I stood and watched him when the Pharisees
Planned to accuse him to Antonius,
And he had done it, in their place, himself.
He'd hurried to the camp, just as he was,
And said it when they came there, point by point,
Repeating their account and adding to it:
'Just say if I omitted anything'.
You know the outcome; many plaintiffs then
Just lost their stubborn heads, did not give in;
He carried off the Roman's high esteem.
  ALEXANDRA: They both were younger then than they are now.
Exuberance in one did please the other,
And all the more because it was at the
Expense of others. Can the Pharisee
Whose tongue is ever preaching anti-Rome
Expect to be important to the Roman?
The man who pulls his beard deflates him, thought
Antonius and laughed; but I must doubt
That he will let that happen to himself.

JOSEPH: You speak as though you wished—
ALEXANDRA: What matters it
To you whether our wishes coincide?
Hold on to yours. It matters much for you
That he returns.
JOSEPH: You think so? If for me,
Then for you too.
ALEXANDRA: I could not tell you why.
There was an Alexandra once before
Who wore a crown in Israel, had reached
For it when it became available,
And had not left it free to crown a thief.
By God, a second one like her exists
(*To Mariamne*) If any Maccabean woman lives
Who keeps her childhood vows!
JOSEPH (*prying*) :   That is the truth!
There once did live that Alexandra, but
Whoever wants to reach her goal must her
Example follow fully, not by halves.
When she assumed the throne, she made her peace
With all her enemies so that no one
Needed to fear her rule, and all had hope.
No wonder that she sat secure 'til death!
MARIAMNE: I think that wretched! Why wield a scepter
If not to satisfy both hate and love?
A stick will do to chase the flies away!
JOSEPH: How true! (*To Alexandra*) And you?
ALEXANDRA: I'm sure she never dreamed
About her tribal ancestor, great Judas,
Or else she would have feared no enemy.
For, from his grave, he still protects his own
Since he can never die in any heart.
How could he die? No one can pray unless
He will admit: it's thanks to him that I
May still kneel now before my God instead
Of wood, or stone, or metal ore!
JOSEPH (*to himself*) :   The king
Was right! I must perform the deed, on both
Of them to be exact, or victim be.
And I must place the crown upon my head
To save it from the executioner.
A world of hatred stares upon me here!
All right; they have condemned themselves today.

This was their last interrogation now.
And if his messenger were only here,
I'd do it, without pity, right away,
For all the preparations are complete.

SCENE V

A SERVANT: The Captain Titus asks that he be heard.
JOSEPH: At once! (*Starts to leave*)
ALEXANDRA: Why not in this room?
SERVANT: He is here.
TITUS (*enters; secretly to Joseph*): What you have feared has
    happened. The people
Does rise up.
JOSEPH: Then do as I commanded:
Quickly arrange the cohort, and march out.
TITUS: That has been done. And now I come to ask:
Do you want prisoners, or do we kill?
My eagle can both seize and tear up flesh,
And you must know what would be best for you.
JOSEPH: No blood may flow.
TITUS: Fine. Then I shall attack
Before they have begun to throw their stones.
To kill, I'd wait.
JOSEPH: Did you see Sameas?
TITUS: The Pharisee who once did almost break
His head upon my shield because, when he
Sees me, he always has to close his eyes?
Indeed, I did.
JOSEPH: And doing what? Speak up.
TITUS: 'Twas in the market place, thousands about,
And he was loudly cursing Herod.
JOSEPH (*to Alexandra*):   Sameas
Did only leave this room one hour ago.
ALEXANDRA: You saw him?
TITUS (*to Joseph*):   You'll come yourself?
JOSEPH: When I can leave.
Meanwhile—
TITUS: All right. I'll go.
ALEXANDRA (*calls him back*): Why did you take away our guard?
MARIAMNE: We have no guard?

ALEXANDRA: Since last night, none.

JOSEPH: Because I ordered it.

TITUS: And since the King, when leaving, said to me:
This is the man who knows what I want done;
What he commands is also my command. (*Off*)

ALEXANDRA (*to Joseph*): And you?

JOSEPH: I thought that Judas Maccabeus
Sufficed for your protection and for hers.
Besides, you've heard what's happening out there.
I need the soldiers. (*To himself*) If the Romans were
So close, then I might fail. Today, I sent
The Galileans.

ALEXANDRA (*to Mariamne*): Do you still think that my
Suspicions have no grounds?

MARIAMNE: I do not know,
But now they touch me too. I find this strange.
Although—A spear thrust from this very wall
Would not at all be more surprising now.

ALEXANDRA: Two thrusts would clear the way right to the
throne;
For, when the Maccabeans are extinct,
Then the Herodians will have their turn.

MARIAMNE: I still should laugh at you if Salome
Were not his wife; I swear it, by my brother,
I'll have her head; I'll simply say to Herod:
As he avenges me so does he love;
For it is she alone. He could not do this!

ALEXANDRA: Your triumph comes too soon. First, we must act!
And I think this rebellion is of use.

MARIAMNE: No, this rebellion is not my concern,
For naught remains to fear if Herod does
Return, and if he does not, then I shall
Accept my death, whatever form it takes.

ALEXANDRA: I'll go. (*About to leave*)

JOSEPH (*blocks her exit*): Where to?

ALEXANDRA: First off, the parapet.
And then, wherever fancy may transport me.

JOSEPH: The parapet is open to you, but
The castle is sealed off.

ALEXANDRA: We're prisoners?

JOSEPH: Until peace is restored, I'll have to ask
That you will please—

ALEXANDRA: You really would presume?

JOSEPH: A stone is blind, as is a Roman spear,
And both may often strike what they should not.
So one must try to stay out of the way.

ALEXANDRA *(to Mariamne)*: I shall climb up and, by a sign, attempt
To let my friends know what is going on.

MARIAMNE: A sign—your friends—oh Mother, Mother! This
Rebellion then is yours, not rabble, stirred?
I hope you are not digging your own pit!

ALEXANDRA *(tries to leave)*

JOSEPH: You will permit my footman to escort
You. Philo!

ALEXANDRA: So this is simply open war!

PHILO *(enters)*

JOSEPH *(whispers to him; then aloud)*: You understand?

PHILO: Yes.

JOSEPH: If it comes to that!

PHILO: I'll wait and see.

JOSEPH: Your head is guarantee!
(To himself) I think that Herod's spirit is with me.

ALEXANDRA *(to herself)*: I shall still go. Perhaps, I can persuade
The soldier, Galilean though he be!
I'll try it! *(Off)*

PHILO *(follows her)*

JOSEPH: I can't help but do it thus,
No matter how suspect this act may seem.
Rebellion forces me. I can not let
Her leave my sight unless I want to make
What must be done impossible for me.
His messenger may come at any moment;
I've given up on Herod long ago.

MARIAMNE: When did King Herod die?

JOSEPH: When did—

MARIAMNE: And how?
You surely know since you presume so much.

JOSEPH: Presume, you say? On what? You puzzle me.

MARIAMNE: On naught, if no protection I shall have
As soon as Rome knows that my life is under
Threat; but too much, if you err in this.

JOSEPH: And who has threatened you?

MARIAMNE: You dare to ask?
You!
   JOSEPH: I?
   MARIAMNE: Can you swear that it is not so?
Can you, by your child's head? You do not speak!
   JOSEPH: You have no right to make me swear an oath.
   MARIAMNE: Accused of this, one volunteers such oaths!
But, woe to you, when Herod does return;
Before we start to kiss, I'll say two things.
I'll tell him that you planned to murder me;
I'll tell him what I swore; now figure out
What fate awaits you when he does come home.
   JOSEPH: What—did you swear? If it's to frighten me,
I'll have to know it.
   MARIAMNE: Hear; it is your doom:
That I shall kill myself with my own hand
If he—oh had I only known—that's right!
Then never would cold courtesy have been
Upsetting, I should have continued then
As I began, and all would now be well!
For at the start, you were a different man.
   JOSEPH: I have no grounds for fear.
   MARIAMNE: Because you think
That it's impossible that he return.
Who knows? And if? But I shall keep my vow
'Though not before I've punished you for this,
Now tremble Joseph; avenged myself the way
That he'd avenge me! Go on, draw at once!
Why not? You do not dare? I believe you!
It does not matter how you try to guard
Me here. I'll find a way to Captain Titus.
Your game is lost since I have seen through it.
   JOSEPH (*to himself*): True, true! (*To Mariamne*) I'll make
      you keep your word; you will
Avenge yourself completely as he would.
You promised that to me. Do not forget.
   MARIAMNE: Thus speaks absurdity! That Herod loves
Me more than I can ever love myself
No one, not even artful Salome.
Your wife, will doubt although, for that,
Her hate of me may double and may try

Vindictively t'inspire you to kill me!
I know that she has prompted this and want
To hurt her where she'll feel it. Let her grief
For you then be my last delight on earth.

   JOSEPH: You're wrong, but still, I have your word, at least!

   MARIAMNE: You say that once again? What strong emotions
What nighttime thoughts and what suspicions you
Stir up inside me, evil criminal!
You speak as though the king had chosen me
As sacrifice and you as ritual priest.
Did he? Is that the truth? In leaving, he
Did drop, I must recall with terror now,
An obscure word. Answer!

   JOSEPH: I shall reply
As soon as necessary; when I know
That he—

   MARIAMNE: No longer can prove that you lie
When, evil coward, you accuse him now
Of an immeasurably monstrous crime
Merely to justify yourself to me.
I tell you that I'll hear you only now,
For he, perhaps before you end your tale,
Will enter here and thrust you to the ground.
Eternal then your silence; so speak now.

   JOSEPH: And were it so? I don't say that it is!
But, if it were? What would that be for you
But confirmation of your sentiment,
But proof that he does love you as no man
Has ever loved his wife?

   MARIAMNE: How strange! Those words?
It seems to me I've heard that said before.

   JOSEPH: I should have thought 't would flatter you to know
That death would not be half so bitter for
Him as the thought that you—

   MARIAMNE: Let's wager then
I can complete the statement you would make.
Bitter the thought of leaving me behind
In such a world where an Antonius rules!

   JOSEPH: Well yes; I don't say that he said this in—

   MARIAMNE: He did say it! He did—What has he done!
I wish that he would come!

HEROD AND MARIAMNE
Deutsches Fernsehen, January 1, 1965
Walter Richter as Herod
Courtesy Westdeutscher Rundfunk

HEROD AND MARIAMNE
Deutsches Fernsehen, rerun August 21, 1970
Antje Weisgerber as Mariamne and Walter Richter as Herod
Courtesy Westdeutscher Rundfunk

HEROD AND MARIAMNE
Deutsches Fernsehen, rerun August 21, 1970
Antje Weisgerber as Mariamne and Alexander Kerst as Titus
Courtesy Westdeutscher Rundfunk

JOSEPH: Oh Mariamne!—
(*To himself*) : How I've involved myself! Yet, all I did,
I had to do! But terror seizes me
That he—I see young Aristobolus.
Accurséd be the deed which casts its shadow
Before it enters life!
    MARIAMNE: So it was more
Than a mad bubble blown by playful brain
Which rises up and bursts from time to time;
It was that way—and now my life begins;
My dream is finished now!

SCENE VI
(*A servant enters; Salome follows*)

    SALOME (*to the servant*)   If you were told
To let in only those who were announced,
I'll take the blame.
    JOSEPH: You, Salome?
    SALOME: Who else?
No evil ghost; your wife, your sad, poor wife
Whom you did court as Jacob courted Rachel
And whom you now— (*To Mariamne*) you wretch, it still was not
Enough for you, was it, that you had turned
My brother's heart from me? Must you now rob
Me of my husband too? Both day and night,
He thinks about you as a widow and
Of me as less than one! All the day long,
He follows ev'ry step you take. All night,
He dreams of you, cries out your name with fear.
Starts from his sleep— (*To Joseph*) Did I not, just today,
Reproach you for it? and now, this very day
When all Jerusalem is much disturbed,
He's not with me, not in the market place—
I asked there for him when he did not come—
He is with you—and you're—alone with him!
    MARIAMNE: She's surely not at fault. It's he alone!
If I had any doubt, it now is gone;
Her foolish jealousy has stifled it.
I was an object for him; nothing more!
    JOSEPH (*to Salome*) : I swear—

SALOME: That I am blind? No! I do see!

MARIAMNE: The dying man who wants his fig tree cut
So that no other man enjoy its fruit
When he has died, ruthless is such a man;
But he, at least, may well have planted it
Himself, and he would know that it would still
Refresh the thief, and the assassin too,
Or anyone who shook it, with its fruit.
In my case, neither fits! And still! And still!
This is the greatest outrage of them all.

SALOME *(to Joseph)*: You speak in vain. Commanded? Who
commanded?

MARIAMNE: Commanded! That does seal it!—Could it be?
Now is the time it could most likely be!
But it can not! There's no emotion of
Ignoble sort to stain my inner self,
No matter what storm rages in my heart.
And to Antonius I now would say
What, on our wedding day, I would have said.
Because I feel that, I am hurt this way;
Else, I should have to bear and pardon it.

SALOME *(to Mariamne)*: And you don't seem to notice me?

MARIAMNE: I do,
For you have done the greatest kindness to me;
For I, who have been blind, do see it now.
I see it clearly, and you've made it clear.

SALOME: You ridicule me? You shall pay for that
On the return of my dear brother whom
I'll tell it all and—

MARIAMNE: What? Oh that. Please do,
And if he listens, then—why not? I laugh?
Is that still far-fetched?—If he listens, then
I promise not to contradict your word;
My love of self no longer is that strong!

SCENE VII

ALEXANDRA *(rushes in)*: The King!
JOSEPH: Inside the city?
ALEXANDRA: No; he's here!

ACT III
Zion Castle. Alexandra's Suite.

(*Alexandra. Joseph. Salome. Herod enters with His retinue.
Sohemus*)

HEROD: I'm back. (*To Sohemus*) It still bleeds? Yes, I know,
    that stone
Was meant for me and only hit your head
Because, just then, you came to speak to me.
This time, your head did serve to shield your king!
If you had stayed where you were—
SOHEMUS: Then I should
Not have this wound, nor then, whatever merit,
If there be any in it. In Galilee,
At worst, that man is stoned who'd even dare
To fight against the king, or even me,
His shadow, or his megaphone, or what
He wants me for.
HEROD: Yes, they are faithful there
To their advantage, after all, and since,
With mine, their own goes hand in hand, to mine.
SOHEMUS: To what degree, you see by this that I
Am here, am in your capital.
HEROD: Indeed,
I am surprised to find that you are here,
For when the King's away, there's greater need
To guard and watch the restive provinces.
What drove you then to leave your station now?
I'm sure, you did not have the wish to prove
To me that you could leave your post without
The slightest danger to it. Nor could you know
That you would catch a stone they meant for me.
SOHEMUS: I have come here to give the viceroy, Sire,
Oral report as quickly as I ought
Of my discoveries of wondrous sort.
I wanted him to know: the Pharisees
Now try to undermine, although in vain,
The ever-stubborn ground of Galilee.
And still, my warning comes too late. I found

Jerusalem in flames and only could
Help put them out.

    HEROD *(extends his hand to him)*   And that you did,
      and with
Your blood.—Well, Joseph, here you are, I see.
I should have looked for you elsewhere.—All right;
But go at once and get me Sameas,
The Pharisee whom Captain Titus has
Been holding captive in the Scythian way.
The stolid Roman drags him all about;
He's firmly bound him to the tail of his
Fast horse and rides about with him because,
In sacred zeal, he spit on him in public.
And now he has to run as no man can
So that he does not fall and drag along
The ground. I should have rescued him when I
Passed by, for, after all, I'm sure, I owe
To him alone the knowledge of the snakes
Who hid before my face before today.
Now I can crush them with my foot at will.

    JOSEPH *(Off)*

    HEROD *(to Alexandra)* : Greetings and message from Antonius:
One can't accuse a river to the court,
And, even less, the ruler of the land
Through which it flows for his not draining it.
(To Sohemus) I should have been here long ago, but, when
Old friends who seldom see each other meet,
They like to spend some time. And I predict
That this will happen to you now, my friend,
When finally I've got you here again.
You'll have to shake the figtree with me as I
Was made to help Antonius who drowned
Morays—the old gourmand!—in streams of wine.
I had to freshen memories for him
And many anecdotes of good old times.
I warn you, be prepared to do the same
For me. Although there's not enough in me
Of him, the triumphator, so that I
Could ever summon you by feigning faith
In some insipid accusations made,
By furrowing my brow like Caesar and by

Putting thunderbolt and light'ning on
Just to be sure—that was his only reason
For doing it—that I would have to come.
So now I'll take advantage of the chance
That has delivered you into my hands
And say, like him, when you begin to speak
About your work: if you conduct it as
You should, it can go on without you for
A while. You come so seldom that it seems
You do not like to come.

SOHEMUS: You wrong me, Sire,
But I have reason not to come too often.

HEROD (*to Salome*): You are here too? So you have learned at
 last
To think, when you encounter Mariamne,
That you are looking in a looking glass
And meet your own reflection face to face.
When you were angry with her, I advised
This often, but it never pleased you. Don't
Resent my joke. In this reunion, one
Can do no wicked deed. But where is she?
They told me she was with her mother now.
That's why I came.

SALOME: She left when she had heard
That you approached.

HEROD: She left? That can not be!
But yes. She left because it's best we meet
Alone.—You want to rage, my heart, when you
Should ask forgiveness?—No, I'll follow her,
For what she feels is right!

SALOME: Delude yourself,
Interpret then her shock to see you well,
Ashamedness for thinking you had died,
The greater one of losing widowhood,
Interpret this as though she were but shy,
A maiden who has known no man before,
But never as confusion caused by sin.
She left in fear!

HEROD: In fear?—Now, look about,
We aren't alone!

SALOME: That does not worry me;

If I bring charge before these witnesses,
It has more chance of being heard, and it
Is harder to suppress.
    HEROD: You place yourself
Between her and myself. Take care, for you
Can be stepped on and crushed!
    SALOME: But not this time,
Although I know how I, as sister, rate
When it concerns your Maccabean wife;
This time—
    HEROD: I'll tell you this; if, on the day
On which I saw her first, someone had lodged
Complaint against her, he would not have found
A very sympathetic hearing here,
But more so, than today. I warn you; hear!
My debt to her's so great, she can't
Do any wrong. I feel that in my heart!
    SALOME: She is completely free?
    HEROD: To wear a mask
She thinks may be deceiving to you, if
She wants t'amuse herself at your expense.
    SALOME: Then—yes, then I must be silent. Why speak?
For, after all, whatever I may say,
You'd always have the answer: Masquerade!
Well, quite successful is this masquerade!
I'm not alone, the world is fooled by it
Along with me; it costs you as much honor
As it has cost me peace; although you swear
That Joseph only did what he was told,
If he—will any one believe all this?
    HEROD: If he—what did you want to say? Speak out!
But no—not yet! (*To a servant*) Go, tell the queen that I
Await her presence.—Does it not seem as though
The whole world were completely free of spiders
Because they all were nesting in my house
So that they could, at once, obscure for me
A bright sky; if it ever would appear,
They'd act as clouds? But yet—it's very strange
That she won't come. She should have kissed me first;
She should have yielded to the moment's force.
And if the ghost would still not leave her, then
She would have bitten her lips 'til they bled!

(*To Salome*) Do you know what you dared? Do you, woman?
I came here glad! You understand? And now—
One time, when I was thirsty, the earth spilled
My cup of wine; before I had the chance
To empty it, there was an earthquake.
I did forgive the earth; I had no choice;
You, I could punish.

SCENE II

(*Mariamne appears*)

HEROD: Kneel to her whom you
Insulted here before these witnesses,
And then I shall not.
    SALOME: Ha!
    ALEXANDRA: What does that mean?
    HEROD: Well, Mariamne?
    MARIAMNE: Sire, what do you wish?
I have been summoned and I have obeyed.
    ALEXANDRA: Is this the wife who swore to kill herself
If he did not return?
    HEROD: You greet me thus?
    MARIAMNE: The King has summoned me to greet him here?
I greet him here. The task is carried out.
    ALEXANDRA: You are completely wrong. You stand accused!
    HEROD: You were to be accused. Before I heard
A word of it, I sent out my request
That you attend; but truly not so that
You could defend yourself against the charge,
But just because I think that it will choke
Quite of itself when you confront it here.
    MARIAMNE: And, to prevent that, I should leave at once!
    HEROD: What, Mariamne? You never were among
Those pitiable souls who, when they see
The back or face of those inimical to them,
Resent or pardon, in accordance with the moment
Because they are too weak really to hate
And are too small for magnanimity.
What has transformed you in your very soul
That you have joined them after all this time?
When I left here, you did bid me farewell;

And this, it seems to me, gives me a claim
Upon your welcome which you would deny?
And now you stand as though the mountains and
The valleys which long separated us
Still did. As I approach, you move away?
Is my return so hateful in your sight?

MARIAMNE: How could it be? It does restore my life
To me!

HEROD:　　　　Restore your life? What can you mean?

MARIAMNE: You can't deny that you do understand!

HEROD (*to himself*): How can she know? (*To Mariamne*)
　　Come. (*Because Mariamne does not follow*) Leave us
　　alone.
(*To Alexandra*) : You will forgive?

ALEXANDRA:　　　　Of course. (*Off; the others follow*)

MARIAMNE:　　　　　　　Coward!

HEROD:　　　　　　　　　　Coward?

MARIAMNE: And also—what other name?

HEROD:　　　　　　　　　Also? (*To himself*) That would be
Unthinkable! She never could forget!

MARIAMNE: He does not care whether of her free will
His wife will follow him in death, or if
The executioner kills her, just so
She dies! And he allows no time for suicide!

HEROD: She knows it!

MARIAMNE:　　　　　　Is Antonius a man,
As I have thought 'til now, a man like you,
Or evil demon, as you must believe,
Since you despair and think that in my heart
No sense of duty, no remaining pride
Would still resist him, if, bathed in your blood,
He came into my presence as a wooer
And urgently invited me to fill the time
Which the Egyptian queen leaves on his hands.

HEROD (*to himself*): But how? But how?

MARIAMNE:　　　　　　　　He would have had to kill
You, after all, before he came to woo me,
And if you feel yourself—I never could
Have thought so, but I see it!—so worthless
That you despair of matching him in your
Wife's heart by virtue of your manly worth,
How can you justify the lack of your

Respect for me when you could fear that I
Myself would not reject your murderer.
Oh, double shame!
  HEROD *(upset)*:   For what price did you learn
This secret? For it was not cheaply sold;
Its guarantee was someone's head.
  MARIAMNE: You knew
Your brother, Salome! Ask the man who told
It to me, what he did receive, but don't
Expect that I shall ever give reply! *(Turns)*
  HEROD: I'll show you now how I shall ask him this!
Sohemus!

SCENE III
(Sohemus enters)

  HEROD: Tell me, is the Viceroy out there?
  SOHEMUS: He waits with Sameas.
  HEROD: Take him away!
I'd given him a letter. He is to do
What I commanded in this letter; it is
To be done at once. You will escort
Him, and you'll see to it that ev'rything
The letter states is done.
  SOHEMUS: It shall be done! *(Off)*
  HEROD: No matter what you may presume, think, know
You did misjudge me after all.
  MARIAMNE: You did,
Of course, impress upon a fratricide
The seal of absolute necessity,
Which one accepts, though shudd'ring, but you won't
Succeed in ever sealing thus my death.
If I am killed, that act is and remains
A sacrilege which could, at most, recur,
But never can a man commit worse crime!
  HEROD: I'd lack the courage now to make reply
If I, no matter what I risked, had not
Been sure that it would turn out in our favor.
But I was sure, and only could be sure
Because I'd gambled everything I had!
I did what soldiers do when they, in war,
Are ready for the sacrifice supreme.

They hurl the standard which is leading them,
On which depends their happiness and honor,
With firm decision in the hostile throng;
But not because they plan to let it go;
They follow it headlong to win it back.
Though tattered then, the victor's crown is theirs
Which desperation won when courage failed.
You called me cowardly. If one who fears
A demon in himself is cowardly,
At times, I am that; but it's only when
My goal has to be reached on crooked paths,
When I must duck and act as though I were
Not what or who I am. Then I do fear
That I might stand erect too soon to gain;
And then, to tame my pride's protests, which, I
Admit, come easily and might cause this,
I do attach something to me that's more
To me than I myself, which must remain
Or fall with me. D'you know what lay ahead
For me when I went off? No duel nor court;
A moody tyrant; I was to deny
Myself before him, which I never could
Have done if—but I thought of you and then
I did not even grit my teeth—and, what
He offered to the man and king in me
When he, with fright'ning silence dragged me,
Not yet exonerated, to the many
Banquets, I accepted like a patient slave!
    MARIAMNE: In vain! For you have wronged humanity
In me, and everyone who's human must
Have share in my most human pain; he need
Not be a woman, nor related to me.
When you deprived me of my brother through
A secret-quiet murder, only those
Who also had a brother could weep while,
With dry eyes, other men could stand aside,
Denying me their sympathy. But all
Have life, and none would wish to be deprived
Of life except by God alone whose gift
It was. All of the human race has to
Condemn a sacrilege like this, has to
Condemn a fate which lets one enter life

But not complete it. You too must condemn it!
And, if my human self has been so hurt
By you, tell me, what should I feel as wife?
How do you stand with me, and I with you?

SCENE IV

SALOME (*rushes in*): What do you plan now, monster? I have
   seen
My husband led away—he pleads with me
That I should beg your mercy—I hesitate
Because I'm angry, do not understand—
And now—I hear such fright'ning whispers here—
They say—They lie.
   HEROD: Your husband has to die!
   SALOME: Before he's had a trial? No, he can't!
   HEROD: He has condemned himself. The letter which
Condemns him now was in his hands
Before he did me wrong and thus he knew
What punishment he should expect
If he did wrong; thus, when he did it, he
Accepted punishment.
   SALOME: Herod, hear me!
Are you quite sure of it? I was the one
Who did accuse him, thought I had the right;
I had a reason for it—that he loved her
Seemed obvious; he never looked at me
Of late; he never squeezed my hand—he was
With her all day whenever possible,
And, in the night, his dreams revealed to me
How very much he had her on his mind.—
All that is true, and more—but, after all,
It does not prove that she returned his love
And even less that she—oh no! oh no!
My jealousy drove me this far—forgive!
And you forgive me too! (*To Mariamne*) I hated you!
Oh God, time goes so fast! They said—Am I
To love you now as I once hated you?
Then break your silence; state his innocence!
And beg for mercy for him as I do
   MARIAMNE: He's innocent!
   HEROD: Of her charge, yes; not, mine!

MARIAMNE: Of yours as well.

HEROD: Then you should have no knowledge!
There's nothing now to pardon him. And if
I have him executed now, without
A hearing first, it is in part for you,
To show that I do value you, regret
The thoughtless word escaping my first rage,
But even more, because I know that there
Is nothing he can say to me!

SCENE V

SOHEMUS (*enters*):   His blood
Is shed. But all men in Jerusalem
Stand petrified and ask: why did the man
Whom you appointed viceroy when you went
Away now have to be beheaded on
Your return.

SALOME (*about to faint*):   Woe unto me! Alas!

MARIAMNE (*tries to hold her up*)

SALOME: Away! Away! (*To Herod*) And she?

HEROD: Calm down, my dear.
Your husband did betray me dreadfully—

SALOME: And she?

HEROD: Not in the way you think—

SALOME: Not so?
But how? You want to save her? If my husband did
So dreadfully betray you, she did too.
For what I said was true, and all who do
Not know about it shall hear. You shall
Now wash yourself in her blood, as you did
In his, or else you never can be cleansed

HEROD: By all that I hold sacred—

SALOME: Specify
His crime to me if it was not this one.

HEROD: If I did specify, I should increase
Its magnitude. To him, I had entrusted
A secret which made possible my life;
He did betray it. Should I do the same?

SALOME: A wretched way out to discourage me!
You think you can deceive me? You believe
In everything I told you, but you are

Too weak to choke your love to death,
Prefer, therefore, to veil the dreadful shame
You cannot purge away. But if you do
Not kill me, your sister, as you did
Her husband, you will fail! (*To Mariamne*) He is dead;
Now you can swear what pleases you, and he
Will not object! (*Off*)
   HEROD: Sohemus, follow her,
And try to reconcile her; you know her.
In former days, she liked advice from you.
   SOHEMUS: Those times have passed; but I shall go. (*Off*)
   MARIAMNE (*to herself*): I probably should not have pleaded for
The man who planned to kill me! But I shudder
To think he left no time for me to try!
   HEROD (*to himself*): He had to go in any case. In the
Next war, he would have had Uriah's place!
And yet, by now, I do regret my haste!

SCENE VI

   A MESSENGER (*appears*): Antonius sends me.
   HEROD: Then I know what
Your message is. I must prepare to fight.
The battle which he mentioned now begins.
   MESSENGER: Octavian has sailed for Africa;
Antonius is hastening to go
With Cleopatra to receive him there,
At Actium, as soon as he arrives
   HEROD: I, Herod, am supposed to be the third!
All right, I'll leave today. Sohemus can
Replace me here, although things are quite bad.
Good thing that he is here!
   MARIAMNE: He leaves once more!
Thank God for that!
   HEROD (*watching her*):   Ha!
   MESSENGER: No, great King, no!
He has no need of you at Actium;
He wants you to prevent the Arabs who
Rebel from joining with his enemy;
That is the service he demands of you.
   HEROD: It's up to him to send me where he has
Most need for me.

MARIAMNE: Once more! That surely does
Resolve it all.
HEROD (*still watching her*): How glad my wife seems now!
(*To the messenger*) Say to him—you know what—(*To himself*)
    Her brow, relaxed
Her hands are folded as in grateful prayer.
That is her heart!
MESSENGER: Will that be all for me?
MARIAMNE: If 'twas a fever, I shall see it now,
The fever of an irritated passion
Confusing him. Or did his inmost self
Reveal itself to me in this clear deed?
Now I shall see!
HEROD (*to the messenger*): That's all for you! (*To
    Mariamne*) Your face
Has cheered. But do not hope too much from this;
One does not always lose one's life in war.
I have returned from other wars!
MARIAMNE (*wants to speak but stops herself*): No, no!
HEROD: This is a greater battle, to be sure.
Than all the others which were fought
For something in the world; but this is for
The world itself, and will decide who is
Its future master: lewd Antonius,
The libertine, or else Octavian,
Whose merit is exhausted when he swears
That he has never been inebriated.
Thick blows will fall in this engagement, but
It is still possible that your wish will
Not be fulfilled, and death may pass me by.
MARIAMNE: My wish? Oh yes, my wish! Yes, that is good.
Restraint, my heart! Do not reveal yourself.
It is no test if he suspects what you
Do feel. If he does pass it, you will be
Rewarded! How you can reward him! Let
Him misjudge you! Test him! Remember
The end when you may give the crown to him
When he, at last, has overcome the demon.
HEROD: My thanks to you! You have relieved my heart!
Although I may have sinned against your human self,
I see quite clearly that I did not sin
Against your love. Therefore, I shall not beg

Your love to offer a last sacrifice,
But I do hope that you will still perform
A last and final duty for me now.
I do not hope so only for myself;
I hope it even more for your own sake.
You will not wish that I should, henceforth, see
Unclearly when I look at you; because
I closed the dead man's mouth myself, you will
Now open yours and make this clear to me.
How did it happen that he gave his head
For you? You'll tell it as a human being;
You'll tell it too because it serves to honor you.

    MARIAMNE: Since I respect my honor, I'll not tell!

    HEROD: So you refuse me what is only fair?

    MARIAMNE: What's fair! So you would think it fair that I
Should throw myself upon my knees to swear
To you: my Lord, your servant did not touch
Your wife; and so that you believe it—for
I don't deserve your trust 'though I'm your wife—
I'll tell you this and that. For shame! No, Herod,
If, later on, your curiosity
Should ask, I might reply. I'm silent now.

    HEROD: If your love had been great and strong enough
To pardon what love prompted me to do,
I never should have posed the question thus!
Now that I know how small your love, I must
Repeat the question, for the guarantee
Your love grants me cannot be greater than
Your love itself. And, I must say, a love
Which places higher value on its life
Than on the loved one seems worthless to me!

    MARIAMNE: I still don't speak.

    HEROD: Then I condemn myself
To kiss no more the mouth which is too proud
To swear to me no other man has kissed it
Until it does so in humility;
Indeed, if I had means to put to death
My memory of you, deep in my heart,
If I, by piercing both my eyes, which are
The mirrors of your beauty which I could
Destroy, could thus destroy your image in
My heart, I should pierce them without delay.

MARIAMNE: Now, Herod, calm yourself. Perhaps you have
Your own fate in your hands this very time
And could choose how to turn it now. For there
Does come a moment when, to every man,
The pilot of his star will hand the reins.
The only disadvantage is that none
Can ever know precisely which it is;
It can be any one that passes by.
I do suspect, this one is yours. So stop.
Perhaps the way you chart your orbit now
Must be your way of living to your death.
Would you decide, beside yourself with rage?
HEROD: I greatly fear that you suspect but half;
The turning point has come; but it is yours!
For I, what do I want? A simple cure
By which I can chase fright'ning dreams away!
MARIAMNE: I do not understand! I bore
Your children! think of them!
HEROD: Your silence does
Arouse suspicion that you do not dare
To tell the truth but do not want to lie.
MARIAMNE: No more of that!
HEROD: No more of it! Fare well,
And, if I do return, do not be too
Upset about it!
MARIAMNE: Herod!
HEROD: And be sure
That I shall not force you again to greet
Me as I did.
MARIAMNE: There'll be no need for it!
(*To heaven*) Eternal One, now steer his heart! I had
Forgiven him the fratricide;
I was prepared to follow him in death,
And I still am. What else can humans do?
You did what You have never done: returned
The wheel of time to the position it
Had in the past; please, let him not do as
He did before, and then I can forget
What did occur, as though he had dealt me,
In fever, with his sword, a deadly blow,
And then, recovered, bandaged up my wounds.
(*To Herod*) : Shall I see you before—

HEROD: If you should see
Me come, then order chains! Let that be proof
For you that I've become insane.
   MARIAMNE: You will
Regret this word!—Restraint, my heart!—you will! (*Off*)
   HEROD: It's true, I went too far. I told that to
Myself along the way. But no less true,
That, if she loved me, she'd forgive me still!
If she loved me? And has she ever? I
Believe she did. But now—How the dead man
Gets his revenge while in the grave! I did
Remove him only to secure my crown;
He took with him what is worth more: her heart!
For, since her brother's death, she's changed
Toward me strangely; never had I seen
The smallest trace of similarity
Between her and her mother, but today
She did resemble her in many ways.
That's why I can not trust her as I did!
That much is sure. But must it then be sure,
Because of this, that she deceived me too?
The guarantee which I found in her love
Is now removed, but there's a second one
Remaining in her pride, and won't such pride,
So great that it disdains to plead its own
Defense, disdain much more to soil itself?
Still, she does know it. Joseph! Why can man
Just kill and never rouse the dead again.
He should be able to do both or neither!
That one will have his vengeance too! He does
Not come, and still, I see him here: 'your wish?'
Impossible! I won't believe it! Keep
Still, Salome! No matter how it was,
It was not that. Perhaps, the secret, like
A hidden fire, ate its way through him.
Perhaps he did betray it, since he thought
Me lost and wanted then to make his peace
With Alexandra, fast, before the news—
We'll see! For I must test her! Had I thought
That she could learn it, I never would
Have gone so far! Now, since she knows,
I must go further! For, since she knows,

I must now fear of her revenge what I
Perhaps did wrongly fear of what I deemed
Her fickleness; for I must fear
That she will celebrate her wedding on
My grave. Sohemus' coming is well-timed.
He is a man who could be in my place
If I were not alive. His coming here
Does prove his faithful zeal in serving me.
I shall commission him now, knowing well
That, if she tempts his human nature, he
Will not tell her. But, should he betray
Me, she will pay a price which—Salome!
Then you were right!—But I must try the test! (*Off*)

ACT IV
Zion Castle. Mariamne's Suite.

SCENE I

(*Mariamne. Alexandra*)
    ALEXANDRA: Indeed, you puzzle me; first, you did vow:
I'll kill myself if he does not return!
Then, when he came, your bitter coldness, your
Defiance too, infuriating him
As much as it pleased me. Now—deepest grief
Again. I'd like to see someone who could explain.
    MARIAMNE: If it's so difficult to see, why try?
    ALEXANDRA: You keep your distance from Sohemus now
With gruffness and a clear aversion. Why?
One sees, he has a problem he would like to—
    MARIAMNE: You think that?
    ALEXANDRA: Certainly. He'd like to tell
Us, but he does not dare, would probably
If he now were to see you plunge into
The Jordan, wonder if you would permit
That he save you; he has good reason too;
You are immeasurably rude to him.
    MARIAMNE: You do think then that Herod could not say
That I had tried to tempt his friend; that I
Had tried to learn his secret, if he has
One, through base flattery! I leave it up

To heaven whether I shall find it out;
My heart tells me that I risk nothing thus.

SCENE II

SAMEAS (*enters; his hands are chained*) : The Lord is great!
MARIAMNE: He is!
ALEXANDRA: You're free and yet
In chains? Another puzzle this!
SAMEAS: I won't
Remove these chains. Jerusalem must be
Reminded every single day that I,
Grandson of Jonas, was imprisoned here.
ALEXANDRA: How come you to be freed? Did you give bribes
To guards?
SAMEAS: I, bribe? The guards?
ALEXANDRA: But then, with what?
You still are wearing your old hair shirt now,
And I must doubt that they would let you go
For a wild bee's nest, such as you, who know
Each hollow tree, could have revealed to them,
Is nothing rare, and honey's plentiful.
SAMEAS: How odd to ask! Sohemus opened up
The gates for me.
MARIAMNE: You mean to say he dared?
SAMEAS: He dared? How so? Did you not order it?
MARIAMNE: I?
SAMEAS: No? It seems to me he said you did;
I may be wrong, for when he entered, I
Was just reciting backwards the last psalm
And only listened to him with one ear!
Well then, the Lord has freed me, and I must
Go to the temple now to thank Him, and
I have no bus'ness here, in David's house!
MARIAMNE: The Lord!
SAMEAS: The Lord! Had I deserved the cell?
The times are past in which the Lord did speak
Directly to his people. We have the law.
It now does speak for Him! Extinguished is
The steam and fire column by which he once
Did designate the paths through desert lands

To guide our fathers, and his prophets too
Are silent with him now!
    ALEXANDRA: Not all of them!
It only was a little while ago
When one predicted fire, and there was one!
    MARIAMNE: Indeed, but he had started it himself
That very night.
    SAMEAS: Woman do not blaspheme!
    MARIAMNE: I don't blaspheme. I only say what did
Occur. The man's a Pharisee like you;
He speaks like you; is mad like you. The fire
Was set to show us that he really was
A prophet, did see through the future, but
A soldier caught him while he set the fire.
    SAMEAS: A Roman?
    MARIAMNE: Yes!
    SAMEAS: He lied! Perhaps, he had
Been paid for such a lie by Herod, or
Perhaps it was by you!
    MARIAMNE: Do not forget yourself!
    SAMEAS: You are his wife, the wife of the blasphemer
Who deems himself to be messiah, you
Who can embrace this man and kiss him
Would do whatever he desires of you!
    ALEXANDRA: You say, he deems himself messiah now?
    SAMEAS: He does; indeed, he told me to my face
When he had me arrested. For when I cried
Unto the Lord: Behold Thy people, Lord,
And send us the messiah whom you promised
To send us in the time of greatest need;
The greatest need is now! he answered me
With scorn and pride: 'He is already here,
But you don't know it. I am the very one!'
    ALEXANDRA: Well Mariamne?
    SAMEAS: Next, he proved with wit
And blasphemy that we are all insane,
That he alone is sane among us all.
He said we did not dwell by the Dead Sea
For nothing; it does not move nor change
Its tide and thus contaminates the world;
It is, he said, a mirror of ourselves.
But he would bring us back to life although,

To do it, he would have to take by force
The stupid book of Moses—ruthless was
His speech—For it alone was to be blamed
If we resemble not the Jordan, our
Clear river which with cheer flows through our land
With skipping movement, but are like the swamp!

ALEXANDRA: He threw his mask away completely!

SAMEAS: Yes!
But then, perhaps he saw me as a dead
Man when he spoke; for, next, he ordered them
To execute me.

MARIAMNE: But he was upset!
He'd found rebellion here!

SAMEAS: I warn you now
To do your duty. Free yourself of him
As he has freed himself of God! By this
Act, you can punish him since he loves you!
I had to think that you had done it when
Sohemus set me free. If you do not,
Then don't reproach the lightning from the sky
As unjust if it now strikes you like him!
I go to make my off'ring.

ALEXANDRA: Take it from
My stable!

SAMEAS: No, I take it where it's missed!
The widow's lamb, the poor man's sheep!
What good's your wealth for God? (*Off*)

SCENE III

SOHEMUS (*enters*):   Excuse me!

MARIAMNE: I
Was about to have you called. Approach.

SOHEMUS: That would have been the first time!

MARIAMNE: Yes, that's true.

SOHEMUS: You have avoided me thus far.

MARIAMNE: Did you
Seek me, and had you any reason to?
I do hope not.

SOHEMUS: At least this one: Regard
Me as most faithful of your servants!

MARIAMNE: I did do that; but now, I don't.

SOHEMUS: Not now?

MARIAMNE: How could you set a rebel free, one whom
The King himself had ordered put away?
Is he still king, or is he king no more?

SOHEMUS: The answer's not as simple as you think!

MARIAMNE: If it's so difficult, you'll pay for it!

SOHEMUS: You have not heard about the battle lost?

MARIAMNE: You claim that they have lost at Actium?

SOHEMUS: Antonius has taken his own life;
And Cleopatra killed herself.

ALEXANDRA: You mean
She had the courage? She who never could
Look at a sword? She shuddered when he once
Did offer it to her as looking glass!

SOHEMUS: It was reported thus to Captain Titus.
Octavian curses that it could not be
Prevented. I myself have read his words.

MARIAMNE: Then death has had its share for quite some time,
And every head rests firmer than it did
Before.

SOHEMUS: You think that's so?

MARIAMNE: Your smile is strange!

SOHEMUS: It seems you do not know Octavian!
He would not ask death if he'd find it loathsome;
He'll hold another banquet for him, serve
Antonius' friends to him, and there
Will be no lack of delicacies then.

MARIAMNE: Do you mean Herod?

SOHEMUS: Well, if he does do
As he had planned—

MARIAMNE: What was that?

SOHEMUS: He said:
I do not love Antonius any more;
In fact, I almost hate him now, but I
Shall stay with him 'til his last moment comes
Although I fear that he will have to die.
I owe it to myself, if not to him!

MARIAMNE: How like a king!

SOHEMUS: Indeed, quite like a king!
Only Octavian would not think well
Of it if Herod did—

MARIAMNE: Who'd dare to doubt it?

SOHEMUS: Then he is lost, or else Octavian
Was much maligned when he was thought the cause
Of the great bloodbath after Caesar's death.
 MARIAMNE: Your firm belief in this result is clear
And also that you're sure of Herod's death,
Else you would not have dared what you did dare.
I shudder too, I must admit it to you,
Before your confidence; you are no fool
And surely would not risk so much without
Good cause. But still, in any case, I am
Still here, and I, I want to show you now
That I want him obeyed, though he be dead.
Whatever he commanded shall be done;
You will ignore not one command; that is
To be our offering for him.
 SOHEMUS: Not one?
I am in doubt my Queen—(*To himself*) Thunder, strike!
 MARIAMNE: As surely as I am a Maccabean,
You will send Sameas back to his cell!
 SOHEMUS: What you wish will be done, and, if you wish
More, if he is to die, as Herod did
State as a threat, then speak, and he is dead!
But please permit a question. I must ask
So that the offering you wish to make
Be perfect, shall I obey in this as well,
Shall I then also run my sword through you?
I also did receive that order from him!
 MARIAMNE: Woe!
 ALEXANDRA: Never that!
 MARIAMNE: And so my end has come!
And what an end! One which consumes all life
From its beginning on. My past dissolves
In me, as does my future—nothing's left!
I have had nothing, do have nothing, shall
Have nothing. Who has ever been so poor?
 ALEXANDRA: I should be ready to believe that Herod has
Committed almost any crime you name,
But this—
 MARIAMNE: You need not doubt. I'm sure, it's so!
 ALEXANDRA: Do you say that?
                         Oh God! I know his reason!
 MARIAMNE:
 ALEXANDRA: Then you must know what you must do!

MARIAMNE: I know! (*She turns a dagger on herself*)

ALEXANDRA (*restraining her*) : You must be mad! Does he
    deserve, deserve
Your being your own executioner?

MARIAMNE: You're right. That would be wrong. He has reserved
That office for himself. (*She hurls the dagger away*) Tempter,
    away!

ALEXANDRA: Surrender to the Romans for protection!

MARIAMNE: I shall prevent no one who wants to save
Himself from doing so!—But I shall give
A feast tonight!

ALEXANDRA: A feast!

MARIAMNE: And I shall dance!—
Yes, yes, that is the way!

ALEXANDRA: Toward what goal?

MARIAMNE: Come, servants. (*Servants come*) Open up the
    halls of state
And summon all who want to celebrate;
Light all the candles which will spend their light;
Pick all the flowers now which are still fresh;
There is no need that anything be left.
(*To Moses*) You did arrange our wedding long ago;
The feast today must be more splendid still!
Spare nothing! (*She steps forward*) Herod, do tremble now,
    although
You never had to tremble in the past!

SOHEMUS (*goes to her*) : I feel your grief as you do!

MARIAMNE: I do not want
Your pity! 'Though you are no torturer,
I cannot doubt that, for you've shown me that,
You are a traitor, and I cannot thank
A traitor, cannot tolerate him in
My sight, although he has his use in such
A world! For, I do not misjudge, if you
Had been the man you seemed, then God need have
Performed a miracle, endowed the air
With speech which it does lack. He could foretell
That when He did create you; therefore He
Made you the very first of hypocrites.

SOHEMUS: I am not that. I was Herod's true friend,
Brother-at-arms, and his companion true.
Before he took the throne, I served him well

And, since he has been king, most faithfully.
But I was faithful only while he had
Respect for me, as human and as man;
As I, for him, as hero and as lord.
He had it, 'til, for the first time with eyes
Downcast just like a worthless hypocrite,
He gave me this command which guarantees,
With heartless cruelty, your death and mine,
By which he left me to the vengeance of
Your people, the anger of the Romans, and
My own deceit, and left you to my sword.
That proved to me the height of his esteem!
    MARIAMNE: Did you express your horror to him then?
    SOHEMUS: I did not, since I thought that I could shield
You; so I did pretend agreement, did
Dissimulate, you'd say, lest he should give
Another the command and kill me then.
A Galilean would have done the deed!
    MARIAMNE: Forgive! You share my situation then;
You too are hurt in your most sacred soul,
Reduced, like me, by him to a mere object!
He is the same as friend and husband both.
Come to my feast. (*Off*)
    ALEXANDRA: So you were biding your time also, just
Like me.
    SOHEMUS: Biding my time? What do you mean?
    ALEXANDRA: I always was amazed to see how you
Would bow before this king who owes his throne
Not to his birth and tribe but merely to
The Roman's whim, the toper's drunkenness.
You bowed as though you had forgotten, as
He has, that you are equal to him still.
But now I see through you; you only wished
To make him feel secure.
    SOHEMUS: You're wrong in this;
I spoke the truth. I do not think that I
Am equal to him and shall never think
It. True, there are some rascals who do serve
Him but protest because he's not his grandson, and
I know that others keep the faith with him
For Mariamne's sake alone; but I
Do not belong with people of that sort

Who rather would obey a child's sword which
Has been inherited than a hero's
Which still is being forged before their eyes.
I always saw the greater man in him,
And was as willing to pick up the shield
My brother-at-arms dropped as I could be
To bend my back to hand a king his scepter.
The crown and the first woman: I begrudged
Him neither, for I felt his higher worth.
 ALEXANDRA: You are a man as well!
 SOHEMUS: I'm proving now
That I have not forgotten it. No man
Is so great that he may make use of me
As his mere tool! One who demands from me
Such services which, whether done or not,
Condemn me to an ignominious doom
Frees me from any obligation to
Himself, and I must show him that there is
A step between a slave and king, and that
A man stands on that step.
 ALEXANDRA: It matters not
To me to know your reason; I'm satisfied
That you're on my side now.
 SOHEMUS: You need to fear
No battle now! He is as good as dead.
Octavian is not Antonius who'd let
His flesh be cut and pardon that because
He must admire the hand's ability.
He only sees the blows.
 ALEXANDRA: And Titus?
 SOHEMUS: He
Agrees with me. I freed old Sameas
Just to make sure that she would summon me
To give her explanation, for that was
The only way to reach the Queen. Now she
Has been informed and thus is ready for
The news of Herod's death, if it should come.
That was my purpose. What a woman! I—
Kill her!—Oh, what a waste her tears would be!
 ALEXANDRA: Of course, a loving husband! Now you must
Persuade her that she should surrender to
The Romans for protection. Do come to

Her feast which marks her break with Herod, be
He alive or dead! (*Off*)
    SOHEMUS (*following her*) :   He must be dead.

SCENE IV

(*Servants appear and arrange the feast*)
    MOSES: Well, Artaxerxes, lost in thought again?
Quick, quick! You do not represent our clock!
    ARTAXERXES: If you had had to do that many years
Like me, you'd feel about it as I do,
Especially, if you dreamed every night
That you still had to do that very job!
I do not even notice when my right
Hand takes a hold of my left pulse, I count,
And count, and count right up to sixty and
Remember then that I'm a clock no more!
    MOSES: Well then, remember now, you aren't supposed
To measure time for us. For that, we have
The sundisk and the sand. You are supposed,
Like us, to use the time to do your work.
It's laziness, that's all!
    ARTAXERXES: Please let me swear—
    MOSES: Be still. You never count while eating, and
Besides, we never swear in this house, and
(*To himself*) If our own king were not half-pagan too,
We'd never have a foreign servant here!
Look the musicians come! Now hurry up! (*Goes to the others*)
    JEHU: Say, is it really true what's told about
Your life?
    ARTAXERXES: Why should it not be true? Should I
Perhaps avow it with a hundred oaths
Again? I was the Satrap's clock, and I
Must say, I was well off, much better than
I'm now. At night, I was relieved, and then
My brother counted; by day, as well, for meals.
I'm honestly not grateful to your king
That he has dragged me here, with other men,
As prisoner of war. It's true, my work
Became more difficult. I had to go
Along to battle, and seeing arrows fly
To left and right and people fall, one can

Lose count so much more easily, of course,
Than in a ballroom where they come to dance.
I shut my eyes, for I'm no hero, but
My father was! An arrow struck him
On his post—he was a clock too, like us,
My brother and myself, we all were clocks—
He called the time and died! What do you say?
That was a man! That took more courage than
The man who shot the arrow had to have.

 JEHU: Have you no sand back home where you come from
That you must do that?

 ARTAXERXES: We? Have no sand?
Enough to cover all Judea with!
It only is because our Satrap has
To have it better than all other men!
And is the human pulsebeat not supposed
To be more accurate, if healthy and
Without a fever, than your sand which runs
Through a glass tube? And what good does a sun
Disk do, unless the sun does shine on it?
(*Counts*) One—two—

 MOSES (*returns*):   Be off! Be off! The guests arrive!

 ARTAXERXES: So that's a feast? I've seen much better feasts!
One, where they ate no fruit which had not come
From foreign continents. Where they punished,
Quite frequently with death, the drinking of
A drop of water. And where humans, wrapped
In hemp with pitch poured on, were used
As torches which did light the gardens in
The darkest night.

 MOSES: Stop that! What had they done
To hurt the Satrap? Tell me what it was.

 ARTAXERXES: Done? Nothing, done! Our funerals were much
More splendid also than a wedding here!

 MOSES: Besides, I've also heard, you eat your dead.
That would fit with the rest!

 ARTAXERXES: Then it's not true,
I guess, that your own Queen did once dissolve
A pearl in wine, a pearl more precious than
All of this kingdom, then gave the wine
To a poor beggar who then drank it up
As though it were not special in the least?

 MOSES: Thank God, it's not!

ARTAXERXES (*to Jehu*): But you did tell me that!

JEHU: Because it seemed to me to honor her,
This tale they tell of the Egyptian queen!

MOSES: Be off!

ARTAXERXES (*points to the roses Jehu is carrying*): But these
are real! Those are so cheap!
We had them made of silver and of gold!
One should send these somewhere where flowers are
As precious as are gold and silver here!

(*Servants scatter. The guests, among them Sohemus, have assembled during the last half of this scene. Music. Dancing.
Silo and Judas move away from the others and come to
the foreground*)

SILO: And what is this supposed to mean?

JUDAS: It means:
The King returns! and he returns today!

SILO: You think that's so?

JUDAS: How can you ask? Could there
Be other reason for a feast like this?
You'd better practice a new bow at once.

SILO: But they said—

JONAS: Lies; deception as always
When we have heard that harm has come to him;
And that's quite natural, for there are many
Who wish him harm! But would they ever dance
Here, in his house, if they were mourning him?

SILO: Then I suppose much blood is to be shed;
The prisons have been filled since the unrest.

JUDAS: I know that even better than you can;
I dragged a number of them in myself,
For this rebellion was so without sense
That one who did not plan especially
To hang himself just had to fight against it.
You know quite well that I do not like Herod,
No matter how I bow and scrape to him;
But he is right in this: the Romans are
Too mighty in comparison to us;
We're like an insect in a lion's jaw
Which must not sting, for then he'd swallow it!

SILO: I'm only sorry for my gard'ner's son
Who threw a stone the other day and hit
The Roman eagle at which he had aimed it.

JUDAS: How old is he?

SILO: How long, I wonder, since
I broke my leg? He was born then; his mother
Could not look after me because of that.
I know—he's twenty!

JUDAS: Then I know he's safe!
(*Mariamne and Alexandra appear*)
The Queen! (*Wants to go*)

SILO: How do you mean? Just tell me that.

JUDAS: All right; in confidence then. Twenty is
Safe. He will not be harmed; but if he were
Nineteen or twenty-one, he'd suffer then.
Next year, it will be diff'rent.

SILO: Do not joke.

JUDAS: I tell you it is so. D'you want to know
Why now? The king too has a son who now
Is twenty, but he does not know the youth,
For, when the mother left, she took the boy
And swore a solemn oath that she'd destroy
Her son herself—

SILO: How monstrous she must be!
A pagan?

JONAS: I suppose. But I don't know.—
Destroy, in such a way, that he would have
To kill his son, you see? Such madness would,
I think, have left her after her first rage;
But he's afraid, and no death sentence has
As yet been carried out if the condemned
Man was the same age as his son would be.
Console your man! But keep it to yourself.
(*They disappear in the crowd*)

SCENE V

(*Alexandra and Mariamne appear in the foreground*)

ALEXANDRA: So you refuse to ask for Roman help?

MARIAMNE: Whatever for?

ALEXANDRA: To make your life secure.

MARIAMNE: My life! Of course! One must make that secure;
Pain has no sting without it after all!

ALEXANDRA: At very least then, give this hour its due.

This is your feast, and you must show
Your guests the cheerful face that they expect!
  MARIAMNE: I am no candle, nor an instrument;
I am not made to glow, nor made to ring!
Accept me as I am. No, do not; please,
Urge me, instead, to whet the axe for my
Neck! No, I mean, urge me to celebrate.
Sohemus come. (*To Salome who enters and walks toward her*)
      You, Salome? Welcome,
Most welcome, even though in mourning clothes!
I hardly dared to count on you.

SCENE VI

  SALOME: I had
To come to learn what's happened here. I am
Invited to a feast but am not told
The reason why it's given. True, I can
Surmise, but I must know for sure. Is it
For Herod who is coming back? Are we
To see him here today? The candles say
It's so; the cheerful music. Say it's so!
I do not ask for my sake! But, you know—
No, no, you do not know; you have forgotten;
Perhaps you even dreamed that she was dead;
Else you would not keep such good news from her;
Your dream deceived you though, for she is still
Hunched over in the corner where she sat
When she gave you her blessing—
  MARIAMNE: What is this?
  SALOME: At any rate, Herod still has a mother
Who worries much about her son and grieves.
And I, I ask you, do not let her pay
Much longer for the crime of bearing me.
Give her the comfort which her heart demands.
  MARIAMNE: I have no comfort for his mother now.
  SALOME: You do not think that Herod comes today?
  MARIAMNE: Certainly not; in fact, I heard, he's dead.
  SALOME: And celebrate?
  MARIAMNE: Because I'm still alive!
Or should one not rejoice to be alive?

SALOME: I don't believe you.

MARIAMNE: Thank you for your doubt!

SALOME: The candles?

MARIAMNE: Well, are they not made to glow?

SALOME: The cymbals—

MARIAMNE: Yes, they have to ring, don't they?

SALOME (*points to Mariamne's elaborate dress*): The jewels—

MARIAMNE: Would become you better, true!

SALOME: All this would indicate—

MARIAMNE: A feast of joy!

SALOME: Which on a grave—

MARIAMNE: It is quite possible!

SALOME: Then—Mariamne, hear a serious word,
I've always hated you, but always had
A doubt whether my hate was justified,
And often came to you in penitence
To—

MARIAMNE: Kiss me; once you even did kiss me.

SALOME: But now I see you are—

MARIAMNE: So wicked that
I shall desert you and join in the throng
Which has begun the dancing over there.
Sohemus, come.

SOHEMUS (*offers his arm*):   My Queen!

MARIAMNE: King Herod must
Have seen me just like this when he gave you
The order for my death. How very strange!
Now everything has come to be that way!
(*To Salome in leaving*) I hope you'll watch. (*She is led to the
        background by Sohemus and both disappear in the crowd*)

SALOME: This woman is far worse
Than I had thought; and that's a lot to say!
She has a many-colored snakeskin which
She uses as her bait. Yes, she does dance!
Well, now my conscience is completely clear;
No one on earth could ever do her wrong! (*Watches Mariamne*)

SCENE VII

(*Alexandra and Titus appear*)

ALEXANDRA: You see my daughter's way of mourning, Titus!

TITUS: She must have had some news from Herod then?

ALEXANDRA: She has received the news that he is lost!

TITUS *(watching Mariamne)* : She dances!

ALEXANDRA: As though not widow but a bride!
She wore a mask until today; and, please,
Remember, Titus, she was not alone!

TITUS: That's very good for her. She'll stay a queen.
If she's among the enemies of Herod,
She will not have to suffer with his friends.

ALEXANDRA: To show this is her purpose at this feast! *(Leaves Titus)*

TITUS: Before these women, I can't help but shudder!
The one cuts off the sleeping hero's head
Whom she first charmed with kisses not
Sincerely meant; the other dances as
Though mad upon her husband's grave, just
To preserve the crown upon her head! I must
Have been invited here to witness it.— *(Watches Mariamne again)*
Yes I do see it, shall tell it in Rome,
But I won't drink a drop at this mad feast!

SALOME: Well Titus, is he so lost that she can
Presume all this already; is it true?

TITUS: If he did not go to Octavian's side
And did not strike Antonius the last
And final blow before his fall, which I
Must doubt, then he is definitely lost!

SALOME: Oh how I wish he had! If she can keep
Her head, I do not know why God gave to
The dogs the blood of heartless Jezebel
To lick! *(Is lost in the crowd)*

TITUS: She goes on dancing, but it seems
Not to be easy for her, for she should flush,
But she turns paler, just as though her thoughts
Were occupied with other things and she
Were dancing like a puppet. I suppose
That Judith must have had some fear as well.
And this one must still feel upon her lips
The final kiss of him whom she does now
So solemnly deny before me here;
Also, she has not seen him dead! She comes. *(Mariamne reappears; Alexandra and Sohemus follow her)*

ALEXANDRA *(to Mariamne)* : I spoke with Titus.

MARIAMNE *(turns suddenly and sees herself in the mirror)* : Ha!

ALEXANDRA:　　　　　　　　　　　　　What is it now?

MARIAMNE: Once in a dream, I saw myself this way!—
So this is why I could not stop before
Until the ruby that was lost was found.
It now gleams very dark upon my breast.
The picture would not be complete without
It; soon the last will follow!

ALEXANDRA:　　　　　　　　　　　　　Mariamne!

MARIAMNE: Leave me alone.—A mirror, quite like this;
It did seem tarnished first, as though a breath
Had touched it; and then, clearing gently like
The images it showed me in succession,
Finally, it gleamed like polished steel.
I saw my life! At first, myself as child,
Surrounded by a gentle, rosy glow
Which then turned redder, darkened more and more.
At first, my features were quite strange to me;
I did not recognize myself until
The third change came; the face had been too young.
Now came the young girl and the moment when
I was escorted through the flower garden
By Herod who spoke flatt'ringly to me:
'There's none so beautiful that your hand may
Not pick it!'—Ha! May he be cursed—he has
Forgotten all of this! Completely! Then
It frightened me. Against my will, I had
To see the future. Then I saw myself
This way and that, this moment last of all!
(*To Alexandra*) Is it not strange that dreams will come to life?
And then the shiny mirror dulled again;
The light turned ashen; I myself turned pale;
Shortly before, I had been blossoming;
Now, I was pale as though my veins had long
Been bleeding underneath this splendid garb.
A shudder seized me, and I cried: Next comes
My skeleton which I don't want to see!
And then I turned—(*She turns from the mirror*)

VOICES IN THE BACKGROUND:　　　　The King! (*General
　　commotion*)

ALEXANDRA:　　　　　　　　　　　　　Who?

SCENE VIII

(*Herod enters in battle costume. Joab. Retinue*)

MARIAMNE: He's death! He's death! Death is among us now!
He comes, as always, unexpectedly.

SALOME: He's death for you! Indeed, you feel it too!
My brother! (*Wants to embrace Herod; he pushes her away*)

HEROD: Mariamne! (*Approaches her*)

MARIAMNE (*repulses him with a violent gesture*): Draw your
    sword!
Hand me the poison cup! You are my death!
Death does embrace and kiss with sword and poison!

HEROD (*turns back to Salome*): What does this mean? A
    thousand candles called
Me from afar and through the dark of night
To say: your messenger has not been caught
By Arabs as you feared; he got there; they
Expect you there; and now—

SALOME: The candles lied;
There was rejoicing here; they thought you dead!
The messenger did not arrive, and your
Old mother has begun to mourn.

HEROD (*looks about; sees Titus and signals him*)

TITUS: It's so!
No one here could believe, I myself could
Not quite, that you would leave Antonius
Before the battle came to Actium,
Would join the Caesar, which was, to be sure,
The prudent thing to do. You must have done
It, as your safe return does prove. Well, I—
Congratulate you!

MARIAMNE (*joins them*): But I must lament
That opportunity did not present
Itself to you to kill Antonius
Yourself. It would have been the best display
For your new lord that you no longer cared
About the old. You could have brought your old
Friend's head; his payment would have been the crown.

HEROD: It's shameful, Titus, that you too think thus
Of me. I went down to Arabia
As ordered by Antonius but found
No enemy. I started then, at once,
For Actium, and it was not my fault
That I arrived too late. If he had held
His own, as I believed he would, then I'd
Have sought (*To Mariamne*) the opportunity to pay

Him for my crown, and with Octavian's head!
(*To Titus*) He did not last that long. When I arrived
He was already dead. No longer did
He need his friend; so I went on to see
Octavian; not as a king, it's true—
I'd taken off the crown—but neither did
I go as beggar; no, I drew my sword
And said: I planned to use this sword against
You, and I might have dyed it with your blood
If things had gone much better there. That's done!
Now, low'ring it to you, I take it off.
Consider now, what kind of friend I was,
Not whose. The dead man's let me go; if you
Should want me now, I'll be a friend to you!

    TITUS: And he?
    HEROD: He said: where did you put your crown?
I'll place another jewel into it.
That province which you lack, take it, today;
Since I have won, and not Antonius,
You'll only feel my generosity.
He never would have taken it away
From Cleopatra; I give it to you.

    TITUS: That—does surprise me. But I praise
Only your star!
    HEROD: Don't praise it, Titus. I
Was spared for graver work! Sohemus, come.
(*Sohemus stays where he is and does not answer*)
Did you betray me? Silence? I know enough!
Take him away then.

    SOHEMUS (*being led away*):   I deny nothing!
But, please believe, I thought that you were dead!
Now do what pleases you! (*Off*)
    HEROD: And after death,
Ev'rything ends, is that it? Yes, Titus,
Had you known the man as I did—you would
Not stand as calmly, quietly as I
Stand here, you'd rage and gnash your teeth
And say with wrath: (*to Mariamne*) What, woman, did you do
To bring him to this end?—Oh, Salome,
You were so right, I have to wash and wash—
Bring me some blood! I'll summon court at once!
(*To Mariamne*) You're silent? Cloaked in your defiance, still?

I do know why! You still did not forget
My love for you! I'd sooner tear my heart
Out of my chest—it's still so, Titus—than
(*again to Mariamne*) Tear you from my heart, which I shall do!
   MARIAMNE (*turns quickly*) : Am I a prisoner?
   HEROD: Yes!
   MARIAMNE (*to the soldiers*) :   Take me then. (*Turns. On
      Herod's signal, Joab and his soldiers follow her*)
I can't be wedded any more to death! (*Off*)
   HEROD: Ha ha! And I once did say to her: two
Who love each other properly can not
Survive each other; and if I should meet
My death on distant battleground, you would
Not need to hear it from a messenger;
You'd feel it as it happened, and would die,
Without a wound, of mine, with me. Do not
Laugh, Titus. Do not laugh. It's true. It is.
But human beings fail to love this way! (*Off*)

ACT V

*Large audience hall as in Act I. One sees the throne and the
judge's table.*

SCENE I

(*Herod and Salome*)
   HEROD: Stop, stop, at once! I've summoned the court here,
And I shall carry out its verdict too!
I who once trembled when a fever struck
Only her chambermaid, shall now arm death
Against her. But let that suffice. And, if
Your zeal does not feel satisfied by this,
It may still fail to reach its goal. I'll have
To think that it's pure hatred only, speaking
From your mouth, and then refuse your words
Of witness, even though I shall admit
Each burning candle and each flower's scent!
   SALOME: Oh Herod, I shall not deny, I did,
At one time, seek to find her faults and tried
To magnify them, just as you did with

Her virtues which you found. But, was the pride
She always showed your mother and showed me,
Was it a reason for our love? She did
Behave as though she were a creature of
A higher sort, which always made me think:
Why does the book exist which tells us of
The Maccabeans' heroism. Her face
Expresses their whole chronicle to me!

   HEROD: You want to prove me wrong but just confirm
My words of judgement!

   SALOME: Hear me out, I beg.
It was that way, I don't deny it. But
If I said more just now than I know, think,
And feel, indeed, if I did not suppress
At least one half of what I could say—since
I am your sister and do pity you—,
My child—you know I love him—he shall live
A year for each hair on his head; and more,
Each day shall bring to him the quantity
Of pain it has of minutes, no, of seconds!

   HEROD: That oath is dreadful!

   SALOME: And yet, it comes to me
More easily than saying this: the night is black!
My eye could be diseased; but it can't be
That, with my eye, my ear too could be sick,
And even instinct, heart, and every other
Organ which supports my senses! And all
Agree so firmly this time just as though
They never could be contradictory!
Indeed if God in heaven had called to me
This night: of which great evil shall I rid
Your earth, you have the choice, I'd not have named
The pestilence, rather, your evil wife!
I shuddered in her presence, for I felt
As though in darkness, I'd put out
My human hand to a demon from hell,
And he was jeering at me for it, was
Displaying his horrid form inside
The stolen body made of flesh and blood,
And grinned at me through hellish flames. Don't think
I was the only one to shudder, for
The iron Roman, Titus, too felt horror.

HEROD: Indeed, and his word is more valid here,
For, as he loves no one, he also does
Not hate. He's just, like spirits without blood.
Go now and leave me. I expect him here.
    SALOME: I never shall forget the dance in which,
According to the music's rhythm, she stamped
Down on the floor as though she knew for sure
That you were lying under it. By God,
I wish I did not have to say it, for
I know how deeply it must anger you
Who sacrificed your mother, sister, all
For her. But it was so! (*Off*)

SCENE II

HEROD (*alone*) :   Titus told me
The very same. And I too saw enough!
Yes, Salome is right! I sacrificed
My sister, and almost, my mother. Would
They not make up for one brother lost?
Not in her eyes.

SCENE III

(*Titus enters*)
    HEROD: Well, Titus, tell me, has
Sohemus now confessed?
    TITUS: To nothing new.
    HEROD: And nothing of—
    TITUS: No, he began to rage
When I commenced to drop the slightest hint!
    HEROD: That was to be expected!
    TITUS: Never had
A wife like yours existed, he said, nor
A man deserved a jewel God bestowed
On him as little—
    HEROD: As I myself! Indeed,
'He did not know what pearls are really like,
So I took them from him.' Thus spoke the thief.
But did that help?
    TITUS: Her heart, he said, nobler
Than gold—

HEROD: Does he know that? Because he's drunk
On it, he praises wine. Is that not proof
That he did drink? Had he excuses? Did he
Explain to you why he betrayed me
To her?

TITUS: He claims, because of horror!

HEROD: Horror?
And would not state his horror to my face?

TITUS: Would that have done him any good? Would you
Have felt you could allow a headstrong man
To live, a servant who received command
And then refused it?

HEROD: Would it not suffice,
In such a case, just to leave it undone?

TITUS: Of course! But if he went further, perhaps
It was because he thought that you were lost
And wished to buy, even at your expense,
The favor of the Queen into whose hands
He had to think his future had been placed.

HEROD: No, Titus, no! Sohemus was the man
To take that step alone which would make him
Be independent of another's favor!
That was why I gave him the order, for
I thought: He'll do it for himself, if not
For you! Indeed, were he a lesser man
And had he not so many friends in Rome,
I could believe it of him, but now—no, no!
He had one reason only!

TITUS: Which he still
Will not admit.

HEROD: He would not be himself
If he admitted it, for he knows well
What is to follow, and he hopes, by his
Denial, to arouse a final doubt in me
Which will, at least, protect her head from death,
If not his own. But he's in error, for
The doubt lacks strength completely; even if
I did not have the grounds to punish what
She did, I'd punish what she was and is!
Ha! If she had ever been what she had seemed,
She never could have changed in such a way;
And I take vengeance on the hypocrite!

Yes, Titus, yes, I swear it by the key
To Paradise which she holds in her hands;
By all the happiness she's given me
And could still give me; yes, even by
The shudder which I feel, reminding me
That I destroy myself along with her:
I'll bring this to an end, no matter what!
    TITUS: It is too late to call to you in warning:
Do not command this! And I know no way
Which could still lead to clarity in this,
And, therefore, I don't dare to say: desist!

SCENE IV

(*Joab enters*)
    HEROD: Have they assembled?
    JOAB: A while ago. I must
Report to you what seems important. In
Prison, they say, they can't get Sameas
To end his life.
    HEROD: I have commanded that
They torture him until he kills himself!
(*To Titus*) He swore, I heard, that he would take his life
If he could not make me to be like him
And could not break in me, what he would call
My pagan spirit. Since he failed at this,
I'm forcing him to do what he has sworn;
He's earned his death a thousand times at least!
    TITUS: I also would have urged that he be killed,
For he insulted me and, in me, Rome,
And one could pardon this anywhere else
Except in this land with its restive people!
    HEROD (*to Joab*): Well, then!
    JOAB: They followed your instructions but
To no avail. The executioner
Tried almost every torture, and, besides,
Enraged by Sameas' stubbornness,
Which he took personally, wounded him.
It is, however, just as though he tortured
A tree and cut into its wood; the old
Man stands as though he did not feel the pain.
He sings instead of screaming or reaching for

The knife they hold in front of him. He sings
The psalm which the three men once sang when they
Were singing in the fiery furnace. With
Each new pain, his voice takes added strength, and
When he stops the psalm, he even prophesies.

    HEROD (*to himself*): They are that way! Yes!—Will she be
      diff'rent?

    JOAB: Then he exclaims as though he had received
As many eyes for strange and wondrous sights
As he has wounds; he cries: The time is now
Fulfilled, and, at this very sacred moment,
The virgin mother of the lineage of David
Places a child into a manger who
Will rouse the dead, upset thrones, and tear down
The heavenly stars and who will rule the world
Forever, throughout all eternity.
The people, who've assembled by the thousands,
Now wait outside the gate, hear this,
And now believe Elijah's chariot
Will flamingly descend for Sameas
To carry him aloft! The torturer
Was so confused by this that he began
To close his wounds instead of causing more.

    HEROD: He must be killed at once; then show him to
The people when he's dead!—Also, summon
The judges and then also call—

    JOAB: The Queen!

    HEROD: You Titus, will sit here with me.
I've also had her mother summoned to
This court so that she will not lack a witness.

SCENE V

(*Aaron and the other judges enter. Alexandra and Salome follow
    and are at once followed by Joab*)

    ALEXANDRA: My King and Sovereign, I greet you, Sire.

    HEROD: Thank you. (*He sits down on the throne; Titus sits
    down next to him; after Herod signals, the judges seat
    themselves in a semicircle around the table.*)

    ALEXANDRA (*while this takes place*): I separate my fate from
    that
Of Mariamne; I reserve myself

As one reserves a torch, for future use! (*she sits down next to
    Salome*)
    HEROD (*to the judges*) : You know the reason why I summoned
    you!
    AARON: We come before you with the deepest sorrow!
    HEROD: I do not doubt that! You are all close friends
And relatives of mine and of my house.
What touches me must touch you too! You will
Be glad to find the Queen who—(*Hesitates*) Spare me that!
You will be glad if you need not condemn
Her, if you may return her to her home
Instead of sending her to Golgotha.
And yet, if necessary, you'll not shrink,
As cowards might, before the most extreme,
For as you share my happiness and sorrow,
You also share my honor and disgrace.
Begin then! (*He signals to Joab. Joab leaves; then he reappears
    with Mariamne. There is a long pause*)
    HEROD: Now, Aaron!
    AARON: My Queen! Our task
Is difficult. You stand before your judges!
    MARIAMNE: Before my judges and before you too.
    AARON: You don't accept our jurisdiction then?
    MARIAMNE: I see a higher court than yours. If it
Permits my answers to your questions, I
Shall speak. If it forbids them, I shall not.
I hardly see you, for, behind you, stand
Spirits who look at me in serious silence.
They are my noble ancestors.
The last three nights, they've come to me in dreams;
And now, they come by day as well, and I
Can understand this means that our dead
Are readying themselves for my reception.
And thus, what lives and breathes pales in my sight.
Behind that throne, on which a king seems to
Be sitting, there, stands Judas Maccabeus:
Do not look down on me so sadly, hero
Of heroes, you'll be satisfied with me!
    ALEXANDRA: Don't be defiant Mariamne.
    MARIAMNE: Mother!
Farewell!—(*To Aaron*) What charge is brought against me here?
    AARON: It is alleged that you deceived your king

And husband—(*To Herod*) That's the charge?

MARIAMNE: Deceived? But how?

That is not possible! Did he not find
Me as he had expected me, at dance
And play? When I heard of his death, did I
Put on mourning? Did I shed tears? Or did
I tear my hair? Then I should have deceived
Him. But none of these was done by me,
And I have proof of this. Speak, Salome.

HEROD: I found her as she says. She does not need
To look for other witnesses. But I
Should never have expected this!

MARIAMNE: Never?

And still, he hid an executioner
Closely behind me. But that can not be!
He found me here when he returned just as
He'd seen me in his mind before he left.
I must deny, therefore, that I deceived him!

HEROD (*breaking out in wild laughter*) : So she did not deceive
     me since she has

Not done but what my intuition and
Presentiment—my thanks, dark warning one—
Had made me fear. (*To Mariamne*) Oh, woman, how like you!
But do not count on any loss of strength
In me along with loss of joy and peace;
Perhaps I still have strength to take revenge,
And—even as a boy, I always shot
A second arrow after an escaping bird.

MARIAMNE: Not intuition, nor presentiment;
You should say fear! You trembled at the thought
Of what you did deserve! And that is human!
You can no longer trust the sister since
You killed her brother; you have done the worst
To me and now believe that I have to
Reciprocate, or even more, outdo,
Your deed! Or did you always, when you went
To face your death in open, honest war,
Provide an executioner for me?
No answer? Since you feel so strongly in
Regard to what befits myself, and since
Your fear is teaching me my duty, I
Shall carry out, at last, what it demands

By leaving you for ever as of now!
 HEROD: Answer! Do you confess, or do you not?
 MARIAMNE (*silent*)
 HEROD (*to the judges*): You see, there's no confession! And I
  have
No proof for you. But did you ever judge
A murderer guilty of death because
He had the victim's gem? It did not help
That he could point to his hands, washed with care,
Nor that he swore to you the victim had
Presented it to him; you sentenced him!
Apply that logic here! She has a gem
Which proves to me with much more force than could
The tongue of any human, that she did
Commit against me the most monstrous crime.
If it were otherwise, it would be like
A miracle that happened many times,
And, thus far, miracles have not recurred.
 MARIAMNE (*moves*)
 HEROD: Of course, she'll say, as did the murderer:
It was a present! She would run no risk,
For, like the woods, a chamber does not speak!
But should her words tempt credence on your part,
I'll place my deepest intuition and
Research into all possibilities
Against them, and I'll still demand her death.
I said, her death! For I don't want to drink
The cup of deep disgust defiance offers,
Nor do I want the daily torture of
The puzzle whether such defiance is
The most distasteful guise of innocence
Or sin's most brazen one. I want to rescue
Myself out of this whirlpool: hate and love
Before I drown, no matter what the cost!
Take her! Away with her! What's this? Am I
Mistaken? Speak! I know. I should hear you!
But speak then! Do not sit like Solomon
Between the mothers with their children. Speak!
The case is clear! You need no more to judge
Than what you see. A woman who can stand
Like her deserves to die though she be free
Of any guilt! You will not speak as yet?

Do you want proof.how firmly I'm convinced
That she deceived me? I can give you that.
I'll simply show Sohemus' head to you!
At once! (*Approaches Joab*)

TITUS (*rising*) :   I don't call this a hearing! Please,
Excuse me. (*Starts to go*)

MARIAMNE: Roman, stay. Because I do.
Who can repudiate it, if I don't. (*Titus sits down again*)

ALEXANDRA (*rises*)

MARIAMNE (*goes to her; sotto voce*) You brought much sorrow
      to me, never did
Your happiness depend upon my own!
If I am to forgive you, do not speak.
You can't change anything! I have decided!

ALEXANDRA (*sits down again*)

MARIAMNE: Judges?

AARON: If anyone of you does not
Consider what the King said just, rise now.
(*All remain seated*)
Then you have all decided for her death!
(*Rises*) You are condemned to death, my Queen!—Do you
Have anything to say?

MARIAMNE: Before my death,
I'd like a word with Titus unless you called
The executioner before the court,
And he awaits me, with his axe, outside.
(*To Herod*) It is the custom never to refuse
A dying man's request. For granting this,
Request, may your life's length increase by mine!

HEROD: The executioner's not here—I can!
And, since you promise me eternity
As my reward, I must and want to grant
It. (*To Titus*) Does this woman not inspire dread?

TITUS: She stands before a man as none may stand!
Therefore, conclude.

SALOME (*comes to him*) :   Please do; your mother is
So sick, about to die. She will be cured
If she should live to hear this.

HEROD (*to Alexandra*) :   Did you speak?

ALEXANDRA: No!

HEROD (*looks at Mariamne for a long time; she remains silent*)

HEROD: Die! (*To Joab*) I place this in your hands! (*Off.
      Salome follows him*)

ALEXANDRA *(watches him go)* :   I have
That second arrow! *(To Mariamne)* You wished it thus!
    MARIAMNE: My thanks! *(Alexandra off)*
    AARON *(to the other judges)* :   Shall we not try to ask that he
Relent? I find this terrible! She is
The last of all the Maccabeans! If we
At least succeeded in obtaining respite!
We could not contradict his will just now,
But, soon, he will become a diff'rent man
Again. And it is possible that then
He'll punish us for not resisting now.
I'll go to him! *(Off)*
    JOAB *(approaches Mariamne)*   Forgive me! I obey!
    MARIAMNE: Do what your lord commanded! do it fast.
I am prepared to go with you whenever you
Are ready. And you know that queens don't wait!

SCENE VI

    MARIAMNE *(goes to Titus)* : Just one more word before I sleep,
        the while
My chamberlain prepares my bed!
You are surprised, I see, that I address
This word, not to my mother, but to you.
But she is like a stranger; we're not close.
    TITUS: I am surprised to have a woman teach
Me how I, a man, must die some day!
Indeed, Madam, your actions frighten me,
And, I admit it, so do you yourself;
But I must honor courage, and you show
That by departing from this life as though
This lovely world no longer even seemed
Deserving of your hasty, final glance.
This courage almost reconciles me with you.
    MARIAMNE: It is no courage!
    TITUS: True, they did tell me,
Your gloomy Pharisees do teach that life
Only begins in death and that he who
Believes them will despise the world in which
Only the sun does shine eternally
While every other light fades into night!
    MARIAMNE: I never listened to them, and I don't
Believe it. No, I know what I must leave.

TITUS: Then you stand there as Caesar hardly did
When, wounded by the dagger at the hand
Of Brutus, too proud to show his pain,
And still not strong enough to stifle it,
He covered up his face before he fell.
But you hold back your pain inside your heart!
MARIAMNE: Not any more! It is not as you think!
I don't feel any pain now, for there must
Be life to feel such pain, and my life has
Died out in me; for, so long have I been
A thing between a human and a shade,
I hardly comprehend that I am still
Able to die. Now hear, what I want to
Confide, but, first, as man and Roman, you
Must promise that you will not tell of it
Before my death, and that you'll walk with me.
You hesitate? Is what I ask too much?
It's not that I'm afraid of faltering!
Also, you can decide whether to tell
Or not when I am dead. I shall not bind
You; nor even tell you what my wish is.
But I have chosen you for this because
You always have looked down into our hell
With cold detachment, like a monument
Of iron which looks down into a fire.
If you bear witness, you must be believed;
We are another race, where you're concerned,
With which you have no ties. You speak of us
As we speak of exotic plants and rocks
Impartially, with neither love nor hate.
TITUS: You go too far!
MARIAMNE: If you refuse your word
To me too rigidly, I'll take my secret
Into the grave with me and thus must be
Deprived of this last comfort, that one man
Will keep my image pure and spotless in
His heart, and that, if hatred goes too far,
He can, for duty's sake, or from respect,
For truth, raise up the veil that covers it.
TITUS: All right, I'll promise this.
MARIAMNE: Then you should know
That I, indeed, deceived Herod, but not

At all the way he thinks. I was as true
To him as he is. Why abuse myself?
I was much truer; he completely changed so long
Ago. Shall I aver that now? I'd sooner
Decide to swear that I have eyes and hands,
And feet. For, if I were to lose those, I
Should still be what I am; but not, if I
Lost heart and soul.

TITUS: I do believe you, and
I shall—

MARIAMNE: Be sure to keep your promise then!
I have no doubt! And now, consider what
I felt when he had hung the sword above
My head a second time, for once I had
Forgiven it when I was forced to tell
Myself: your shadow looks more like yourself
Than his distorted inner image of you!
I could not stand that any more; how could
I? So I took my dagger and, when stopped
In rash, attempted suicide, I swore:
If you would be my executioner
In death, you shall be that, but while alive!
You now shall kill the woman whom you saw
And only see me, as I am, when I
Am dead! You saw me at my feast. A mask
Was dancing.

TITUS: Ha!

MARIAMNE: Today, a mask stood there
Before the court, and, for a mask, they now
Are sharpening the axe which will kill me!

TITUS: I'm deeply shocked, my Queen, and don't accuse
You now of any wrong, but I must say:
I was deceived myself when I saw you;
I was as filled with horror and disgust
As I am now with shudd'ring admiration.
If this befell me, how could the appearance
Not obscure your nature to him whose heart
Was moved by passion? He was like a stream
So tossed that it can't give a mirror-image.
Therefore I feel deep pity for him too
And so must think this punishment too harsh.

MARIAMNE: A punishment at my expense! And I

Shall show him, when I throw away my life,
That it was not for love of life that
I resented dying like an animal.

TITUS: Let me take back my promise.

MARIAMNE: Even if
You were to break it, you would cause no change!
A man can cause another man to die;
The strongest can not make the weakest live.
And I am tired, even envy stones,
For, if it is life's purpose that one learn
To hate it and prefer eternal death,
That is achieved in me. I wish that they
Would carve my coffin out of granite which
Never does crumble and would lower it
Down to the very bottom of the sea
So that my very dust would be removed
From all the elements for evermore.

TITUS: Our world consists of mere appearances!

MARIAMNE: I see that now, and that's why I shall leave!

TITUS: My testimony was against you too!

MARIAMNE: I had invited you to have it thus!

TITUS: But, if I were to tell him what you said—

MARIAMNE: Then he would call me back, I have no doubt!
And, if I came, I should have this reward:
Henceforth, I'd tremble before anyone
Who might approach; I'd think: have care! He well
May be your own third executioner!
No, Titus, no, I wasn't playing games!
For me there's no return. If there were one,
Do you believe I'd not have found it when
I said goodbye for ever to my children?
If, as he thinks, defiance were the cause,
My guiltless sorrow would have broken it,
But thus, my sorrow now embitters death!

TITUS: Oh, if he felt that and came on his own
To kneel before you!

MARIAMNE: Yes, and then he would
Have overcome the demon. I could tell
Him all! For it would be undignified
To bargain with him for a life which has
To lose its last remaining value through
The price I'd need to pay for it; I should

Reward him for the victory he won.
Believe me, I could do it!
    TITUS: Herod, have
You no suspicion?
    MARIAMNE: No! He has sent him! (*Points to Joab*)
    TITUS: Let me—
    MARIAMNE: Titus, did you not understand?
Do you still see defiance as the thing
Which closed my mouth? Can I live on? Can I
Continue life with one who even lacks
Respect for God's own image in me? If,
By keeping silent, I could conjure up
My death and even arm it, why should I
Now break that silence? Should I just exchange
One dagger for another? Why? And could
It have been any more than that?
    TITUS: She's right!
    MARIAMNE (*to Joab*): Is ev'rything prepared? (*Joab bows*)
(*Looking toward Herod's quarters*):   Herod, farewell!
(*Toward the earth*) And now I greet you, Aristobolus!
I'll be with you in the eternal night!
(*She walks toward the door; Joab opens it. One sees armed men
    who form ranks in a respectful manner. She exits. Titus
    follows her, then Joab. Solemn pause*)

SCENE VII

    SALOME (*enters*): She's gone, and still my heart is very calm!
Another sign that she deserves her fate.
And thus, I've won my brother back at last,
And Mother has her son again. It was
A good thing that I did not leave his side!
The judges still might have dissuaded him!
No, Aaron, don't consider prison, for
She would not stay a month! Only the grave
Can hold her, for he has no key to that.

SCENE VIII

    A SERVANT: Three kings have journeyed from the East, and they
Bear many gifts of priceless value here.
They're just arriving at this moment, and

We've never seen such an unusual sight
Nor stranger costumes than the ones they wear.

SALOME: Lead them inside. (*Servant off*) I'll tell him that at
    once.
As long as they are with him, he won't think
Of her! And very soon, she will be dead! (*Goes into Herod's
    quarters*)

(*The servant leads the three kings. They are dressed in exotic
    costumes, and so, that they differ in regard to every detail of
    appearance. A large retinue, of whom this is also true,
    accompanies them. Gold, incense, and myrrh. Herod
    enters immediately after them with Salome.*)

FIRST KING: Hail, King, to you!

SECOND KING: Your house is greatly blessed!

THIRD KING: May it be blessed for all eternity!

HEROD: I thank you, but, just now, your greeting seems
Quite strange to me!

FIRST KING: Has not a son been born
To you?

HEROD: To me? No. My wife just died!

FIRST KING: Then we shall not stay here.

SECOND KING: Then there must be
A second king besides.

HEROD: But if there were, there'd be
None here.

THIRD KING: But then there must be still a second
Royal family residing here.

HEROD: But why?

FIRST KING: That's right.

SECOND KING: Indeed, it must be so.

HEROD: But I know no such house!

SALOME (*to Herod*):   In Bethlehem
A branch of David's house survives.

THIRD KING: In Bethlehem?
And you say David was a king?

HEROD: He was!

FIRST KING: Then we shall make our way to Bethlehem.

SALOME (*still addressing Herod*): But his descendants are all
    beggars now!

HEROD: I'm sure! Else—

SALOME: I once met a girl who was
Of David's house, called Mary, I believe.
Considering her background, she was lovely.

She was engaged then, to a carpenter,
And hardly dared to raise her eyes to me
When I asked her her name.
    HEROD: Did you hear that?
    SECOND KING: No matter, we shall go!
    HEROD: But will you first
Explain what brings you here?
    FIRST KING: Our rev'rence for
The King of Kings!
    SECOND KING: Also the wish to see
Him to his face before we meet our death.
    THIRD KING: The sacred duty to lay at his feet
What's precious here on earth to honor him.
    HEROD: But who has told you of his birth?
    FIRST KING: His star.
We did not start this pilgrimage together;
We did not know each other, for our realms
Are in the East and West; and oceans lie
Between them and high mountains too.—
    SECOND KING: But we had seen the very same bright star,
And the same wish had seized each one of us.
We traveled the same road and now have met,
At last, together at our common goal—
    THIRD KING: And whether he be king's or beggar's son,
The child whose entry into life this star
Illuminates will be raised high; no man
Will breathe on earth who does not bow to him!
    HEROD (*to himself*): The old book says that very thing! (*Aloud*)
      May I
Offer a guide to Bethlehem to you?
    FIRST KING (*points to the sky*) We have one!
    HEROD: Good! And, if you find the child,
Will you inform me of it, so that I,
Like you, may go to pay respect to him.
    FIRST KING: We shall do that! Let's go! To Bethlehem! (*Kings
      off*)
    HEROD: They will not do it!
    JOAB AND TITUS (*appear*)
    ALEXANDRA (*follows*)
    HEROD: Ha!
    JOAB: It has been done!
      (*Herod covers his face*)
    TITUS: She's dead! Indeed! But I must carry out

A far more terrible assignment now
Than did the man who executed her!
I have to tell you she was innocent!
    HEROD: No, Titus, no! (*Titus wants to speak; Herod stands*
        next to him) For, had this been, you should
Not have allowed her death.
    TITUS: But only you
Could have prevented it. I do regret
To be worse than an executioner
For you, but, if it is a sacred duty
To give the dead, no matter who they are,
A burial, then still more sacred must
The duty be to cleanse her name of slander.
It is this duty which commands me now.
    HEROD: All you can say proves only this to me:
Her magic charm was faithful 'til her death!
I need not blame Sohemus! How could he
Resist her brilliance while she was alive;
As her light faded, she still dazzled you!
    TITUS: Does jealousy extend beyond the grave?
    HEROD: If I were wrong, if from you came words
Of anything but pity now, one of
Such depth that it could not be more, then I
Should have to warn you that it was
Your witness which condemned her too,
And that it was your duty then, to tell
Me if the smallest doubt came to your mind!
    TITUS: My word prevented that, and, more than that,
She felt she absolutely had to die.
If I had only moved one step away
From her, she would have taken her own life.
I saw the dagger hidden in her dress,
And, more than once, her hand began to twitch.
            (*Pause*)
She wanted death and had to die, for she
Had suffered so much and forgiven it
As she could bear to suffer and forgive;
I looked into her very deepest soul.
Let him who would demand still more of her
Not quarrel with her but the elements
Alone which had so fused inside her that
She could not go beyond this. But let him

Show me a woman who endured still more!
HEROD *(moves)*
TITUS: She wanted you to kill her, and playing
Her suicidal game, which did deceive
Us all, she did pretend to bring to life
The ugly image of your jealousy.
I found that too severe, but not unjust.
She wore a mask for you; this mask was to
Incite you to attack her with your sword. *(Points to Joab)*
And you did this by killing her yourself.
HEROD: She said this. But vengeance made her say it!
TITUS: It's true! I testified against her; how
I'd like to doubt her!
HEROD: And Sohemus?
TITUS: When
I saw him on his way to meet his death—
He started his when she had finished hers—
He seemed to find it comforting that now
His blood would blend with hers, although
In death, and only on the block and knife.
HEROD: Ha! There, you see!
TITUS: See what? Perhaps he did
Love her in secret. But, if that was sin,
It was his only; never hers. He called
To me: I now shall die because I spoke;
If not for that, I'd die because I could
Still speak, for that was Joseph's fate. In death,
He swore he was as innocent as I!
I heard him!
HEROD *(shouting)*:   Joseph? Does he seek vengeance?
Is earth now opening? Do the dead rise?
ALEXANDRA *(stands before him)*: They do!—But no! Come now,
    Don't be afraid!
There's one at least who will stay in her grave!
HEROD: You wretch! *(Controls himself)* Then be it so! And
    even though
Sohemus did then but commit one crime—
(Turns to Salome) Still, Joseph who inspired suspicion in
Him, Joseph was still lying when he was
About to die. And he—why don't you speak?
SALOME: He followed ev'ry step she took—
ALEXANDRA *(to Herod)*:   He did!

But surely only so he'd find the chance
To carry out your order to him which was
To kill both her and me—

HEROD:　　　　　　　　　　　　　　　Is that the truth?

(*To Salome*) And you? You did—

ALEXANDRA:　　　　　　　　　　Almost precisely when
He altogether stopped pretending with
Us, Mariamne made the solemn vow
That she would kill herself if you should not
Return. I shall not hide the fact from you
That I did hate her for this vow!

HEROD:　　　　　　　　　　　　　　　　Dreadful!
And—you could wait to speak?

ALEXANDRA:　　　　　　　　　　　　　　　I did!

TITUS:　　　　　　　　　　　　　　　　　I know
It too; it was her final word to me,
But I should never have revealed the vow;
My aim was cleansing her, not hurting you.

HEROD: Then I—(*his voice fails*)

TITUS:　　　　　　Compose yourself! It pains me too!

HEROD: Indeed! You—her (*To Salome*) —and ev'ry one who was,
Like me, the blinded tool of treach'rous fate.
But I alone have lost what never in
Eternity can be on earth again!
I've lost? Oh, lost!

ALEXANDRA:　　　　　　　　　　　Ha, Aristobolus,
My son, you are avenged, and I in you!

HEROD: You triumph? You believe that I shall now
Collapse? No I shall not do that! I am
A king, and I shall never let the world (*gestures as though he
　　　were breaking something*)
Forget it. Rise up then, Pharisees,
Rebel against me! (*To Salome*) You, why do you move
Away from me already? Probably
I still have the same face; tomorrow, though,
It may occur that my own mother has
To swear that I am not her son!—

(*After a pause, softly*)　　　　　　　　　　　And if
My crown were jeweled with the stars which blaze
Up in the sky, for Mariamne, I
Should give it up, and, if I had it, all
The globe as well. Indeed, if I could free

Her from the grave by burying myself
Alive, I'd do it, yes, would dig the grave
With my own hands! But I can not! So I
Shall stay and firmly hold what I still have!
That is not much, but there's a crown among
My things, which now will have to take the place
I had assigned to her, and he who'd reach
For it, to take it from me—that is now
The case, there is the lad, the wondrous child
Of whom the prophets spoke so long ago,
And on whose entry into life, a star
Does shine. But, Fate, you did miscalculate
Quite badly, if you thought to smooth his path
By crushing me under your iron foot;
I am a soldier; I shall fight you too!
And, even if I'm down, I'll bruise your heel!
(*Quickly*) Joab!

  JOAB (*approaches*)
  HEROD (*with restraint*) :   You'll go to Bethlehem and tell
The captain whom I've put in charge down there
That he should find the wondrous child—no, he
Will not find him; not ev'ry one can see
The star, and these kings are as false as they
Are pious!—No, he is to kill at once
The children who were born last year—each one;
Not one of them shall stay alive!

  JOAB (*steps back*) :   Yes, Sire.
(*To himself*) I know the reason! But Moses lived in spite
Of Pharaoh!

  HEROD (*still with a loud, clear voice*) : I shall check tomorrow!
  —But
Today is Mariamne's—(*He collapses*) Titus!

  TITUS (*tries to support him*)

PART THREE

Gyges and His Ring

Introduction to
Gyges and His Ring

SUMMARY OF HEBBEL'S SOURCES

PLATO'S *REPUBLIC*

Gyges, the ancestor of the famous Lydian, was a shepherd in the service of the king. One day, there was a great storm, and an earthquake split the very area where he was with his sheep. In the chasm, he found a horse made of brass, inside of which there lay a naked corpse which wore a ring. Gyges took the ring and put it on his finger. He discovered one day that he became invisible whenever he turned its bezel inward. He then contrived to become a messenger to the court, and, using the ring, seduced the queen. With her help, he killed the king and seized the throne.

HERODOTUS, *HISTORIES*, I, 7-12

Candaules, a descendant of Alceus, the son of Heracles, was the last Heraclid ruler of Sardis, which his family had ruled for five-hundred-and-five years. Candaules loved his wife so much that he considered her the most beautiful woman in the world. He raved to Gyges, his favorite bodyguard, about her beauty. Finally, he told Gyges that he must see her naked. Gyges pointed out that stripping a woman of her clothes was equivalent to stripping her of her honor and asked the king to abandon the idea. But the king insisted that Gyges hide in her bedroom while he was present and see the queen. The queen saw Gyges leave but said nothing to Candaules. On the next day, she told Gyges that he must either kill Candaules and take her and the throne or die himself. Gyges begged her not to force him into such action, but when she insisted, he agreed to attack Candaules in his sleep. He killed the king and succeeded him as ruler and as husband.

ANALYSIS

As in *Herod and Mariamne,* the time of this drama is one of transition between old and new. The arrival of the new era is clearly shown with the coronation of Gyges at the end of the play. Candaules is the transitional figure, without being aware of this function. The old time began with the Heraclid Dynasty, some five hundred years ago, and the Lydians have tried to preserve its traditions, for instance, the festival games, the gigantic sword, the inhumanly heavy crown. Candaules, an iconoclast like Herod, feels that these traditions are of the past and that modern times call for different customs. He is the first to admit that he is no Heracles and better suited to the lighter crown and sword than to Heraclean gear. We learn from his servant Thoas near the end of the drama that he has never seen Candaules use arms. This seems to be less because of inability to do so, and certainly not out of cowardice, but much more because he realizes that life is short enough (as he states in the first act) without ending any lives even earlier by putting men to death. Although he is not presented as a man of culture, we must note his respect for life, which is especially noteworthy in a product of a civilization which he himself describes to Gyges as strong-armed and barbarously bellicose.

To Candaules' problem as "modern" king in a traditionalist society is added his desire to impress his friend and favorite, Gyges. The Greeks have always considered themselves superior in culture and courage to barbarians and Gyges, the Greek, must be impressed, so thinks Candaules, by the virtues of Lydia. When he urges Gyges not to participate in the festival games lest he be killed at once, Candaules is trying to convince Gyges that the Lydians are superior to the Greeks, although his tone does not necessarily convey total approval of this area of superiority. At the same time, he speaks as though he looks down on the Greeks, who are clever, but not as clever as they think; they are manly, but certainly not as courageous, strong and ferocious as the Lydians! It does come as a shock to Candaules, therefore, that Gyges carries away all the prizes at the games. Perhaps in part to restore his feeling of superiority, perhaps merely because of the sight of Lesbia and the wine he has drunk, he then tells Gyges that he must see Rhodope in order to believe his enthusiastic descriptions of her beauty. His wife is a jewel, an ornament, a precious possession to Candaules; he can not see her as a human being; has no human relationship with her; and is annoyed by the fact that she will not show herself in public and will not remove her veil. All he sees in his offer to Gyges is a display of his friendship, his trust in Gyges and the desire to prove honestly that he possesses the finest treasure a man can have. As Hebbel indicates in his prefatory verses, the ring is but an instrument in this; Candaules would have been no different in his desire to show off his wife even if there had been no ring. Within the plot, however, we can add Candaules' wish to play with the ring to his motivation.

Candaules must have been taken aback when Gyges suddenly became visible in Rhodope's room! Since Candaules is incapable of deceiving a friend (a wife is not a friend to him), however, he assumes that Gyges was so moved by Rhodope's beauty that he did this without realizing it. When Gyges explains the next morning that he did this deliberately, Candaules is shocked. But, no matter what Gyges says, he does not want to kill him; he merely wants him to leave the court and thus end the unpleasant incident.

When Candaules goes to Rhodope, he first succeeds in reassuring her, especially when he turns out to have the diamond which she had worn during the night and which she has missed this morning. He has almost succeeded when he adds what he considers final reassurance; he tells her that Gyges is leaving. He insists that she has been jealous of Gyges for no good reason, since a friendship between men is of a different nature than the physical affection between man and woman. With these remarks, he underlines again his failure to understand his wife as a human being, and he also pinpoints Rhodope's suspicions; she is sure at once that Gyges was the intruder. This does not become clear to Candaules, however. He is not as sophisticated as his wife in matters of tact and intuition and does not know how her mind works, if indeed he thinks that she has a mind.

Yet Candaules is by no means merely a blustering boaster.
When Gyges later comes to tell Candaules that he must kill him,
Candaules immediately offers his heart to Gyges' sword. Candaules
realizes now that he has tried to destroy the old traditions of
his world without having anything to offer it in return, and that
such destructiveness must be punished by death. He is ready to
accept this punishment without fighting. He only agrees to the
duel with Gyges because he wants to show Rhodope that he did
not give her up lightly. In spite of his boasting and swaggering
in previous scenes, Candaules dies as a great man, for he has
realized his guilt and dies to affirm and restore world order and
harmony.

Candaules is a more positive hero than Herod, who refused
to acknowledge his wrong but decided rather to do his utmost
to force the world to conform to his image of it (at the end of
Herod and Mariamne). In Herod, Hebbel portrayed the tragic
hero who avers in the face of tragedy that he is right and that
the world is wrong. In Candaules, he portrays the hero who
conforms to world order by dying to restore it and affirming it
in death. Both types of tragic heroes are discussed by Hebbel in
his theoretical essay.

If we compare the heroines of the two dramas, we find that
Mariamne was the more alive, more human of the two. Both
will their own death, but Mariamne is the stronger of them in
forcing Herod to have her killed without ever explaining herself
to him. She is the more complex character because she choses
to "play" for Herod the role he has assigned her in his mind
and yet shows us through Titus what she really is like; she is an
honest human being on whom her husband's narrowmindedness
imposes a role. Her development is shown in her decision to
assume the role at the cost of her life. Rhodope stays the same
throughout. She does not develop; her mystic purity, symbolized
by her veils, is her main characteristic. She is always veiled as a
human being, whether or not she actually wears her veils. Her
death comes as no surprise to us, but must be a great shock to
Gyges, who talked about their marriage as though it would be
consummated after he had defended the country against its at-
tackers. Her death is not the result of her development but is
totally consistent with her approach to life and her rigid code
of purity. She is almost a superhuman being, and it seems fitting
that Gyges' crime against her purity is referred to as a sacrilege.
She is mystic in her very origins, somewhere where India and

Greece blend—even this is veiled. In her attitude toward her slaves, she is humane but not human in her vast superiority to these mortal women; her attitude toward Candaules also seems superhuman. She has some human moments, to be sure: when she believes that Candaules may love her as a person and not as a possession, and when she thinks, as Candaules has almost convinced her, that there had been no one in her room during the night. At this moment, she almost comes to life. She also seems human when, moved by his sensitivity and delicacy in addressing her, she concludes at the end of the scene in which she sends him to kill Candaules that Gyges would not have taken her from her homeland to expose her to such a situation.

Gyges is an interesting character, both noble and human. He is a Greek, highly cultured and civilized, artistic and sensitive, and yet a man of prowess, character, courage, and strength. Candaules is noble by instinct, Gyges, by training or, perhaps more accurately, by tradition. Both are great and good men; both do wrong. Gyges spies on Rhodope for a number of reasons. He is just awakening to women, thanks to having seen Lesbia; he is flushed with his manliness after winning all the honors at the games; he has had a fair amount of wine to drink; his friend Candaules wants him to see Rhodope, overwhelms him with the urgency of his wish. Yet, as soon as he is in Rhodope's room, Gyges realizes the enormity of his offense; her beauty stirs him, not merely as a man, but as a human being, as an idealist. Realizing, this time by instinct rather than tradition, that this is indeed a sacrilege, he wants to be killed at once. He makes himself visible because he expects that Candaules will be angry enough at this breach of trust to kill him. Candaules' failure to kill him makes him appear weak in comparison to Gyges, as does his later refusal to kill him when he asks Gyges, who has confessed why he made himself visible, to leave Lydia. This is consistent, however with the Candaules who let Gyges kill the tiger, even though he could have done it easily for himself. Here, his generosity and greatness almost appear culturally motivated, while Gyges, appearing like a young hothead, seems to be ruled by instinct. Finally, the duel of the two must be mentioned. Gyges tries to force Candaules to kill him when he informs the king that Rhodope will marry the survivor. Although he wants to live to marry Rhodope, Gyges wants a hard battle and is ready to die at Candaules' hand. Still, one wonders whether Candaules does not repeat the tiger ploy in this final battle. After all, he has made very clear that he must die to restore world order.

The final question confronting us is that of the fate of Gyges. He had expected to conquer Lydia's enemies and to live with Rhodope as man and wife. He can not have been totally without suspicion as to her plans when he found her at Hestia's temple rather than Aphrodite's. Gyges must either be killed in defending Lydia or survive as a man with a duty to perform, with all joy gone out of his young life. Although Candaules is Hebbel's hero and carries out Hebbel's dramatic theory of tragedy, Gyges is perhaps the most tragic of the characters.

Hebbel himself was quite surprised at the way in which the tragedy developed beyond his intentions:

> Of course, the play is intended to be Greek only in the sense in which Troilus and Cressida or Iphigenia are Greek; I don't think much of adding new wine to old bottles and don't think that an experiment of that sort has ever been successful. But I hope that I did not miss the point of intersection at which the ancient and modern atmospheres meet, and that I have resolved a conflict which could only have come into being in ancient times and which is depicted in the colors proper to them, that I have resolved this conflict in a universally human way which can be understood by every age. Also, I had a strange experience when I wrote this drama. In my other dramas, I was always conscious of a certain background of ideas, which was by no means the reason why I wrote . . . which, however was to be regarded like a mountain range which bounded my landscape. This time, I lacked it completely, I was only challenged by the anecdote itself, which, with some modifications, appeared to me extraordinarily well suited for the tragic form, and now that the play is finished, suddenly, to my own surprise, there rises, like an island out of the ocean, the idea of ethics as the one which brings everything about and connects it all . . .[1]

The appearance of the ethical theme should come as no surprise to the reader of Hebbel's plays, however. Holofernes, Herod, and Candaules all seem to be one and the same character in their function and in their ambivalent nature, one and the same character as envisioned by one and the same writer at

---

1. Letter to Friedrich Uechttritz, December 14, 185

different stages of his own life. All three do the same wrong, for they all must upset world order because they are individuals. Hebbel wrote in his diary:

> *Life* is the attempt of the stubbornly defiant *part* to tear away from the whole and to exist by itself, an attempt which succeeds as long as the strength lasts of which the whole has been deprived by the individuation of the part.[2]

Judith, Mariamne, and Rhodope are similar stages of development: titan virgin, exemplary human being, and apotheosis of womanhood. For these characters, tragedy is the vehicle for a return to world harmony. Judith gives herself and kills to restore harmony but will have to sacrifice her own life if she is punished as a woman for overstepping her feminine limitations; Mariamne dies to assert human dignity after she has tried to be a wife at the expense of her tradition. Rhodope does nothing to assume guilt but becomes defiled, according to her tradition, through the fault of two men. But, because she causes one's death, she too has assumed guilt, for which she expiates by dying. There seems to be no way to avoid this assumption of guilt and of expiation in Hebbel's view. By defining life in this way, he has explained why this must be so: life itself is individuation—separation from the whole—and the restoration of harmony to the whole—to the universe—is as inevitable as is the death of the individual.

---

2. February 2, 1841.

Gyges and His Ring

Over the picture I saw, I extended a colorful rainbow,
Radiating a kinder light, much softer than sunshine,
But it was only to shimmer ever so gently and never
To serve as a bridge for man's fate which arises alone from the
*   heart.*

DRAMATIS PERSONAE

CANDAULES, *the King of Lydia*   LESBIA, *a slave*
RHODOPE, *his wife*   HERO, *a slave*
GYGES, *a Greek*   THOAS, *a slave*
                CARNA, *a slave*
                LYDIANS

The action is prehistoric and mythical; it takes place within twice twenty-four hours.

ACT I

Great Hall. Candaules and Gyges enter. Candaules is putting on his sword. Thoas follows with the crown.

CANDAULES: Today, you'll see the best of Lydia!
Although you Greeks are known to be subservient,
Since that's your only choice, I know you bear
The ancient yoke with gnashing teeth and jeer
At all your lords. Besides, not easily
Does one invent aught in this world which you
Would not immediately seek to better,
And even if it's just to add a wreath,
You'd add it, claiming it your whole invention.
    (*Thoas hands him the crown.*)
The new one, I insist! What good is this?
Did you, perhaps, give me the wrong sword too?
Indeed, by Hercules, whose feast this is!
Has premature senility beset you?
    THOAS: I thought—
    CANDAULES: What then?
    THOAS: It's been five centuries
Since your great ancestor did found these games,
And no king has appeared in diff'rent garb;
But when you last did try suppression of
The ancient holy symbols, terrified
And in astonishment the people watched,
Resenting it and saying so!
    CANDAULES: You think
I should remember this and hence improve.
Is that your point?
    THOAS: My Lord, I've never held
This diadem without a shudder and

Could never touch the handle of this sword
Which all the sons of Hercules did wield!
But I regard your newer jewels just
As I do anything which glitters, shines,
And which one owns if one can pay for it.
They do not call to mind Hephaestus who
Did forge the weapons of Achilles, the divine,
Using the very flame with which he steels
The thunder bolts of Zeus, nor do they bring
Thetis to mind, whose daughters had to fish
For pearls and corals for him lest he lack
For ornamental decoration; no,
For, after all, I know the man who's forged
The new sword and then made the crown you like.
    CANDAULES: Well, Gyges?
    THOAS: Lord, my loyalty moves me to speak.
If I am daring, it is for your sake.
Believe me, Lord, the many thousand men
Who here converge, though they be clothed in wool
Better than mine and used to better fare,
Are just as foolish, just as pious as
Am I. Your head, together with this crown,
And so your arm, together with this sword
Are, for them, but two halves of one entirety.
    CANDAULES: They all think thus?
    THOAS: Yes, by my head, they do!
    CANDAULES: That must be changed at once! Take this away,
And do as I've commanded.
(Thoas off with the old crown and sword)
    GYGES: You've hurt him!
    CANDAULES: I know. But tell me now, what could I say?
'Tis true, he's right. The king may rule here, just
Because he wears the regal crown. Its worth
Is based upon its rust. Woe to the man
Who'd polish it and thus decrease its worth!
What good is it if one let go just once
And showed that kingship, solely based on old
Tradition, seems too much to bear, refused
To be accepted like a minted coin
Which no one weighs, to share inviolate
Immunity with ancient statues which
Unreasoning tradition keeps in shrines.

It can not be undone!
(*Thoas brings the new crown and sword*)
That's better now.
(*Puts on the crown*)
That fits! And ev'rything my realm produces
In gems and pearls, from mines and ocean's base,
Is represented here, no more or less.
That gem which is not native to our land,
Though beautiful, is strictly banished here.
But, to be sure, I left some space for such
As might be found a hundred years from now.
You understand?
(*To Gyges*)
The other crown is fit
For a titanic head, resembling what
Your sculptors like to give my ancestor,
When he, in lion skin, wielding a clumsy axe,
Is called upon to help to frighten children
Away from mossy edges of deep wells.
(*He puts on the sword*)
This sword weighs slightly less than does the old,
But one can wield it anywhere if there
Is need, not merely under open skies
Where giants like to hurl gigantic rocks.
(*He draws the sword and swings it*)
It also works in narrow, human space.
So, Thoas, spare yourself a third attempt;
I heard the second fail today.

THOAS: Forgive
Me, Lord, but know: a change of weather is
Not ever felt by younger bones; the old
Bones always are the first to feel such change. (*Off*)

GYGES: He leaves in sorrow.

CANDAULES: Yes, he's said to think
That now I shall be hit when thunderbolts
Next strike, and he is sure they will, unless
The earth would open and consume me first,
Unless the minotaur himself appears!—
They are that way, but do not think the less .
Of them for that! Well now, today you'll see
Them at the games.

GYGES: I wish to join with them.

CANDAULES: What's this, my friend?
GYGES: My Lord, I'd like to join.
CANDAULES: No, no; I want you sitting by my side
So that they'll see you in my high esteem,
And how I want them all to honor you.
  GYGES: If you would honor me, let me compete.
  CANDAULES: You do not know the Lydians, my friend.
You Greeks are clever, letting others spin,
The while you weave. But such a net, no thread of which
Is yours, though you still have the net in hand,
How easily could it be closed, and then
The whole world would be caught! If only
The fisher who's to rule it all just had
A slightly stronger arm! But there he fails!
You have no art by which you could reel in
The fibers of our nerves; so we pretend
To be much blinder than we really are,
And, to amuse ourselves, step in your nets;
A little jerk would free us anytime.
  GYGES: We also celebrate these games.
  CANDAULES: That's true.
Among yourselves! The Dorian will fight
With the Ionian, and, if at last
Boeotians interfere, you think, of course,
Ares himself is watching what you do,
Remembering each blow und shuddering.
Friend Gyges, even if you'd won each prize
They had in Greece, my warning still would hold:
You should not even try to win our least,
For wild and bloody is such battle here.
If you, the Greek, my fav'rite, tried to win
A single silver poplar's branch today,
The kind of which thousands are to be won,
This competition you would not survive!
  GYGES: Now you've agreed, and now you cannot keep
Me from it anymore!
  CANDAULES: You see it thus?
Then I must hold my peace!
  GYGES: My Lord, I came
Not just to ask. (*He pulls out a ring*)
          Take this! It fits a king!
You see a ring, see nothing in it now.

You wonder that I'd dare to offer it.
You'll take it like a rose a child might give
So that you'll not offend the simple mind
Which offers it. Not that it pleases you;
It is quite plain, that's true, and simple too.
And still, you could not buy it with your realm,
Nor take it from the owner by sheer force,
In spite of all your regal might, unless
He willingly would give his ring to you.
When worn this way, (*Signs and gestures*)
                   so that the metal shows
Upon your hand, it merely ornaments;
Perhaps not even that. But turn it now
So far that this small ruby, dark and red,
Can freely shine in all directions, then
You suddenly will be invisible.
You'll walk the earth like gods within a cloud.
So don't refuse it, for I'll say again
It is a regal ring, and I planned long
Ago to give it to you now; you are
The only one who may possess this ring!
     CANDAULES: We've also heard of most unusual things;
We've heard of magic, practiced by a woman,
Medea was her name, whose spells were said
To charm even the moon down to this earth.
But never have I heard about this ring.
Where did you ever get it?
     GYGES: From a tomb.
I found it in a tomb in Thessaly.
     CANDAULES: You broke a tomb and desecrated it?
     GYGES: No, my King, no! I found this had been done.
I merely crawled in when I had to hide
From robbers who pursued me in far
Greater number than I could fight when I,
In search of high adventure, recently,
Was wand'ring through the desolated woods.
The urns had been upset when I found them,
The broken pieces lay in sad confusion
And, in the pale glow of the ev'ning sun
Which penetrated through cracks in the wall,
I saw a little cloud of dust which moved
And rose before me as the last remains

Of those dead buried here. This moved me so
That I long held my breath within me lest
I should, by chance, inhale, against my will
The ashes of my forefathers or peers.
    CANDAULES: Well? And the robbers?
    GYGES: They had lost my tracks,
Or so it seemed, for fainter did the echo
Of their voices become; and I thought then
That I was safe, although I did not leave
My shady hiding place in which I was
Still kneeling quietly. Then, suddenly,
This ring had caught my glance, this ring
Which sparkled with its stone like something live,
Almost reminding me of a snake's eye
As it lay there, shining and cold amid
The ashes, and I wondered whose long since
Disintegrated finger wore it once.
Then, just to see if it had been a man's,
I put it on. But hardly finishing,
I heard a shout outside: 'Stop! He must be hidden
In here. Here, in the tomb, come comrades, here!
We have him now!' Quickly, the band appeared;
And I, lest I be slaughtered, helpless as
An animal, once it's been driven in
A cave, leapt out and thrust myself into
Encounter with them, my sword raised high. The sun
Was just about to set; its rays shone forth
Like those around a candle's flame before
It dies, a final, most intensive light.
But they, as though the night had fallen
For them alone, ran past me, and they cursed
Most bitterly and stood about the tomb.
They searched it closely, and, not finding me,
They loudly jeered: 'It does not matter much;
He probably had nothing but his stubborn eyes
Which challenged us with brazenness of glance.
We'll let another man blow out his eyes!'
Then, once again, but slowly and annoyed,
Yes, peering at me, staring in my face,
They went past me and still did not see me!
    CANDAULES: And then you thought—
    GYGES: Not of the ring! Not then!

I did believe a god had saved me by
A miracle. I threw myself upon my knees
And said to the invisible divinity:
I don't know who you are, and if you don't
Reveal your face to me, then I can not
Make off'ring to you, of your fav'rite beast.
But still, to show my gratitude to you,
I'll offer you the wildest of the robbers,
I swear it here, no matter what the price.
And then, I hurried after them, and mingled
In their band, and terror gripped me when
They did not only fail to see me there
As if I were but air, but when they spoke
And passed their bread and wine right through myself!
My glance was dulled and moving fell upon
The stone set in the ring; it sparkled red
And bright to meet it from my hand, and, in
Its constant movement of reflection and
Refraction, looked much like an eye which bled
And smoked. I turned the ring in self-defense,
One might say, out of fear, for it still shone
As though it were a star, and I then felt
As though I'd looked into th' eternal source
Of light itself, and its abundance made
Me blind. In the same way, as music of
The spheres is said to make its list'ner deaf.
But then I felt that someone took strong hold
Of me and heard: 'What's that? Who hid him here?
The joke is good!' from all the robbers all about.
And now, ten fists reached for my throat at once;
Ten others started tearing at my clothes,
And if the clumsiest of them did not
Attempt to take the ring, I'd surely lose—
A wretched end seemed absolutely sure.
But suddenly, they cried: 'He is not poor;
Our catch is good; just look, that's shiny gold.
There even is a stone; let's take that first.'
But then, in the same breath, their cry
Did change: 'A god has come to us!'
And all of them were lying at my feet.
    CANDAULES: When they were pulling at the ring they must
Have turned it once again and shuddered then

When, like a cloud formation, you dissolved.
  GYGES: It must be so. But now, at last informed
Of its mysterious power, I, with pride
And daring, turned it one more time and cried:
'A god indeed, and you will all repent.'
Then I attacked them; they were terrified
As though I held the thunder in my hands
And were accompanied by thousands of
New deaths. Indeed, they hardly could maintain
The strength and courage needed just to flee.
But I pursued them hotly, just as though
The Furies had chosen me to serve them thus;
So not a single one eluded me.
And then I tried to put the ring back in
The tomb, but though I'd marked my path with blood
And corpses too, I could not find it then
Nor in the morning when I tried again.
And so the ring was mine against my will.
  CANDAULES: That is a matchless treasure!
  GYGES: I told you,
A ring fit for a king. So take it, King!
  CANDAULES: Not till the battle's done!
  GYGES: Lord, I have not
Worn it again; nor shall I ever wear
It. You can't be miserly about the wood!
My pyre does not demand a forest; no,
A single tree suffices! Trust my arm;
Perhaps it even spares this tree for you.
  CANDAULES: Give it to me; I'll test it!
  GYGES: I shall arm!
    (Both off)

The Queen's Chambers.

Rhodope enters with her servants, among them Lesbia and Hero.

  RHODOPE: Rejoice, dear maids! Today's the day for joy!
You may be glad! As much as I must scold
You all on other days when you eavesdrop,
And would have had to scold you yesterday,
Dear Hero, when you climbed into the tree,
If not, to punish you, a branch had broken,
In spite of your light weight, because it was

Too weak for all your curiosity—
HERO: Oh Queen, if you saw that, you also know,
I'm sure, that of the many trees I chose
The one that had the thickest foliage.
  RHODOPE: The thickest? That may be! But certainly
The one located closest to the wall.
  HERO: It was the very thickest! I was in,
What one can only term, a night of green.
It almost frightened me to go and leave
The golden day behind me and to creep
Unseeing in its night.
  RHODOPE: Why do it then?
  HERO: Certainly not to be a few feet closer
To Mount Olympus! No, indeed, I left
That to the nightingale which sang above.
I wanted—no, please do not laugh! I can't
Forget the rocking cradle, and I hoped
To rock up there.
  RHODOPE: And that was really why?
  HERO: And, by the way, but really only by
The way, quite by the way, to look outside,
Beyond our garden, just this once, because
I'd really love to know whether a lake
Surrounds it just as gloomy Carna claims
Persistently.
  LESBIA: A lake!
  HERO: Do you know better?
  LESBIA: But have you ever heard it splashing here?
And is a lake as still as you can be?
  RHODOPE: I won't ask any further, for I know
You won't do it again. For never did
A girl enjoy a gentler fall, but still,
I've never seen a girl appear so shocked!
  LESBIA: Yes, all her limbs went limp!
  HERO: But I need not
Have fallen, for there was a stronger branch,
And close enough for me, but it was cradling
A nest with tiny birds; I did not wish
To come so close that I might frighten off
The baby brood which just began to try
Its naked wings.
  LESBIA: So that was why you fell?

But they still tried their wings, you probably
Reached over as you fell to find support.
    RHODOPE: You may tease as you like; this is the day
Which frees you from the confines of the house.
Do what you like; look outside all you want.
    HERO: And you?
    RHODOPE: Don't look to me! What you may do
Is merely not forbidden to me. So,
Today, I can't serve as example for you.
    HERO: You still will not attend the feast, my Queen?
    RHODOPE: So that I shan't disturb your gaiety!
It's not our custom and would seem to me
As though I were to eat and drink and be
Without hunger and thirst. Also, to me,
Our way appears superior to yours,
For never without shudd'ring have you come
Home from these feasts which seem to lure you so,
And I prefer the girl who feels the deepest
Shudder and then will not go back again.
I don't mean to reproach you, no, not that;
But I am glad that Lesbia who has
Grown up among you shares my views on this.
    LESBIA: Would you forgive me if, today—
    RHODOPE: What's this?
What's to forgive? You wish to go with them?
I'm sorry that I spoke this way, now you're ashamed
To be the daughter of your native land.
You have good reason to be that; I am!
Go on, and tell me later how it was!
    HERO: I'm sure young Gyges will participate.
His is that pleasant voice.
    RHODOPE: You say, you know
His voice?
    HERO: I do, but nothing more as yet.
Today, we are to see him, and she too
Is going just because of him.
    LESBIA: I still
Can stay and make a liar out of you.
    HERO: I know you won't.
    CANDAULES (*enters*):   Rhodope, greetings, Queen.
Do you know who I am? The guard of statues,
A border-barrier king who measures ells

But never touches swords and is to blame
That twenty-four new other greater feats
Have not long since outdone the labors twelve
Of Hercules! And if you don't believe this,
Simply ask Alcaeus who's enraged.
You don't know him? I've only known him since
This day! And do you know how I make people
Happy? I say: Come lad, here is a seed.
Just plant it in the earth and water it
With regularity, day after day,
And then be sure that when your hair's turned white
You will eat cherries, fruit of all your work!
And whether they be sweet or sour you will learn!
The witness I can name for you is Agron,
Worthy Alcaeus' worthy friend who looks
Just like him though his beard is not as white.
    RHODOPE: You are quite happy!
    CANDAULES: And why not! Although
Alcaeus plans to offer me open
Rebellion if I ever dare to show
My face to him, as I now do to you,
While I am wearing this new diadem!
Agron plans to protect me, and you'll be
Surprised to learn how mild his plans for me!
In gratitude, I am to promise not
To doff the crown again, also to bear
A sword, so heavy, drawing it exhausts me!
    RHODOPE: How do you know all this?
    CANDAULES: Not from a spy,
And even less, from some deceiving friend!
From them themselves, from their own mouths, I heard!
    RHODOPE: You make fun of my question.
    CANDAULES: No, I don't!
I am completely serious! I stood
Near them, while they exchanged these vows, and nicked
The table with their nails, and gnawed their lips
As though they bit some wild and alien flesh;
I'm sure they meant it all! There is a kind
Of invocation of the judgement of
The gods in this: one thrusts at me, the other
Defends; and Justice can decide the end.
    RHODOPE: You listened then? I can't believe you would!

When I am somewhere where I'm not expected,
I make a sound so that they'll notice me
And make no statement I'm not meant to hear.
And you—oh, no! A king could not do this!
    CANDAULES: Of course, he wouldn't! But you'll never guess!
Look at this ring. What could its value be?
    RHODOPE: Who gave it to you?
    CANDAULES: It's from Gyges' hand!
    RHODOPE: Then it must be of greatest worth to you!
    CANDAULES: It is! But you can't tell me why. You'll be
Amazed! It makes its wearer invisible!
    RHODOPE: Invisible!
    CANDAULES: It does. I've tested it!
Don't climb again, dear Hero! Only birds
Will hide in leafy trees.
    RHODOPE: Oh, Lesbia!
    CANDAULES: Now I can walk through ev'ry door; no lock
Nor bolt can bar my way!
    RHODOPE: How terrible!
    CANDAULES: For ev'ry criminal, you mean.
    RHODOPE: Oh, no!
Much more indeed for ev'ry decent man!
(*To Lesbia*) Can you still breathe in peace, not die of shame,
Now, that you know? My Lord, please throw it out,
Please hurl it in the deepest river! He
Whom Destiny intends to have the power
Of gods is born a demigod. Give it
To me. We have a saying that what can
Destroy the world is hidden here and there
On earth. This has been there since gods and men
Still walked together and exchanged tokens
Of love. This ring is one of those, I'm sure.
Who knows whose finger once was honored with
It by a goddess, knows what kind of bond
It was to seal. Does this not frighten you,
Appropriating for yourself her gift
Thus summoning her vengeance on your head!
Its very sight is dreadful! Give it to me.
    CANDAULES: But for a price! Only if you as queen,
Will then appear at today's games.
    RHODOPE: I can't.
You went to your remotest borders to find

A quiet bride and knew well how she was.
The knowledge pleased you that, before you came,
Only my father had laid eyes on me,
And, since our marriage, no one has but you.
    CANDAULES: Forgive me! I just think a jewel which
One does not show—
    RHODOPE: Can not attract a thief!
    CANDAULES: Enough! Your 'no' is nothing new to me!
Although the fresh wind's blowing ev'rywhere
And lifting veils, you'd tie yours to your face!
(Music) Now the procession's here. The king must lead!
    RHODOPE: With rebels too! Today, I'm sorry that
I may not go with you.
    CANDAULES: My thanks! But have
No fear. Provisions have been made for them.
    RHODOPE: They have?
    CANDAULES: Indeed. But not because I fear
Them; only, I would have to punish them
And do not want this. Life is all too short
For man to have to earn his death, and so
I will not sentence anyone today.
    RHODOPE: You too are going now.
    LESBIA: I'll stay my Queen.
    RHODOPE: Oh no! No nurse sang at your cradle that
A man's face would bring certain death to you!
(Lesbia, Hero, and the rest off)
They don't know how to dream. The best of them
Considers my sole joy a sacrifice! *(Off)*

Open Space

*Much populace. The King on a throne. Lesbia, Hero, etc.,
on a balcony to one side. The games have just ended.
General movement. Groups begin to become distinguish-
able: wrestlers, boxers, charioteers, etc. All of these wear
silver poplar wreaths. Wine is served. Music is heard. The
feasting begins.*

PEOPLE: To Gyges, hail!
CANDAULES *(looks into the background)* : He won at discus too?

The third time? I should be offended now!
There won't be any prizes for my people!
(*He gets up from the throne and goes to meet Gyges, who enters
    from the back accompanied by the jubilant throng which
    makes way for the king*)

CANDAULES: You certainly are modest, friend; you just
Take all we have!

GYGES: My Lord, today, I fought
Not as myself, but as a Greek.

CANDAULES: The worse
For us if you are the new type of Greek.
That will necessitate our looking for
Old dragons' skins to stuff, of which 'tis said
That they've been rotting in the corner of
Some shrine since Hercules has gone. Besides,
We should restore the ghost of Hydra too
And other monsters which could frighten you!
You do not hear me!

GYGES: Yes, I do.

CANDAULES: I see
You are distracted, eye those girls, and they
Have noticed it. Just look at them! The small
Girl now begins to tease the taller one.
You're blushing! Shame on you!

GYGES: I'm thirsty!

CANDAULES: Well,
That's something else, of course. A man who fights
Like you deserves a satisfying drink.
And though I don't, I shall drink with you. For
I like the feasting after games the best! (*Signals a servant*)
Come here.

(*The servant brings a chalice with wine*)

CANDAULES (*pours some drops on the ground*) : The root comes
first and then the branch!

(*He drinks and is about to hand the chalice to Gyges, who is
    looking at the balcony again.*)

CANDAULES: Come!—Ah! The question here is black or brown,
Is that it?

GYGES: Lord!

CANDAULES: How does the wine please you?

GYGES: I have not tasted it.

CANDAULES: So you know that?

Let me remind you of your thirst! Come, drink!
I'll promise you that she will stay up there
Until you've told me what is on your mind.
    GYGES *(drinks)*: That's cooling.
    CANDAULES: Woe, your star's descending now.
(The girls move away but are still seen)
Well, it was time! Just see them twist! They walk
As though they were to wind around a thyrsus
Which suddenly has shot out of the ground,
Climbs skyward arrowlike and faster still
And drops a million grapes upon the earth.
But wine is meant for wingéd creatures only,
Not for the world in which one limps and crawls!
Wine turns it topsy-turvy. For example,
Take that old man; he'd mount the tiger fast;
He'd crown his wrinkled brow with flowered wreaths,
As did Dionysus when he went to
The Ganges! But that's what I like.—She's pretty?
    GYGES: I don't know whether what I like is pretty.
    CANDAULES: Say yes with confidence; her eyes like coal
Which only glows but throws off sparks and plays
In colors with the gentlest breath so that
One does not know: is't black or is it brown;
And then, as though this everlasting shimmer
Coursed through each drop of blood within her
Exchanging modesty and quiet flame,
It lends her blush a charm beyond compare.
    GYGES: You do for me completely what the wind
Does but in part. It moves the veil; you raise it.
    CANDAULES: I don't do it so you will kneel to her,
Oh no! If I should lead you to another,
Though she is lovely, you'd just wipe her like
A speck out of your eye, a speck which dulled
The mirror for you!
    GYGES: You think it's thus my Lord?
    CANDAULES: Of course! But stop! A treasure one can't show,
One should not praise! One would be ridiculed.
Who would believe in pearls in a closed hand!
    GYGES: I—
    CANDAULES: Gyges, even the shadow of my wife,
Seen in the moonlight—Now you smile.—Let's drink.
    GYGES: I did not smile.

CANDAULES: You should. For after all,
Who could not boast this way? If you spoke thus
To me, I'd say to you: show her to me,
Or hold your tongue!
GYGES: I trust you.
CANDAULES: Come, now.
A man should trust his eyes and not his ears.
You trust me? Hah! This silly child excites
You so, and now—well, that's enough; I do
Not wish to boast to you with idle talk
As I've been doing for a long time now.
You are to see her!
GYGES: See her!
CANDAULES: Yes, tonight!
I need a witness to the fact that I
Am not a fool, and vain, and self-deceiving
When I boast that I kiss the greatest beauty,
And I chose you for this!
GYGES: Oh please, not that!
Consider: for the husband it's disgrace;
But for the wife, and such a wife as she,
Who, even in the day—
CANDAULES: She'll never know!
Did you forget the ring? And I shall not
Be happy 'til your mouth tells me I am.
Come, ask yourself whether you'd like a crown
If you could only wear it in the dark.
Well, that is how I feel about her. She's
The queen of women, whom I must possess
The way the sea possesses pearls, and none
Suspects how rich I am, and, even when
I die, no friend can write about this on my tomb,
And I shall lie, a beggar among beggars.
So don't refuse me this; do take the ring!
(*He offers Gyges the ring, but the latter does not take it*)
And now night falls; I'll show you to her room,
And when I go in, enter it with me!
Just follow me!
(*He takes Gyges by the hand and pulls him along*)
                     This I demand of you!
You do owe this to Lesbia, you know;
Perhaps the vict'ry will be hers!
                          (*Both off*)

ACT II

Hall. Early morning. Thoas enters.

THOAS: I simply have to speak to him once more!
The things I had to overhear last night!
I certainly did not intend to spy,
And yet I come home loaded down, as though
I were the bloodiest tyrant's legged ear
And hardly dared to go back to my lord!
Rebellion! Enemies about to strike!
Election of a new king! Can it be?
I feared a lot but not as much as this!
Be quiet. I hear steps. Indeed, who wakes
As early as an old man, before dawn?
Young Gyges! Ah, if you knew what I have
Just learned, you would not walk stooped over, friend.

(Off)

GYGES (*enters*): I'm here again. What do I want here now?
I cannot bear it in the open air;
There is, out there, a lulling, heavy scent,
As though all flowers were in bloom at once
To suffocate humanity with scent,
Indeed, as though the earth exhaled itself.

THOAS (*enters*): Awake already, Carna? Lord, forgive;
I took you for another! Not asleep?
Ambition does not let you rest, I guess.

GYGES: Ambition!

THOAS: Well, you won so many wreaths
There, at the games—

GYGES: The laurel tree needs not
Fear me at all. I only planned to show
That one can have strong bones and marrow in
Them too, although one does not need to tear to shreds
The zither's strings when merely touching them.
Now ev'ryone has been informed of this,
Including those who've always doubted it,
And that suffices.

THOAS: Why aren't you asleep?

GYGES: Why aren't you drinking then?

THOAS: Perhaps you just
Awoke so early?

GYGES: Yes, if I have slept!

THOAS: That's what I'd like to know. For if he heard
What I heard—well, I trust he did not hear! (*Slowly off*)
   GYGES: She's still asleep. Ah, what a joy 'twould be
To waken her. The nightingale which just
Begins its own sweet song while half asleep
Might—and—He comes! What will he think of me!
   CANDAULES (enters) : She is awake and acts as though asleep!—
You, Gyges? Here again? Or is it still?
But no, I have your word!
   GYGES: Here is the ring!
   CANDAULES: So early and so fast?
   GYGES: It is your ring.
   CANDAULES: You do not dare to keep it any longer?
   GYGES: Why not? But to what purpose? Take it now.
   CANDAULES: This tells me even more than did your sigh
During the night.
   GYGES: My Lord, forgive me that!
   CANDAULES: Nonsense! It symbolized my triumph, friend.
   GYGES: Were you the only one to hear it?
   CANDAULES: No!
She started up and screamed—you claim you missed
All that? Well, then I do not need to ask
You anymore whether I won my bet!
   GYGES: I did not miss it!
   CANDAULES: Well, then just deny
That you were quite confused. And I have still
Much better proof of your confusion, for
You even turned the ring and didn't know it.
   GYGES: I did not know!
   CANDAULES: She trembled when she heard
The sound and cried to me: 'get up, get up;
A man hides in that corner, wants to kill
The King, or me! Where is your sword?' I then
Pretended I was startled too and rose;
And suddenly you stood before my eyes,
Most clearly shown by brightest lantern light.
Is that enough? Are you struck dumb by this?
   GYGES: I wanted to be visible!
   CANDAULES: Now you say that
Just to decrease my triumph! If I had
Not placed myself between you and her eyes
Before they focussed on you, I should have

GYGES AND HIS RING
Deutsches Schauspielhaus Hamburg, May 21, 1960
Director: Gustaf Gründgens
Gustaf Gründgens as Candaules
Photo by Rosemarie Clausen

GYGES AND HIS RING
Deutsches Schauspielhaus Hamburg, May 21, 1960
Director: Gustaf Gründgens
Gustaf Gründgens as Candaules and Sebastian Fischer as Gyges
Photo by Rosemarie Clausen

GYGES AND HIS RING
Deutsches Schauspielhaus Hamburg, May 21, 1960
Director: Gustaf Gründgens
Joana Maria Gorvin as Rhodope and Sebastian Fischer as Gyges
Photo by Rosemarie Clausen

To kill you now!

GYGES: I knew this well, my Lord.
I turned the ring so hastily because
It was my wish to force you to this act.

CANDAULES: What Gyges?

GYGES: Yes, for sacrilegious seemed
This brazen deed!

CANDAULES: But you had my permission.
Indeed! But at that fev'rish time, I thought

GYGES: You had no right to give it to me, so
I wished to punish you and me as well.
I knew you'd hate to kill me!

CANDAULES: How could you!

GYGES: And even now, I shudder in my soul
As though a crime had been committed here
For which the lip lacks a defining term,
But conscience does not lack the pang of guilt.
Enraged, I would have hurled before your feet
The awful death ring you'd forced back on me,
Instead of using it once more to flee,
Had I not been concerned about the Queen.
I felt she must be spared such terror and
Eternal shadows in her very soul.
I never thought to spare you, King—forgive,
Me, for my mind was fev'rish—the deed!

CANDAULES: You are a fool!

GYGES: A fool! I had to leave;
I felt, if I had stayed, an insight, new
And greater, would have come to her, the kind
Which Artemis received when she knew of
Actaeon's spying; so would she know mine.
I'd never flee this way if I had killed!

CANDAULES: And still, you had not killed.

GYGES: Who knows? The gods
Will turn away from taint. What if the golden
Aphrodite now did turn away,
Offended, from her dearest daughter who
Was desecrated by a stranger's eyes!
She does not want to, waits, because she hopes
Quick retribution is to be exacted.
Oh Goddess, go on smiling; I shall pay!

CANDAULES: So speaks the Greek.

GYGES: My Lord, please grant to me
A last request.
  CANDAULES: A thousand if you wish,
But not the last! That would be premature!
  GYGES: Accept me as your sacrifice; I give
My youthful life to you. Do not refuse!
There still were many years I could have lived,
Your life is to be lengthened by them if
You will receive them from Zeus' altar now!
So follow me, that I may hold your hand
With one and my sword with the other as
Is the sacred custom for such off'rings,
And, with a smile of triumph, I shall die!
  CANDAULES: I almost must regret what I have done!
Here, madness, and suspicion, there!
  GYGES: Why wait?
How often have young men been offered for
A warlord whom the shades of death just touched;
How often, for a madman in a rage?
Why not a sacrifice for one who's blessed?
Why not for you so that you can give joy
And feel it too for many years to come.
I'm not deprived of anything. What do I have;
What can I get, tell me. But you can gain
A great deal, for the gods are envious,
And so perhaps, the jealous fate will cut,
But all too quickly, the gold thread of life
For you while spinning mine deceitfully
So I'll outlive you. Come, anticipate
This fate, and give the permanence to joy
Instead of sorrow! Cross your fate! At once!
  CANDAULES: No more of this! You know how much you mean
        to me!
And if I were to turn into an old
Man now, with dried out lips and wilted veins,
I'd never borrow life's fresh warmth from you!
  GYGES: And yet, you would run no risk doing this,
For, if I could now blend my blood with yours,
No matter what its warmth, it would not change!
  CANDAULES: You still show your confusion at this hour,
And don't know what you say and what you do.
  GYGES: Forgive me, Lord.

CANDAULES: I'm not reproaching you.
You are intoxicated as though from
The scent of wine; the morning wind will blow
It all away.   (*In leaving*) At least, I hope it will. (*Off*)
GYGES: Why did I give the ring back now? I should
Have disappeared, never been visible
Again. Then I could be eternally
Around her; then I'd see her as only
The gods do now! For they save some things for
Themselves: a charm of beauty even she
Has never seen, a flash in solitude,
A last, and very secret, magic spell,
That is for them, and could be mine as well!
Of course, I never could escape their rage
If secretly I were to nip from such
A cup which only runs and foams for them.
The air would stir with sound, and Helios
Aroused by angry Aphrodite's signs
Of flame, would send, from his sure-arrowed quiver,
The very surest of his arrows, and,
Thus hit, I'd surely fall, but it would be
Of no significance to me, for as
I breathed my very last, I'd turn the ring
Once more while lying at her feet, raising
My eyes to hers for the last time, and, from
Them drinking in—her soul—to quench my thirst
While my soul slowly left my body; thus,
I'd be content to take my final breath.
(*Thoas enters accompanied by Lesbia, who is veiled*)
THOAS: To Gyges, to his fav'rite, the King
Desires to give the lovely slave he likes!
GYGES: The King makes fun of me, and I do not
Deserve such treatment nor submit to it!
THOAS: The gift is choice and generous of course,
But I have no doubt that the King is serious.
GYGES: Be silent, you who are most uninformed!
His royal seriousness mocks me most cruelly!
THOAS: Speak up, young maiden, come, tell him yourself
Since he will not believe what I have said.
GYGES: Say nothing!
THOAS: Then you'd scorn the royal gift?
GYGES: Yes!

THOAS: Gyges! But you must know what you do!

GYGES: The King first killed me and then placed a jewel,
Designed for life, into the corpse's hand.

THOAS: I cannot understand you, but I shall
Report what I have heard.—Return with me.

LESBIA: You won't see me again! Forgive me, please,
For speaking. I'm sure my speech sounds harsh,
Offends your ear.

GYGES: Not so, my lovely child!
If you would stand behind the plane tree there
And speak this way, a passionate young man
Would say: a nightingale which more than sings!

LESBIA: But you are no young man!

GYGES: I'm even less!
You can see that. 'Tis true, I've come to think,
I'm not the clumsiest at wielding arms,
And have accomplished something here and there,
No longer can be punished like a child,
And even might be called on to defend
The house if there's no better man at home.
But these are boyish dreams! Come, beat the boy;
He must have drunk some wine tonight.

LESBIA: Bring me
A laurel branch so I can beat you first
And then wind you a wreath.

GYGES: So you have dreamt
It too? Perhaps it even could be true?
And still this scorn?

LESBIA: This scorn? Where is this scorn?

GYGES: Do you not stand here now?

LESBIA: That hurts!

GYGES: I do
Not mean it thus!

LESBIA: You've killed some men before;
Could you restore any of them to life?

GYGES: You're very beautiful! Of course! A blend
Of roses and of lilies which in colorful
Profusion are swayed together by the game
The teasing wind plays, so one can't tell them
Apart. You blush, also turn pale. And at
The same time too!

LESBIA: What do you know of me?

You've dreamt it! No, I look quite diff'rent!
I'll startle you! (*She starts to remove her veil*)
    GYGES: No, No! (*Stops her*)
    LESBIA: Back to the Queen!
She was not glad to give me up. She'll take
Me back most willingly!
    GYGES: Then please tell her
That Gyges did not even look at you!
    LESBIA: Oh shame!
    GYGES: Not that! You know how often I
Kept looking yesterday, and that was my
First chance.
    LESBIA: And probably each time, I was
Just being silly! I'm ashamed to say
I only realize it now! But I
Must blame my friends, for they kept teasing me.
    GYGES: What I saw seemed most charming to me!
    LESBIA: Of course!
What we find charming, we don't wish to see!
Old man, let's go!
    GYGES: Why do you hasten so?
I am your master now. But do not tremble;
There is but one demand I'd make of you,
And then I'll let you go.
    LESBIA (*to Thoas*): Then go alone.
    GYGES: No, stay! But no! Just tell the King my thanks!
I'll take his gift and show him that I do
Appreciate it.
    THOAS: Very well! (*Off*)
    LESBIA: And now demand!
    GYGES: You are to stay here long enough so that
You'll smile again.
    LESBIA: That will not be so soon!
    GYGES: And, in the meantime, talk a bit with me.
You are close to the Queen; surely 'tis true,
She won't enjoy a peach unless you bring it.
Tell me about her now.
    LESBIA: Her?
    GYGES: Well, then speak
Of other matters if you like. The park
In which she walks, perhaps the flowers
She likes the best. Or tell about yourself.

I'd like that too. Do you resemble her?
Speak fast, and, all the faster, you'll be dear
To me! In height? Not quite! Still less in form!
But still, your hair is just as black as hers,
Though not as full. It crawls about her face
As night does crawl about the ev'ning star.
How else do you resemble her?
(*Lesbia moves instinctively*)

                                                       No, stop!

Stand still. Her walk is quite unique. When you
Are walking, I can see where you are going;
You want some fruit or want a drink of water.
But when she moves, we must look to the sky
To see if Helios is not about
To lower his gold chariot so that
He can receive her and can drive her off
Into eternal bliss and happiness.
    LESBIA: Yes, she is beautiful!
    GYGES: You close your eyes,
My girl? Do open them; it seems to me
They sparkle just like hers!
    LESBIA: (*forcing a laugh*):   Perhaps they do
Right now!
    GYGES: Did my words hurt your feelings, child?
    LESBIA: Now that I've laughed, am I allowed to leave?
    GYGES: But not without a gift! My lovely child,
I want you to remember me with love!
I am quite rough, and often wound so fast
And unsuspectingly with piercing words;
But never have I left such wounds unhealed.
    CANDAULES (*enters*): Well now?
    GYGES: My Lord, you've come at the right time!
    CANDAULES: Then I should find two happy people here.
    GYGES: Not yet. But soon! (*To Lesbia*)
               Give me your hand, my dear.
How soft it is! How hard is mine and full
Of ridges from my sword and spear! They do
Not suit each other! Yours would find a rolled
Rose petal painful, but mine would repel,
And even dull, the very sharpest thorn.
Yours trembles now as though it had been welded
Into mine. No fear, my child, I shall not keep

You, that's not my intention. As the King
Knows well, I do not merely understand
His word; his hint is just as clear to me.
It saddened him that you have been so well
Endowed by nature; not at all, by luck,
And he wants me to be good luck for you.
I shall be that. (*Releases her*)
               I now declare you free!
    LESBIA: They say that freedom is a precious gift;
I do not know, for I was stolen as
A child. But one must thank the donor for
A gift, and so I thank you for my freedom.
    GYGES (*to Candaules*) : Are you now satisfied?
    CANDAULES: I am surprised!
    GYGES: And since you don't know where your father lives,
And where your mother weeps for her lost child,
Go now to live in my house 'til you find
Them. It is yours. I'll only take my sword. (*Lesbia off*)
    CANDAULES: What are you doing, Gyges?
    GYGES: Lord, my thanks
For doing this good deed through me. It will
Remain your deed.
    CANDAULES: It seems you wish to see
The grandson of great Hercules today.
Be careful now! He is not fast asleep.
    GYGES: Could I offend you now?
    CANDAULES: Forgive me—no.
But go at once, take from my treasury
Doubly the worth of what you gave away.
You've made me angry; I still feel the hurt!
    GYGES: Forgive me, if I can't obey you now.
But everything's become a burden to me,
And, since the lovely slave was added now
By you, to all the gold and precious stones,
I used her beautiful white neck to hang
On it all of the treasures which I had!
I have not need for them, just need my sword.
But, if you want to show me further favor,
Grant me the heads of all your enemies!
I shall collect them, find them all.
    CANDAULES: You've changed, my friend. You're like a diff'rent
      man!

GYGES: I have, my Lord.

CANDAULES: You love!

GYGES: Love? I could
Have beaten up that little girl with ease!

CANDAULES: Rhodope is the one!

GYGES: Lord, I just can
Not serve you anymore.

CANDAULES: Then go if you
Insist! It hurts me, but I can not keep
You here. But since you won't accept my gifts,
I can not keep what you have given me.
Here is your ring!

GYGES: Give me your sword for that!

CANDAULES: I thank you for your generosity! (*About to exit*)

GYGES: One more thing! (*He takes out a jewel*)
            Take it!

CANDAULES: What?

GYGES: You know it well!

CANDAULES: Rhodope's di'mond!

GYGES: Which I took along
Because, around her neck—forgive that now;
I have repented!

CANDAULES: Furies, have you come?
Oh, it is true, you have the lightest sleep!

GYGES: You're angry with me!

CANDAULES: No, not with you. But
Go now. For we must never meet again. (*Off*)

GYGES: No never. Now to leave. But where to go?
Where was I going when I met the King
Of Lydia? Have I forgotten? No!
I'd felt the urge to go to the old Nile
Where yellow men with slanted eyes are said
To build eternal houses for dead kings.
Well, on that road, I shall continue and
There take the place of one who's tired of it. (*Off*)

ACT III

Rhodope's chamber. Hero and other servants at work.

RHODOPE (*enters*): Why have the mirrors not been draped
   with veils?

HERO: The mirrors, Queen?

RHODOPE: And what about these doors?
Who opened them so wide?

HERO: Madam, we thought
You'd like to see the sunlit happy day
And to inhale its fresh and clean perfume

RHODOPE: Who told you that? Enough! Close them at once,
And turn all mirrors to the wall.

(Hero closes doors and turns mirrors)

RHODOPE: It's so!
I've tried in vain to tell myself that I've
Deceived myself. Return, I beg, oh night,
And hide me in the thickest of your veils!
I have been tainted like no other woman!

HERO: But you can not refuse this rose which I
Did pick for you before the sun had risen.

RHODOPE: Away with it! It would wilt in my sight!

HERO *(leaving with her companions)*: I'm only Hero and not
   Lesbia!

RHODOPE: Eternal gods, could this have come to pass?
I've brought you many pious offerings
With purity of heart from childhood on.
The first lock of my hair did fall to you
Before I ever knew that you held in
Your hands all blessings fit for human life.
As a young woman too, I never failed
To serve you; rarely did a wish rise up
To your high place with my burnt offering.
With modesty and fear, I sought to press
Under my consciousness each wish which might
Have just begun to stir within my heart.
Sincere was my desire just to pray
For your regard and never for your gifts;
I wanted to be grateful, not to beg.
Nor did I, as a woman, wait to be
Reminded by a dream of sacred duty,
As did the daughter of the Tyndarids.
For I did decorate the altar of
My own desire. And still—why dedicate
The best part of one's goods to you
If you would not with mercy shield a man
Where he alone can not protect himself.

242 Three Plays by Hebbel

The lion who leaps out at hot noon time,
When rage or hunger drives him, can always be
Controlled by man with sword and courage, and
No brave man cries to Zeus for lightning then.
But that the coward snake not creep to him,
When he, exhausted after battle, sleeps,
That is your work, for night is yours alone!
And I—and I—have I been so accursed,
Accursed since birth, so that your strength is chained
Down at the Styx, so that you gave success
As to a pious deed—to sacrilege—
Against me—which no one would dare commit
Against the very lowest of my slaves?

HERO (enters) : The King.
RHODOPE: Already? Then my death comes too!
Yes, it will veil me in the night of nights,
Of which our mortal night is but a shadow;
Why tremble now? I've longed for just that night.

CANDAULES (enters) : Will you forgive me?
RHODOPE: Lord, I know, you have
No choice. The hour matters not. Why ask?

CANDAULES: I can not understand you.
RHODOPE: King, be frank!
You'll find me ready.

CANDAULES: Ready? But for what?
RHODOPE: I know what you must do and thank you for
The speed with which you do it. If you were
To hesitate, it would become my duty.
You have investigated, seen, and judged;
I see it in your face; and now, I'm next.

CANDAULES: You must misunderstand—
RHODOPE: Have you not come
For final vengeance?

CANDAULES: No, by all the gods!
RHODOPE: Then none who was alive last night has died?
CANDAULES: For what?
RHODOPE: No one committed sacrilege?
CANDAULES: I know of none!
RHODOPE: Why have you come to me?
CANDAULES: Do I not have the right to come after
Last night? Were you your usual self? Did you
Not act as though you were still sitting by

The tree, a lily in your hand, and then
Deny to me the only kiss I asked?
   RHODOPE: You will be grateful for it.
   CANDAULES: But, no fear!
'Tis true, I wanted you as much as on
The morning after our first night; but you
Just need to wave your hand, and I shall leave;
Indeed, I'll hurry off with greater haste
By far than if I'd seen a modest naiad
Arising from her bath from just the spring
Which I had quietly approached to drink.
   RHODOPE: Stay!
   CANDAULES: No! Not for the length of just one breath
If it upsets you. And it does do that,
I feel it now. I'm sure, this is the hour
For that which you so sweetly term, inner
Reflection; and I do not wish to spoil
This hour. If Aphrodite with a smile
Of grace, to bless this morning walk, had given
To me for you the golden belt which she
Would never give away and seldom lends:
I still would bring it here some other time.
   RHODOPE: Stop now! That sounds too sweet and worries me,
For, as my nurse already told me, if
A man comes to his wife too tenderly,
He surely has offended her in secret.
   CANDAULES: That is my case. I have offended you,
For I do know what you are like and know
You can't be diff'rent. Since your father rules
Where India and Greece their customs blend,
Your veil is part of your own self for you.
And still, I keep on pulling it away,
And yesterday, I tried to take it off.
Well, I regret this now and swear to you—
That drove me here—Never again by force!
(*Rhodope laughs*)
   CANDAULES: For never did I long, as I do now,
To keep from you not only suffering
Which digs into the marrow and leaves scars,
No, also to destroy the smallest shadow
Which, cast upon your soul, could bring you grief,
Indeed myself, if I were such a shadow!

I shall protect you as the faithful lid
Protects your eye. It does not only close
To ward off grains of sand but also when
A sunbeam is too hot or strikes too fast.
    RHODOPE: It is too late!
    CANDAULES: Too late for what, dear wife?
    RHODOPE: I—no, I shall not, can not tell him this.
Let him surmise, and, if he does surmise,
I'll kneel before him wordlessly and still
And point first to his sword and then, my breast.
    CANDAULES: Did bad dreams frighten you?
    RHODOPE: Bad dreams? Oh no,
There were none left for me. Not worthy was
My person of such warnings. Yes, the star
Which crashes down does have a shadow by
Which man is warned; the quick sword gleams; but I
Was hit—Candaules, speak; you want to ask—
Please ask me quickly.
    CANDAULES: I? Well, yes. I'd like
To hold your hand.
    RHODOPE: No, do not touch it, please!
No water ever can remove its stain!
    CANDAULES: Oh, Gyges!—Well, if you refuse your hand,
Your cheek tells me enough to understand:
A fever burns within you. But the best
Physicians wait before your door. Why is
It closed, the while a morning, abounding in
The splendor of the Horae, is knocking like
A beggar. Open it now, and you'll be healed! (*Tries to open door*)
    RHODOPE: No, stop! 'Twere better now to open up
A tomb! The sungod would not turn from urns
With greater outrage to his purity
Than from the woman who has been your wife.
    CANDAULES: You wretch!
    RHODOPE: Tell me, was there not in our room—
Answer me!
    CANDAULES: A murderer? No, there was not!
Just ask yourself, would he escape my sword?
    RHODOPE: If you had seen him—
    CANDAULES: Would I not have seen?

The light had just been lit that minute and
It shone quite brightly.

RHODOPE: So it seemed. And still,
I heard some sounds which did not come from you
And not from me.

CANDAULES: My dear, the night is full
Of sounds and strangely alien noises. One
Who does not sleep hears much.

RHODOPE: There was a clatter.

CANDAULES: A termite!

RHODOPE: But it sounded like a sword
Just striking lightly.

CANDAULES: That may be. What sound
Exists which Nature, in a playful mood,
Did not embody in some animal
As its own voice? Just tear your dress apart,
And don't forget the sound it makes, and then
I'll get an insect which sounds just like it.

RHODOPE: I also heard a sigh.

CANDAULES: Do murd'rers sigh?

RHODOPE: That's what disturbs me!

CANDAULES: 'Twas the cool night wind;
It sighed, when, in the hope of touching you,
Your mouth and cheeks, it only found the wall.
There are some trees which can absorb all sounds,
As there's a stone that drinks the light of day
To give it back in darkness, and such trees
Do sing and chatter, even groan, at night.

RHODOPE: You see it thus? There's more! I lack a jewel!

CANDAULES: I know; it is a di'mond, is it not?
This one?

RHODOPE: You have it? You?

CANDAULES: Who else? You see!

RHODOPE: My thanks to you, eternal gods; forgive
The doubts of a poor heart which deemed itself
So innocent and yet undone! You are
With us like air and light!

CANDAULES: Furies, be gone!
There!

RHODOPE: Put it in the temple treasury!
I owe the gracious gods a splendid gift,

And, most of all, I owe the marriage goddess;
Her doves are to be fed the softest grain
Today from golden baskets, and they are
To quench their thirst from marble basins now!
And you, Candaules, you—

CANDAULES: The youth may kiss
The hand his love touched just before she left,
Thus summon her to mind and memory.
The man requires more.

RHODOPE: Oh, day of joy!
Am I so dear to you. Forgive, I beg,
My wronging you in thought. I always feared
Possessive pride, instead of love, was the
Emotion which did bind you to my side,
And that the envy felt by others was
Required for you to keep alive your love.
Now I no longer fear this.

CANDAULES: Never shall
You fear again! I know what poison did
Consume your heart. You thought I slighted you
To be with Gyges. And it's true. I did
Become a hunter just because he hunts.
And yet, this did not interfere with your
Own wifely rights, for what joins man to man
Is not the same relationship as man's
With woman. Does a kiss require courage?
But, even though your fears are very foolish,
I'll spare no medicine for your quick cure,
So I shall tell you now what should relieve
Your mind: Gyges, my favorite, departs.

RHODOPE: What's this?

CANDAULES: Today!

RHODOPE: Impossible!

CANDAULES: Do you
Not want this any more? You seemed to wish it!

RHODOPE: How could I have forgotten just because
I was so glad!

CANDAULES: Forgotten? What?

RHODOPE: Your hand!—
'Twas he! That's whom I saw before my eyes
As though his fiery outline had remained
Within the air! How terribly my fear's

Confirmed! He has the ring—Give it to me!

CANDAULES: The ring is my possession!

RHODOPE: Did you not
Remove it even once since you received it?
Did you not lose it, miss it even once?

CANDAULES: Oh wretched one, why torture yourself thus?

RHODOPE: He shuns my question! You sent him away?
So suddenly, just like a criminal?
Why so?

CANDAULES: I did not say! He wants to leave.

RHODOPE: He wants to leave? What forces him to go?

CANDAULES: I do not know it, and I have not asked.

RHODOPE: You do not know it? I can tell you why!
He's sinned against you as no man before—
And you must punish as you never have!

CANDAULES: Rhodope, come, don't say that! Surely he
Is noblest of the noble!

RHODOPE: If he were,
How could you let him leave with such great calm?

CANDAULES: Because, I know, the very best can spread,
Against his will, not blessing, but a curse!

RHODOPE: Is that his case, and has he felt it too?

CANDAULES: And if he did not, still, his mind is proud;
He strives for greatness and may dare all things.

RHODOPE: You think this?

CANDAULES: There's no throne too high for him,
And, if he leaves and does not tell me why,
Just wait, he will return here with a crown,
And then he'll smile and say: 'this made me leave!'

RHODOPE: Oh?

CANDAULES: Dearest wife, the night disturbed you and
The shock—

RHODOPE: Perhaps!

CANDAULES: You heard all sorts of things—

RHODOPE: Which were not there! I almost do believe
You, for—I do recall—I did see wrong!
You never did remove the ring last night;
You neither lost it, never missed it once.
And still, I thought—I looked most carefully,
And it was morning; I saw ev'rything—
It was not on your hand! And so one sense
Here testifies against the other, and

The blind eye does support a deafened ear.
Forgive me, I did torture you, allow
Me now some solitude to find myself.
(*Candaules wants to speak*)
  RHODOPE: Indeed! Indeed! Forgive me, Lord, and go!
(*Candaules off*)
  RHODOPE: So it was Gyges! That is clear to me!
He had the ring—that's clearer still!
Candaules knows, he must—that is most clear!
And now, instead of seeking monstrous vengeance
For monstrous crime, he lets him flee. And thus
One riddle solves another riddle; this
Is one to rid me of my senses, if
I fail to solve it. For my husband sees
His wife dishonored—? Only that? No, killed!
But killed? No, rather damned to kill herself
Unless her violator's blood be shed
In expiation. Now, the husband is
A king, bears Justice's sword and needs not borrow
The dagger of the furies, has, indeed,
To punish such crime; it's his sacred duty.
If not his love is spur enough, he has
To offer the gods sacrifice, though he
Deny it to me. And this husband, king, now fails
To draw his sword and dagger; lets the sinner
Escape! But he shall fail! I do not lack
Of servants tried and true. I did not come
To this house as a slave but as a queen!
My escorts were befitting royalty.
I now shall summon my old faithful friends
To stop the flight of him who so transgressed.
And then I'll tell Candaules: I am here;
And there, your favorite; this dagger is
For me unless you use your sword on him!
  LESBIA (*enters*): Forgive me please, my Queen!
  RHODOPE: For what, my child?
For your return to me? Oh no, forgive
Me rather that I let you leave my side.
I felt—I did not know myself what I
Was doing, but I thought the King had told
Me that you wished to go, and then I lacked
The courage to say no because, alas,

I had refused him so much in the night.

LESBIA: Then I am free no longer? May again
Be counted as one of your servant girls?

RHODOPE: Oh no, come to my heart as my dear sister.

LESBIA: What has occurred? You are more moved than ever!

RHODOPE: A dreadful thing for which there is no name
Because, before I find a name, it is
Transformed and still more dreadful than before!
Indeed, I now could kiss the first view of
This nightmare grinning at me since the far
Worse second form now dawns in revelation!

LESBIA: Can I do anything for you? I ask
A foolish question, I suppose.

RHODOPE: You can
Not kill, my girl, and only one who could
Could help me now.

LESBIA: My Queen!

RHODOPE: That is the truth!
You stare at me and can not understand
That such a word can issue from my mouth.
Yes, Lesbia, Rhodope speaks thus who
So often warned you girls, prevented you
From interference in the offices of death
Although the object might have been a spider!
I've not forgotten that, but that was when
I washed myself in the fresh morning dew
And dried myself in the warm sun; but now
I cry for blood; now there's so little left
Of me, only enough so that the gods will seek
Their vengeance for my former, better self!

LESBIA: And does the King know nothing? After all,
The King of Lydia must have avengers!

RHODOPE: It seems that way! And still—well, I shall know
It soon. Go, Lesbia, and summon Carna.

LESBIA: You mean, you want a message given to him?

RHODOPE: No, that is past!

LESBIA: But you will want your veil!

RHODOPE: No, no!

LESBIA: I'm frightened now! That's the first time! (*Off*)

RHODOPE: He can not sacrifice his friend, and so he'll spare
His wife. He could not bear this otherwise!
(*Lesbia enters with Carna*)

RHODOPE: Carna, you know what oath you took that day
On which your lord, my royal father, gave
His daughter to your keeping at the golden gate.
Although I wore my thickest veils and sat
Up high upon my elephant, I did
Observe quite closely what took place, nor have
I, to this day, forgotten a word you spoke.

    CARNA: Nor I, my Queen, as I now hope to prove!

    RHODOPE: Then find Gyges, the Greek, and say to him
That I desire to see him.

    CARNA: You?

    RHODOPE: Make haste,
So that he does not flee; pursue him if
He has already fled, and bring him back.
He must confront me ere the night has fallen!

    CARNA: I'll bring him here, dead or alive, my Queen!

    LESBIA: What do I hear? It's Gyges?

    RHODOPE: Gyges, yes!

    LESBIA: You say he has offended—

    RHODOPE: Violated
What is most sacred! He has brought upon
Myself the very worst of curses, that
Which all the gods hurl with aversion since
It only strikes those mortals who are free
Of guilt. And he has taught me how to kill!

    LESBIA: Not he! I swear it!

    RHODOPE: Swear? How can you?

    LESBIA: Queen,
I too experienced something, and I know
That he would sooner lose his very soul
Than hurt you.

    RHODOPE: Really?

    LESBIA: Yes. I must tell you
Something about him too. How bitterly
His words did hurt me when I heard them, but
I'm almost glad about them now! I am
To tell you that he did not look at me!
He loves you! Can that be?

    RHODOPE: So he loves me!
Then it is certain!

    LESBIA: What?

    RHODOPE: You fool, tell me

How can one love what one has never seen?
And when could he have seen me face to face?
(*Puts her hand in front of her eyes*)
Now tell me, girl: has he the right to live?

ACT IV

Rhodope's chamber.

RHODOPE: Oh, for a moment of oblivion!
Why keep repeating this bad riddle, since
It will be solved so soon? I should now do
What all my girls would do to pass the time.
They listen to the birds and argue then
About what bird has which call and whether it
Be red or green.—What sound was that just now?
Is Carna back with him? All quiet, still.
There can have been no sound!—How I have changed!
When did I ever ask from where sounds came?
I never knew what fear was. Even fire,
No matter how deep red its rising flames,
No matter how it menaced as it spread,
Gave me no fear; I knew there was a group
Of faithful watchmen who invisibly
Surrounded and protected me, the King's
Dear daughter, with their blood and life!—But now—
A footfall! They are here! Yes, Carna is
As clever as he's brave. I'd heard that, but,
Today, I'll see it. No, not yet! Perhaps,
He'll never come! Dear gods, you can not be
So cruel! I do not ask you to extend
Your hands to hold me back from the abyss;
I only wish to see who tries to force
My fall. The more I think about it all,
The less I understand my husband. For
I did hear as a child, a violated
Woman does not have the right to live,
And, if I shuddered at this thought when young,
I now have felt the reason for the law;
She can not live and does not want to live!
Is he alone exempt from this? Or is
His wish to kill the criminal behind

My back because he hopes to hide the crime
From me? My thanks, eternal gods, that too
Could be. If Carna finds him dead with a
Cold dagger in his burning heart, then I
Shall know whose hand has taken this revenge,
And I shall never ask where Gyges is.

LESBIA *(enters)*: He comes, my Queen.

RHODOPE: I am expecting him.

LESBIA: A throng of men, all bearing arms, has closed
Behind him, as an iron bolt snaps shut.

RHODOPE: I am quite sure that Carna's competent.

LESBIA: Must it be thus?

RHODOPE: It must be he or I!
Perhaps, it's both of us!

LESBIA: You strike me dumb!

RHODOPE: Tell Carna that he should send for the King;
I'd like to have a single word with him.

(Lesbia off)

RHODOPE: Now, you below who won't prevent an act
Of sacrilege but punish just the same,
Rise up, rise up, and guard my threshold, for
A bloody sacrifice is certain here!

GYGES *(who has entered in the meantime)*: You've had me
        summoned to your presence, Queen.

RHODOPE: And you know why! You know it, for you tremble;
Can you deny it? Your color changes, and
Your heart beats audibly within your breast.

GYGES: Did not your husband tremble just like me,
Did he not change his color, and did not
His heart beat audibly as mine does now?
Recall the hour when he was first allowed
To look into your face, and ask yourself:
Did he not then resemble me completely?

RHODOPE: Resemble you?

GYGES: Of course, my Queen! I'm sure
He stood before you blind and dizzy, and,
When consciousness returned, without a word,
He tore his crown off like a wreath which in
The hair has wilted suddenly and threw
It down, behind his back, despising it.

RHODOPE: He? Ha! Not he!

GYGES: And then you smiled when you

Saw what he did, and this gave him enough
Encouragement to come a half step closer.
But then his knees failed to support him; they
Desired to do a nobler service, and,
Before you knew it, he knelt thus to you! (*Kneels as he speaks*)
    RHODOPE: You'd dare?
    GYGES: Why not? It was this way. You stretched
Your hand to him, instinctively, perhaps
To hinder this, perhaps to draw him up.
He took this hand, shyly and tenderly,
Which had become nothing but fingertips
Before he'd ever touched it with his hand.
You did do that? Oh, speak!
    RHODOPE: Rise, rise, I say!
    GYGES (*rising*) : But it struck him like lightning; he felt,
As though, up to this time, he had been lost
Among the human race, as though he'd been
A cold and sober shade, returned from Hades,
Had only now received the living blood
Of men, had imitated, never felt
Their laughter, tears, rejoicing, sighs,
Their very breathing; never had suspected
Why the human breast does rise and fall.
But now he burned with the desire to share
This life and drank the image of you with
His eyes which usually reflected what
They saw indiff'rently, like quiet pools,
Then turned away. But now they hardly could
Forgive their trembling lids. He slowly glowed
While drinking in your beauty 'til he himself
Turned into somber fire as your white hand
May glow if you hold it before a flame,
But you recoiled before your red reflection.
    RHODOPE: No further!
    GYGES: Oh, no further! Is there more?
I too can feel what he has felt, can feel
It just as fully, glowingly as he,
But how he wooed and won you, that is his
Own secret which but one can have alone,
And this one man is he and not myself!
But now you know why I was trembling so;
A blissful shudder took a hold of me;

A sacred terror shook me to the core
When suddenly I stood before you and
Saw: Aphrodite has a sister; But
Tell me, please, why you have had me called.
   RHODOPE: To die!
   GYGES: How's that?
   RHODOPE: Don't you deserve to die?
   GYGES: If you condemn me, then I'm sure I must!
   RHODOPE: This very hour!
   GYGES: I am prepared to die!
   RHODOPE: You feel no shudders which would grip a man,
Yes, any man, and doubly so, a youth?
Perhaps, because a woman speaks this sentence,
You tend to doubt its bitter seriousness
Since womankind, to you, means only wives
And mothers. But, I warn you, there's no hope
That even the mildest woman would reverse
This. She, who would forgive a murder, might
Plead for her murderer if he had left
Her breath to do so. But, a shame which
Makes her loathe herself, from tip to toe, such shame
Indeed has to be cleansed with blood alone:
The more completely she is woman, just
A modest woman, in all things, the more,
The deeper hurt a man can cause in this!
   GYGES: It's dreadful!
   RHODOPE: Now, at last, you shudder. Hear
The rest. If you were not now standing judged
Before me, guarded by ready swords beyond
My door, you weren't, willingly or not,
The promised, certain sacrifice to Hades,
I'd open my own veins before the sun
Has set; although my hands would tremble, I
Would cleanse myself with my own blood! For all
The gods already have averted from me
Their faces though in pity; golden threads
Which bind me to the stars and hold me upright
Are tearing now, and dust pulls down with might.
And, if I hesitate, the toad will hop
Into my room and call me its own sister!
   GYGES: My Queen, there's much that I could answer you,
And I could shake much sand out of my hair

Which was blown into it by raging storm!
But I don't wish to. Just believe one thing:
Although it's only now I clearly see
What I have done, I felt strong urge to pay
For it as soon as it was done. And, if the King
Had not then barred my path to Hades, I
Should be a shade among the shades; you'd be
Avenged, although not reconciled as yet.
    RHODOPE: My husband did not let you die and knew—
    GYGES: No matter! Yes, the strange emotion which
He felt deprived me of the merit of
A voluntary death, but you will have
Your sacrifice! Farewell! Your swords stay clean!
    RHODOPE: No, stop! Your fall must not be at your hand,
Nor murderer's, but through your highest judge.
The King comes now; let him decide your fate!
    GYGES: The dying man, no matter who he is,
Is granted a request. You will, I know,
Not take this wretched right away from me.
You can not do that! Therefore let me go.
(*Rhodope makes a gesture of refusal*)
I have done all I could. Let come what may,
It is not my responsibility.
(*Candaules enters*)
    RHODOPE (*goes toward him*) : I did not err. A man had hidden in
My room.
    GYGES: Yes, King. What I but hinted at,
Because I lacked the courage it required
To make confession to you, is now revealed.
I stand before you now deserving death!
    CANDAULES: Gyges!
    GYGES: With these—these eyes of mine, I did
Commit a sacrilege which hands can not
Outdo, indeed, can not begin to equal,
Not even if I were to kill you both!
    RHODOPE: It's so!
    GYGES: Of course, I swear, I didn't know;
Women are strangers to me. But, like a boy
Who tries to catch a rare, exotic bird
And throttles it because he does not know
How delicate it is and only wants
To touch it, so I have destroyed the jewel

Of this world not knowing what I did!

RHODOPE: His words are noble! Woe to him and me
That this can't help!

GYGES: If the Castalian spring
From which the fav'rites of the gods do drink,
Which gleams with play of colorful reflection
As though it had been strewn by Iris' hands
With rainbows plucked apart, now if this spring
Which has its origins on Mount Parnassus
Is dulled by a thrown stone, it starts to rush
And, wildly rushing, rises heavenward.
And then, no nightingale, no lark can sing
On earth, and, there up high, the sacred choir
Of muses becomes silent too, and then
True harmony can not return until
A raging stream will grind the brazen one
Into its darkest depths. And this compares
To what occurs inside a woman's soul.

CANDAULES: Gyges, I am no scoundrel.

GYGES: Lord, you are
Rhodope's husband, her protecting shield,
And must avenge her.

CANDAULES: I'm, above all else,
A man who will not let another die
To expiate a sin I have committed.

GYGES: Oh, King, what would you save?

CANDAULES: Myself!

GYGES: He's mad!
Ignore him! Do not listen!

RHODOPE: Lord and husband,
What did you say? I can't believe your words
If you do not repeat them.

CANDAULES: Speak for me.
Do not excuse me; no, just tell her how
This came to pass.

RHODOPE: Is that it? Oh, good gods,
How you must laugh at me! I have accused!

CANDAULES: Speak, Gyges. (*Off*)

GYGES: Queen, oh, if you only knew
How much he's always praised you, and how I
Did dully listen to his flaming words
Because each bird which flew out of the bush,

And thus escaped my arrow while he spoke,
Distracted me—if you could only tell yourself
How much this inattentive childishness
Of mine, which he thought must express half doubt
Or quiet disbelief, seemed challenge, though
It merely came from my distracted mind;
If you had only seen us once when we
Were walking in the woods, had looked at him,
Completely flaming, and myself, because
I was so innocent, expressing lack
Of understanding, hunting colored stones
While he was pointing to the rising sun,
I'm sure you would no longer feel enraged!
He, priestlike, tried to light the very flame
Which does consume him, honoring his god,
Within the stranger's heart; and if a priest,
Uncautious in his burning passion, does
Unveil the sacred mysteries, because
He hopes to rouse dull senses with more speed
And to dethrone false idols much more surely,
Is this so grave a crime one can't forgive?
    RHODOPE (*gestures unwillingness to go on listening*):
And did he abdicate the husband's rights to you?
    GYGES: Don't call it that!
    RHODOPE: It was not as I thought
That you had simply lifted up his hand when
He and you were drinking wine and just removed
The ring. He gave it to you of his own
Volition and, perhaps, he brought you here!
    GYGES: Can you believe this, Queen?
    RHODOPE: You are a youth—
You think so nobly—
    GYGES: But was I his servant?
Has ever he demanded that I be?
No, Queen, do not seek to excuse me thus;
Your sentence stands! And do not think that it
Is cruel, for it is mild. I took the path
I never should have taken, but, with it,
I took along my curse as well. And so
I have matured and ripened unto death;
I've seen that ev'rything life has to offer
Is wasted, and, if I did fail to find

My death that night and thus to wash, with my
Own blood, your desecrated threshold, it
Was not my doing, for I sought my death.
If I had just insisted on my death,
Then, in your soul, there would still tremble now
A shudder when you saw the murderer
Who'd made your breathing all the sweeter, and
Your husband would be kissed with fiery love
Because he'd saved his very grateful wife.
    RHODOPE: And subsequent events would then reveal
Most terribly and clearly that the gods
Are not in need of human arms for vengeance
If guilt, which finds no expiation since
It hides in darkness, stains the world.
But they are merciful; this sacrilege
Has veiled itself in darkness quite in vain.
It still shines through the dark! For water will
Not be transformed to flame when thirsty mouths
Do touch it. And the fire will not be put
Out by the breath of hungry men who blow
Upon it burning in the hearth. No, indeed,
The elements need not announce to man
That Nature is enraged within its core
Because it has been violated in
A woman, for we know what happened!
    GYGES: And
We know what has to happen. Just forgive! (*Wants to leave*)
    RHODOPE: No, stop! Not that!
    GYGES: What else can I do now?
    RHODOPE: You'll have to kill him!
    GYGES: What?
    RHODOPE: You must! And I—
I'll have to marry you.
    GYGES: My dearest Queen!
    RHODOPE: Go then!
    GYGES: And kill him!
    RHODOPE: When you say to me:
You are a widow now! then I'll reply:
You are my husband now!
    GYGES: But you have seen
The way he left here. Not a word in his
Behalf! He simply left it all to me,

And I—I am—
RHODOPE: You have to do it, as
I must demand it! Neither of us may
Stop to ask whether it's hard or not.
   GYGES: If he has been no husband, he is still
A friend like no one else! How can I kill
The man who was too good a friend to me?
   RHODOPE: You argue, but it is in vain.
   GYGES: But what
Can make me kill him if your charm does not?
I do love you! I feel as though I had
Been born a paralytic, and your glance
Were healing me so I could move at last!
My senses which, like sleeping watchmen, failed
To see 'til now, or hear, are rousing one
Another now in blissful wonder and
Are holding on to you, while, all around
Those forms, which were defiant and so sharp
So that they almost scratched the eye, now melt
As cloud formations do before the sun.
And, like a dizzy man who fears to fall
In the abyss, I could reach for your hand
And put my arms about your neck so that
The nothingness will not devour me now!
And yet, I could not buy this highest place
If his blood be the price that's set for it,
For, even drunk with bliss, I would remember!
   RHODOPE: Of course, it's true! You can refuse me still!
But leave me then.
   GYGES: What are you thinking, Queen?
   RHODOPE: About a deed, resolved in silence, done
More silently—go.
   GYGES: That's your plan?
   RHODOPE: Perhaps.
   GYGES: You could?
   RHODOPE: You need not doubt! I can and will!
   GYGES: But by the gods whose throne is there on high
And by the Furies, listening below,
That may not be; it never shall occur!
   RHODOPE: Then you agree?
   GYGES: You'll wake me from my sleep,
Won't you, when he appears to me in nightmares,

A smile for me, his killer, on his face,
Until I scream with horror?
    RHODOPE: Stop! No more!
    GYGES: And you will also kiss my lips of course
So that I can recall, although afraid,
Why I have killed him. But you turn away
As though the very thought aroused your fear!
Swear that you will!
    RHODOPE: I shall become your wife.
    GYGES: Why do I ask? I have not conquered yet.
    RHODOPE: Will you do battle then?
    GYGES: Indeed, my Queen!
You do not think that I could murder him?
I'll challenge him to fight for life or death.
    RHODOPE: And if you lose?
    GYGES: Then do not curse my name.
I can't just kill him.
    RHODOPE: Don't I lose with you?
    GYGES: But if I should return?
    RHODOPE: You'll find me at
The altar; I'll wait, equally prepared
To place my hand in yours or else to take
The dagger in my hand and, with it, cut
The bonds which fetter me to him—if he
Should win.
    GYGES: Before the sun has set, all will
Be known. And now, farewell, my Queen.
    RHODOPE: Farewell.
And if it pleases you, hear one more word:
I know you would not have led me from home
To treat me thus!
    GYGES: Is that your thought, Rhodope?
That means, I would have been more jealous and
More envious, and would have been afraid
Because I am a lesser man than he!
And still, I'm glad you think this; yes,
That is enough for me, more than enough! (*Off*)
    RHODOPE: And now, my bridal gown and shroud of death!
    LESBIA (*rushes in and throws herself at Rhodope's feet*)
Oh, gracious Queen—Forgive me!—And, my thanks!
    RHODOPE (*raising her up*): You will not thank me very long,
        poor child!
Yet, in the end, yes, Lesbia, you will!

ACT V

Open Space. The King appears. Thoas follows.

CANDAULES: You follow ev'ry step I take. What do
You wish, old man. Is courage lacking you
To speak to me because my tone to you
Was somewhat harsh? Go on, speak up! I shall
Be patient, listen, even though you were to need
So much time that, in it, green grapes turn ripe,
Turn purple even while you speak and speak.
   THOAS: My Lord, have I accused a man before?
   CANDAULES: No, Thoas.
   THOAS: Have I ever been suspicious?
   CANDAULES: Certainly not.
   THOAS: Or picked up heated words,
The kind hurled to the ground in bitter rage,
And thrown them in your ear and kindled them?
   CANDAULES: No, never that!
   THOAS: I shall not do at seventy
What I refused to do at twenty years,
For I have served your house for more than fifty.
   CANDAULES: I know, my faithful servant.
   THOAS: Earth keeps on
Creating, whether kings are killed or crowned
By men; it does not let the trees become
Extinct, nor berries dry out, and it would
Never withhold its springs if to it had
Been given human blood, one time, to drink.
   CANDAULES: Yes, I agree.
   THOAS: That's right then? Ev'rything would stay
The same, I mean, as far as I'm concerned,
For that's the bliss of slavery that a
Red moon up there affects us very little,
And that we're calmer watching sacrifice,
Like hungry dogs who hope to snatch a bite.
We never anxiously need ask if it
Does prophesy a good or evil thing.
   CANDAULES: What do you want to say old man?
   THOAS: Your father
Always kept me by his side; whether
He went to banquets or to war, he would
Not go without me; one day, I would hand

The wine to him; the next, his shield and spear.
And I arranged his funeral, the pyre,
And, with my stiff old fingers, I did place
The whitened ashes in the dark brown urn.
He'd wanted it done thus. Why, do you think?
    CANDAULES: The grapes are turning red.
    THOAS: You are like him,
Perhaps—I've never seen you draw your sword;
He did that often, liked to draw, at times
Without good reason, I admit that too;
And still, 'twas good—perhaps you're just like him.
So I wish you his fate.
    CANDAULES: Is it not mine?
    THOAS: Who knows? I would include his end with that.
Forgive me, Lord. My head is not so quick.
I comprehend but slowly, don't invent,
And he who calls me stupid does no wrong!
But able men have come to ask advice
From me and when I seemed surprised they said:
'A man of seventy, though never bright,
Who's kept his senses knows much more about
Some things than does a very clever youth.'
Well now, I have my senses still, I think;
So listen now.
    CANDAULES: I do.
    THOAS: Don't torture me
By asking for my reasons; do not think
That I am wrong, although I may fall silent
Because I lack a Why of proper weight
Just when you might desire to weigh my words.
For, after all, you can disperse, with but
A single arrow, birds whose flight displeases
The King for whom the seer has questioned them,
And some have done this very thing in rage.
And yet, the tragic future they predicted
Comes just the same. So do not say to me:
'What do you want? He's brave, faithful, and good!'
I know this too; yes, I can swear to it.
But still, I have to warn you all the more:
Beware of Gyges, King!
(Candaules laughs)   That's what I thought!
But I'll repeat it still. Beware, oh King.

But understand me properly. I'll say
This also: He will never take your crown;
He will defend you with his final breath.
And still, he is more dangerous to you
Than all who, yesterday, with angry looks
And words, did plot against you, for, indeed,
They will not harm you any more as soon
As he is gone! So rid yourself of him
As soon as possible, for, if he stays
And walks about among them any more
And freely shows the wreaths he's won, I know
That much can happen.

CANDAULES: You mean?

THOAS: I more than know!
I see and hear what's going on these days!
They whisper and compare and shrug their shoulders;
They form a fist, exchange their secret nods!
You have offended them too deeply. Will
The Greek who stumbles suddenly across
Your crown tomorrow morning, which they'll
Place before his feet tonight, refuse to take
It still? Then he would be a fool! It does
Suffice that he would never rob you; but
He may inherit it; he'll be your heir; he will;
His signs are excellent beyond belief!
They used to think the less of him because
He played the zither, and they thought, as I
Thought too, the only birds who have sweet throats
Are those who've had their talons clipped too short;
But now, because he sings so well, they see
Him, not as Phoebus yet, but as his son!

CANDAULES: And that surprises you? He conquered them!
How could a human being do that to them?

THOAS: All right! But he is really good and true,
So heed me. It may still turn out quite well
Unless the gods should visit punishment,
And, in a year, you'll reconcile us all!
(*Gyges appears*)
He comes. Lord, did I speak in vain? Don't smile!
Saltpeter penetrates the thickest walls,
Why should time's salt have failed to season me?
(*Withdraws to the background*)

CANDAULES: You've reached me better than you think, my
    friend!—
Well, Gyges?
    GYGES: Lord, I've searched and looked for you.
    CANDAULES: And I for you. Now tell me quickly what
You bring to me.—You're silent, turn away?
Whatever it may be, I am prepared!
    GYGES: If you had but allowed my sacrifice!
    CANDAULES: I never shall regret that I did not.
But even if I had, to what avail,
Since her suspicion had already been
Lit inextinguishably by your sigh.
But don't reproach yourself for this; what man
Alive would not have sighed like you last night?
    GYGES: It was an evil day when Lydia's King
Encountered Gyges, who had come from Greece.
    CANDAULES: I do not curse the day.
    GYGES: You could have killed
That tiger as he lay in wait for you,
And I, instead of saving you from death
With my unnecessary arrow, merely
Deprived you of a mastershot.
    CANDAULES: That's true;
I'd seen him, and I was prepared for him;
But then I saw your shining eyes, your cheeks
So flushed, and how you panted for the chance.
I thanked you and suppressed a quiet smile
Inside.
    GYGES: He always was so generous!
When I did not suspect it also! How—
    CANDAULES: I also did see at first glance, if there
Were even greater danger, you'd repeat the deed
With even greater courage. Well,
The lack of opportunity is not your fault.
    GYGES: Lord, say no more. It is just as you said.
I would have risked my blood to save a hair
Of yours. And still, I now have to demand
—It is a curse which forces me—your life—
    CANDAULES: My life!
    GYGES: Unless she is to die instead!
But if your eyes tonight still look upon
The ev'ning star, then hers will nevermore.

CANDAULES: If you don't kill me, she will take her life?
GYGES: So she insists. That's why I must be here.
CANDAULES: No other sacrifice can satisfy?
GYGES: I offered all I could, but she refused.
CANDAULES: Then she'll refuse to take her leave of me?
GYGES: I fear she'd flee before you to the grave.
CANDAULES: Then take my life!—That startles you, my friend?
GYGES: You'd give it willingly?
CANDAULES: A sacrilege
Demands penitent acts, and he who does
Not smile while he's performing them does not
Show penitence!—Do you not know me well,
Or think so little of me that you are
Surprised or shocked by this? You could not think
That I would force her rosy fingers, which
Are much too delicate to pluck a flower,
To take a dagger, and to test with it
If she can find her heart?
GYGES: You even take
The light protection of your garments off
And offer me your heart!
CANDAULES: I'm showing you
The closest path to reach your goal and smooth
It for you so that you can praise something
About me when you come before her face.
The spring of life you seek flows here, my friend.
You have the key to it. Now open it!
GYGES: Not for the world!
CANDAULES: For her, my friend, for her!
(*Gyges makes a gesture of refusal*)
CANDAULES: But, I recall, today, you wished to spill
Your own young blood at your own hands. I think
That I shall show the same degree of courage;
So go to her, and say my last fare well,
And tell her all is well; I'm lying dead.
GYGES: No, no, I came to fight!
CANDAULES: You are that sure!
You think you can't be vanquished if you fight
Against me?
GYGES: You know me better!
CANDAULES: Yes, that's true,
And even if I won, I'd still have it

Ahead of me! Is that not aloe's scent?
Indeed, the wind already bears it to
Us from the park. The aloe opens only
When the night approaches. Then it is time!
    GYGES: This wretched ring!
    CANDAULES: You think, 'twere better if
It had stayed in the tomb. Yes, that is true!
Rhodope's fears did not deceive her, and
Your shudder's warnings were not meaningless.
It was not forged for playing idle games
Or senseless jokes; indeed, perhaps the fate
Of all the world depends on it. I feel
As though I had the privilege to look
Into the future most remote. I see
The battle of young gods with ancient ones;
Often thrust back, god Zeus is climbing now
Toward his father's golden throne; he holds
The dreadful scythe, and, from behind, there steals
A titan, wearing heavy chains. But why
Does Cronos not see him? He's fettered now,
Is even maimed and overthrown. Does that
One wear the ring? He did, friend Gyges, yes;
Gaea herself had given it to him!
    GYGES: Then let the man be cursed who brought it here!
    CANDAULES: But why? No, what you did was right. Were I
Like you, I would not have been tempted thus.
I'd have returned it quietly to night,
And all would be, just as it was before.
So do not try to see my crime as less because
You served as tool. The guilt's completely mine!
    GYGES: But guilt of what?
    CANDAULES: She must be judge of that!
But now I strongly feel how wrong I was,
And what's exacted from me, I deserve.
The simple words my trusty servant spoke
Have taught me this. One should not always ask
What something is but also what it means.
I know for certain that the time will come
When all will think like me. For what's contained,
In veils and crowns or even rusty swords,
Which is eternal? But the tired world
Has gone to sleep believing in the things

Which it has won in its last battle, and
It holds them firmly. He who wants to take
Them from it wakens it. So let him test
Himself, before he does, to see if he
Is strong enough to bind the world when it,
Half roused, flails all about and if
He's rich enough to offer more if it,
Unwillingly, abandons baubles. Heracles
Could do it; I can not; too proud to be
His humble heir and much too weak to do
What he did, I have stirred the ground which bore
Me, and it vengefully now grinds me down.
    GYGES: No, no!
    CANDAULES: It's so! And must be just this way!
The world requires sleep, as you and I
Need ours; it grows, like us, and gains in strength
When it apparently has died and tempts
Some fools to jeer. Yes, when a man thus lies;
His arms, so used to toil, relaxed and idle;
His eyes sealed tightly shut; his mouth is closed
With lips clamped shut, perhaps still holding fast
A wilted rosy petal, just as though
It were the greatest treasure; that must be
A most peculiar sight for him who does
Not sleep. But if one were to come who might
Not know of human needs because his birth
Was on another planet and would cry:
'I have some fruit and wine for you; come, rise
To eat and drink!', what would you do to him?
'Tis true, if you did not, still in your sleep,
Choke him by taking hold and squeezing hard,
You'd say: 'But this is more than food and drink!'
And you'd continue sleeping until day
Which does not waken one man or another,
No, rather calls them all to live again!
I have disturbed the earth that brazenly,
And now I am in Briareus' hands,
And he will crush this stinging insect pest!
So, Gyges, if the wave of life moves you
This way or that, it will raise you, and higher
Than you would think. But you must trust it and
Not be repelled when crowns appear. Only

Make sure you don't disturb the sleeping world!
And now—
GYGES: The sun sinks! Now it has to be.
CANDAULES: Thoas! (*He takes off his crown*)
THOAS: What is it, Lord?
CANDAULES: You wished to see
Me fight, and I shall grant this pleasure now.
But for it, you must hold the crown and give
It to the one of us who will survive.
(*To Gyges*) If it be you, I don't begrudge it, and,
I know, they will be glad to see it on
Your head!—What? You don't want it? Be ashamed!
Then it might well go to a lesser man!
GYGES: My Lord, please swear, you'll fight the best you can.
CANDAULES: I have to show her that I will not lose
Such beauty easily. So I do swear.
And you?
GYGES: She lives or dies with me. I must!
Although I'll think with ev'ry blow I strike:
I'd rather kiss, I still shall not strike less
On that account
CANDAULES: Then shake my hand for the
Last time. Now be a tiger for me, and
I'll be your lion. Here will be our woods
In which we often did enjoy the hunt.
(*Both draw*)
GYGES: Just one more thing I was ashamed to tell:
She'll marry me if I should conquer you.
CANDAULES: Ha! Now I understand her!
GYGES: Then resist!
(*Fighting, both go off to the left*)
THOAS: He falls!—The Heraclids are gone from earth!

―――――――――――――――――――――

Hestia's Temple.

*In the center, one sees a statue of the goddess. Rhodope enters
from the right in solemn procession, Lesbia, Hero, Carna
with her. It is evening. Torches.*
RHODOPE: Friend Carna, is the pyre being built?
CARNA: It has been built!
(*Rhodope enters the temple and kneels before the statue of the
goddess*)

HERO: She speaks of pyres, not
Of bridal chambers!
LESBIA: That surprises you?
There has to be a dead man here before
There'll be a bride. Come now, we all know that.
HERO: I'm trembling, Lesbia. She asked, when I
Was dressing her, did any poison berries
Grow in our garden—
LESBIA: What?
HERO: And whether I
Could bring her some of these and promised me
A pearl for each I'd find, and even for
A hundred of them, but I'd have to find
Them for her very quickly!
LESBIA: Did you?
HERO: I refused.
And then she smiled and said: 'I thought as much.
Tomorrow I shall show you where they are.'
But it seemed strange to me.
LESBIA: It is most strange.
HERO: Then she sent me away, but secretly
I spied and saw her cut her arm as though
Experimenting I should call it, but with
A dagger which looked very sharp.
LESBIA: Hero!
HERO: I saw red blood!
LESBIA: How dreadful!
HERO: True, she has
Some alien gods she worships besides ours;
We do not know them, hence fail to understand
Mysterious customs!
LESBIA: No! Where is the flute
And where the reed? Who sings to Hymen here?
Where are the dancing choirs? I have been blind!
She's come here, planning never to return!
My Queen, I must beg your forgiveness! Is
A feast prepared?
HERO: Not to my knowledge!—No!
LESBIA: Oh, cursed be the stubbornness which made
Me stay away from her this very day!
Oh, goddess, she is yours this very hour;
Please change her mind! It is too late for me!

HERO: Yes, chaste and pure and holy one, please do!—
It's strange that she chose somber Hestia
Before whose glance the greenest wreath would wilt
Instead of ever-cheerful Aphrodite
To be the witness of her marriage feast.

　　LESBIA: Alas, it all points to calamity!

(*Gyges appears*)

　　HERO: Oh Gyges!

　　LESBIA:　　　　　　Take him, I beg! Don't do this thing!

　　GYGES: I feel as though the blood which streamed from him
Had been my own. I am as cold as death.

　　HERO: How pale he looks!

　　GYGES:　　　　　　　　This is the altar—I
Have looked for her at quite a diff'rent one—
Her girls are standing there—and she is here—
What happens now?

　　THOAS (*enters*):　　　　　I'm bringing you the crown!

　　GYGES: It is the Lydians'; it is not mine.

　　THOAS: And I first brought it to the Lydians;
And now I am their messenger to you!

　　PEOPLE (*outside*): Hail, Gyges, hail!

　　RHODOPE (*rises and turns*)

　　PEOPLE (*crowding in*):　　　　To Gyges, our King, hail!

　　THOAS: But don't be proud that you were chosen thus;
Our neighbors have attacked our land; our people
Wants you to lead us!

　　GYGES:　　　　　　　　　　How—

　　THOAS:　　　　　　　　　　As I had thought,
He was too mild, and no one feared him. Now
They are upon us!

　　GYGES (*puts on the crown*)　　I shall pay his debt.

　　RHODOPE (*who has slowly approached Gyges*): But first your
　　　own debt, Gyges!

　　GYGES:　　　　　　　　　　You, my Queen,
Will be the prize awaiting me when I
Have totally destroyed the enemy—

　　RHODOPE: No, no! From me you'll get no stay.—We can
Not stand before my father; let us stand
Before the altar of pure Hestia,
In front of her, give me your hand and join
Me for eternity as I join you.

　　GYGES: If you had been a witness to his death,

You would hold sacred now my hesitation
Even to touch your dress before I've done
At least this much for him! To whom had this
Rich world so much to offer as to him,
And still he left as others enter it.

RHODOPE: If he so nobly entered the dark world
Below where no one stains himself with guilt
Again, then I shall gladly meet him there,
Yes, even on the threshold of that world.
With my own hand, I'll give him Lethean bliss,
Indeed deny myself the blessed drink.
But I ask you to end at once.

GYGES: So be
It then; but I do promise you, dear shade:
I shall go forth as soon as we are wed.

RHODOPE: I too have made a promise.

GYGES: Oh my Queen,
A man who puts aside the cup of such
Great bliss, as I have done, were it but for
An hour, would deserve your promises.

RHODOPE: Be still, you are in a most sacred place!
(*They walk to the altar*)

RHODOPE: Oh Hestia, oh keeper of the flame,
Which does consume what it can't purify;
I owe it to this youth that I can once
Again appear before your face. Now, as
The people raised him up to be the king,
Before your witness, I become his wife.
(*She gives her hand to Gyges*)
Take as my wedding gift to you the crown
Which even now adorns your head, and give
Your bride the death ring as her token now.

GYGES: The King still wears that ring upon his hand.

RHODOPE: Then it already has its rightful place.
(*She releases Gyges' hand*)
And now step back and keep your promise, just
As I'll keep mine! I'm purified at last,
For only he who may has looked at me,
But now I thus (*She stabs herself*)
                            divorce myself from you!